Fear is the Mind Killer

How to Build a Training Culture that Fosters Strength and Resilience

Kaja Sadowski

Cover design by Courtney Rice

Cover photo and author photo by Dannielle Collings (nionvox.com)

ISBN: 978-1-9990663-0-7

Printed in the United States, United Kingdom, and Australia by:
Ingram Book Group LLC
One Ingram Blvd., La Vergne, TN 37086

This book is intended to assist experienced instructors of martial arts and self-defence with evaluating and improving their existing programs and to supplement their prior knowledge and training. It is not an instructional guide to martial arts or self-defence techniques, nor does any part of it constitute legal or medical advice. Training for martial arts and self-defence carries inherent risks of physical and psychological injury. Readers are ultimately responsible for their own safety and the safety of their students and training partners. If you are unfamiliar with any of the skills, techniques, or training methods described in this book, seek out professional, hands-on instruction.

For Jordan, with love

Acknowledgments

This book wouldn't exist without Guy Windsor. Ever since he sat across from me in a sushi restaurant two years ago and very pointedly asked why I hadn't written a book yet, he's been an invaluable source of support and accountability. I'm grateful for the degree to which I've been able to draw on his experience as both an author and an instructor throughout this project.

As a martial artist and a teacher, I stand on the shoulders of giants. Without the mentorship, experience, and patience of my own teachers and colleagues, there wouldn't be much for me to write about. I am especially grateful to David Randy Packer, who first showed me that failure and chaos aren't the enemies of growth, but its biggest drivers. Courtney Rice built the school of my dreams with me and is also responsible for the stellar cover design on this book.

This project also owes a lot to Maija Soderholm, Rory Miller, John F. Irving, Jessica Finley, and Andrew Somlyo. Every one of them is an example of the kind of instruction and culture-building that I advocate in my writing. Each of them has also contributed to the content of this book by helping with background research, letting me build on their drills, or giving me feedback on sections that fit within their expertise.

The lonely, exhausting writing process was made a lot less lonely and exhausting by my fantastic beta readers. Thank you to Ash Banks, Paige Knorr (who's also a great proofreader), Eva Sadowski, and Josef Sadowski. My copy editor, Eva van Emden, was a joy to work with. If you need a meticulous, thorough, and friendly freelancer who can adapt to the scale of any project, I highly recommend her.

Putting together Appendix I: Sample Exercises was its own labour of love. I benefited immensely from having a small army of playtesters who were willing to print off my instructions, teach the drills to their students exactly as written, and send me video of the results. My thanks to Mike Cherba, Ken Dietiker, Edward Hines, Nicholas McWilliams, Alex Spreier, Tanya Smith, Dan Weber, and Shanna Zak for helping me make sure that what I wanted to teach was actually on the page.

I owe an equally large debt of gratitude to everyone who supported me through the long process of publishing my first book. My fellow coaches and students at Valkyrie Western Martial Arts Assembly gave me both a safe haven and a laboratory for my teaching experiments. My supporters on Patreon gave me the financial means to hire a professional editor and publish this book at a level of quality I could be proud of. My amazing partner, Jordan Both, helped keep me sane, fed, and even occasionally well-rested right up until the publication date.

Thank you all.

Introduction

Martial arts make you stronger. Not just physically, but mentally. It's a fundamental truth of what we do and I haven't met a martial arts or self-defence instructor who didn't believe it. It's one of the main selling points of the lessons we teach — especially in a society that's grown averse to violence as a part of everyday life — and a driving force behind our own training. The point of what we do isn't punching, or kicking, or stabbing, or hitting people with sticks, but the transformation that takes place inside the person practising those skills.

As they work through the physical and emotional challenges their art presents, they become a better person. They become more confident, more willing to stand up for themselves and others, more resilient, and more capable in the face of adversity or danger. One of our primary goals as instructors is to make our students greater than they were. It might be the most important thing we do.

But how, exactly, do we do it? What alchemy happens over the course of hundreds of hours of training that turns a student into the best version of themselves? How do they develop the bone-deep faith in their own capabilities, the willingness to tackle challenges head on, and the ability to persevere through pain and fear, that characterize true strength? Physical skill alone doesn't do it. If it did, we could all just as easily be teaching golf or synchronized swimming.

The magic of fighting is in how it brings us up against our greatest fears and limitations. It makes us engage with pain and discomfort. It puts us in the viscerally uncomfortable place of facing another human being who is trying to hurt us. It makes us confront some of our biggest social taboos around touching and hurting other people. Facing these things and coming out the other side is a transformative experience like few others.

It's also not something that can be forced. No teacher can make a student push past their fear or discomfort, or take on a big challenge, against their will. It's an internal choice that they have to make and making that choice is what changes them. Our job is to give them as many opportunities as we can to choose the harder path and to create an environment where that choice is easy. That means understanding how to challenge students appropriately and removing the obstacles that get in the way of tackling those challenges.

The single biggest obstacle they face is not lack of talent, or lack of fitness, but fear: fear of failure, and the embarrassment and exclusion that comes with it; fear of breaking a social taboo and being punished for it; fear of being hurt or — even worse — hurting someone else. When our students are afraid they hold themselves back. They run away from challenges. They make themselves weaker and smaller and less effective out of sheer self-preservation. To help them become strong, we must first help them become fearless.

That's a bit of a tall order, because most of the fears that our students bring to the training floor are rational. They're afraid of being mocked or excluded when they fail because that's what happened the last time somebody saw them screw up. They're afraid of being punished because they've been punished in the past. They're afraid of being hurt because they've been hurt already. They're afraid of hurting others because they've been raised to believe that's the worst thing they could ever do.

So we can't teach them fearlessness by dismissing what they feel. They have good reason to believe these things and pressuring them to ignore their misgivings just teaches them to ignore their own instincts about danger, which could cause them a world of hurt later on.

Instead, we need to show them that there's nothing to fear here. If the training floor is a space where they will not be humiliated for failure, or punished for non-conformity, or broken beyond repair, then their fears have no reason to exist. If they feel safe, they'll actually be willing to take risks. Someone who's terrified of making a false step will never willingly step outside of their comfort zone, because the consequences feel too great. Someone who feels like they've got a safety net, and who's experienced what it's like to fall and have others catch them, will push themselves so much further and learn so much more.

I've learned this firsthand. Since I was twelve years old, I've played and trained in communities that valued mental strength and fearlessness above almost everything else. For twenty years, I've run with climbers, mountaineers, backcountry skiers, snowboarders, martial artists, and cops.

I've taught rock climbing in every venue from indoor gyms to several-hundred-metre outdoor rock faces, run field courses in basic mountaineering and crevasse rescue, and taught countless group classes, private lessons, and workshops on historical swordplay, unarmed striking and grappling, and self-defence. I've participated in hundreds of hours of tactical training simulations with the Force Options Training Unit of my local police department. I've faced all kinds of fears, from the existential dread of balancing above a sheer three-hundred-metre drop down to a crevasse-ridden glacier, to the gut-churning discomfort of staring down an authority figure in full uniform and daring them to take you down.

All of these have been easy to deal with compared to the fear of failure. For many years, I trained in environments where it wasn't really safe for me to make mistakes. The climbing community was where I first realized this fact. I was one of very few women and I had to prove that I belonged. Girls weren't supposed to climb as well as boys, or to be tough enough to suffer through the extremes of long alpine routes and epic mountaineering trips. Most people assumed we were just there to socialize or get dates until we proved otherwise.

I couldn't afford to show anyone that I was afraid. I couldn't afford to slow down, or take rests, or fail to complete a route cleanly. If I did, it would only confirm the assumption that I wasn't good enough. I'd stop being invited on trips, stop getting credit for my achievements, and get pushed to the margins of my community. I'd felt it start to happen when I faltered and seen it happen to other women when they proved to be anything less than exceptional.

At first, that fear of failure made me a great learner. I was so driven to prove myself that I trained constantly. I took on harder challenges as soon as I could. I got very good at ignoring pain and even injury, and at blocking out any sense of fear or danger. My skills improved quickly and I soon impressed everyone I trained with.

That was where the trouble began. Once I'd established myself as a competent climber, I couldn't afford to make mistakes lest that image be shattered. Years of ignoring pain and injury led to elbow tendinitis and a dislocated shoulder that never set right after I popped it back into place and tried to finish the route I'd just fallen from. I alternated between routinely taking life-threatening risks, and backing off easy climbs and cancelling trips at the last minute because I was so terrified of messing up and embarrassing myself. My progress didn't just stall — it cratered.

At the same time, I was struggling as a teacher. I was great at communicating technique and would have tiny women out-climbing their gym rat boyfriends by the end of a two-hour lesson, but I couldn't get the mental stuff to stick. I'd be gentle with my students until they got a handle on the basics and then I'd shift gears to the "tough love" approach that I'd internalized. I pushed them to be competitive, to ignore when their bodies weren't happy, and to prove that they were tough enough to belong. Though I didn't realize it at the time, I was creating an environment that didn't cultivate mental strength and fearlessness but simply filtered out those who didn't already possess these qualities, or who had valid reasons to be afraid.

It didn't escape my notice that most of the people who were failed by this approach were like me: women, members of the LGBT community, and other minorities. They were people who felt like they couldn't afford to make mistakes or show weakness, which meant they couldn't afford to really learn or grow either.

I didn't understand what was happening yet. I only saw that something changed for a lot of my female and minority students around the one-year mark. Beginners were pretty evenly matched in terms of physical capability, interest, and mental fortitude. At the intermediate level, women and minority students started dropping out in startling numbers. Their stated reasons varied: maybe life got too busy for them to be able to prioritize climbing, or they got injured and couldn't bounce back, or they just weren't having fun anymore. Whatever the explanation, the pattern was the same. Initial enthusiasm and competence gave way to hesitation, fear, and withdrawal.

I saw the same pattern in martial arts. At the fencing school where I started learning swordplay, beginner classes were evenly divided between genders. The lowest rank of the school was still pretty balanced, but the second rank saw a precipitous drop in female participation. The number of women to achieve the third rank was in the single digits by the time the school reached its tenth anniversary, and there were no female instructors. When I left in 2011, a few women were teaching, but they were still substantially outnumbered and most were in junior roles. Things haven't improved since then. That school's demographics aren't unusual — in fact, they're almost exactly average for the community — and its problems are endemic in martial arts and self-defence.

There's a gap between the psychological growth that we expect to see in our students and what actually happens. A substantial portion of the people we train just don't make the transition from well-founded caution to fearless confidence. Instead, they either stagnate at the intermediate levels of their art — technically competent enough to keep up with training but lacking the mental skills they need to progress to the next level — or they drop out after the initial rush of beginner's progress has faded.

There's a critical component missing from their training environment: they're not getting the combination of safety and challenge that they need in order to flourish. We see it hit minority students the hardest, because they're the most likely to have valid fears that keep them from taking big risks, but the truth is that it's affecting everyone.

When I started running a new school with my colleagues, David R. Packer and Courtney Rice, our main goal was to tackle this problem head on. With over fifty years of combined martial arts experience between us, we were confident that we could handle the technical side of teaching. The real challenge would be facilitating internal growth. We'd all seen enough schools fall short of their ideals that we couldn't pretend that this growth would just happen on its own. And so, we took on the project of environment- and culture-building with the same rigour we brought to building a curriculum.

By the time Valkyrie Western Martial Arts Assembly (Valkyrie WMAA) became a full-time school with a permanent location, we'd found a successful formula. Our school had developed a reputation for both inclusivity — especially of female, queer, and trans students — and for running some of the most challenging classes and most realistic self-defence training around.

Guests from other schools routinely remarked on how comfortable everyone looked in classes and how willing they were to throw themselves at challenges as a result. They saw students who'd spent their entire lives behind a desk gamely take on cartwheels, handstands, and complex gymnastic movements that were difficult even for competitive athletes. Our smallest fighters would routinely pick fights with opponents twice their size and come out smiling — if not necessarily victorious.

The fearlessness we've managed to cultivate in so many of our students is the result of careful engagement with every part of our training culture. We took the lessons we'd learned over decades of teaching physical skills in a range of demanding environments and used them to put together a toolkit for facilitating mental growth. I've been putting it into daily practice for the past five years, and the transformations I've seen have been incredible.

Students who walked in the door uncertain they could ever bring themselves to hit somebody have found a love for boxing sparring. Students who'd walked away from martial arts entirely because they were sure they weren't cut out for it have made more progress in months than they'd previously made in years. Self-described "couch potatoes" have gone from barely making it through a warm-up to bugging our coaches for more challenges and extra opportunities to train. When we introduce high-stress training tools and adrenaline into classes, our biggest challenge is tempering everyone's enthusiasm and keeping a lid on their energy, and not coaxing reluctant students to try a scary thing.

Our long-term students have been tested in everything from informal sparring to competition to real-life self-defence, and they have succeeded. They know their own minds and bodies well enough to have a realistic understanding of what they are capable of and how they will act under pressure; they have the tactical ability to adapt to changing circumstances; they know how to handle adrenaline, fear, and pain without losing control; and they know how to mitigate the long-term consequences of the scary stuff. They are truly resilient and they carry far less psychological baggage and physical scarring from their training than those of us who learned through stubbornness and luck.

The methods we use to get them there aren't specific to any martial arts system. Instead, we've created an environment where they can learn the right lessons. Where psychological stress and social pressure don't push them down and force them out, but are harnessed to help them embrace challenge and move beyond fear.

This book lays out those methods, and provides a model for turning any training space into a community that not only welcomes all comers, but turns everyone who shows up and puts in the work into a genuine badass.

It starts with an overview of sport science and coaching theory that highlights the importance of allowing students to fail, and of using chaos and play as drivers of growth. We'll look at how building a healthy relationship to failure is integral to both skill development and psychological resilience, and we'll address where perfectionist approaches to training often leave our students lacking essential tools.

The three "pillars" that follow will break down how to effectively integrate failure, chaos, and genuine challenge into every level of your training environment:

- Policies and high-level structures that reduce the personal cost of failure for students and allow you to get on with teaching

- Classroom tools that build the trust necessary for students to lean into failure; allow flexibility, variation, and fun without sacrificing control of the group; and cultivate the self-reliance and internal regulation students need to get the most out of their training

- Stress testing and stress inoculation tools that put the right kind of pressure on students, and allow them to experience high-stress situations that build their confidence in their own skills without unreasonable risk

These are followed by two sections that focus on specific student populations that greatly benefit from this approach, and on mitigating some of the cultural factors that make it more difficult for them to succeed:

- Addressing the social pressures and myths that stack training environments against women

- Accommodating and challenging students with a history of violence and psychological trauma without causing harm

The final appendices compile suggested exercises and further reading to give you additional tools for expanding your teaching practice.

The goal of this book isn't to push you toward a particular fighting style or body of techniques, or to tell you how to teach a given skill. Instead, it provides guiding models for how to think about the training culture that you've built and how to structure it to create the conditions for success. You'll learn how to apply your existing skills, knowledge, and teaching methods in ways that allow your students to grapple with failure, test themselves regularly, and come out of each class a little stronger and more resilient—and a little less afraid — than they came in.

Failure: The Keystone of Learning

So much of the rhetoric of toughness teaches us that failure is something to fear. If we fail, we die. There's a banner in our police training gym that proclaims, "Losing is not a force option." Similar language shows up all the time in demo videos and sales pitches for every self-defence group, martial art, and fitness community you can imagine. When a colleague joined an online fitness forum years ago, he was told, "To fail once is to fail always." New swordplay practitioners looking for training tips hear, "Practice doesn't make perfect; perfect practice makes perfect."

The idea that failure is the domain of the rank beginner, and a flaw to be overcome as quickly as possible, is baked right into our understanding of how to train. If you look at any martial domain, you'll see where it can become twisted by the fear of failure.

In traditional martial arts, solo form practice shifts away from exploring and internalizing fundamental principles and becomes a tool for perfecting one single interpretation of a given sequence. In Historical European Martial Arts (HEMA), a desire to preserve and enliven the material that survives in a handful of manuscripts becomes a slavish adherence to one reading of a single segment of text or image. In self-defence instruction, an awareness of the consequences of making the wrong tactical choice leads to a false narrowing of options to a single cure-all technique or mindset.

In all of these cases, the problem isn't that the teacher's motivations are somehow corrupt, but rather that they've lost sight of the line between the overarching goals of a discipline and the day-to-day goals of its instructors—between legacy and practice. Traditional arts aim to pre-serve a living tradition and inculcate respect for its tenets; historical re-creation aims to piece together an accurate picture of the past and its arts; self-defence aims to keep its students as safe as possible in as many contexts as possible. That's the big picture, and failing to meet any of those goals is a serious problem.

Our actual path to those goals, though, is motor learning. We're all teaching physical skills, and the growing body of knowledge on how to develop them shows that being able to fail—often and in a bunch of different ways—is the key to getting better and staying on top. Without room for failure, progress stalls and skill retention drops off, and people stop learning very well at all. In fact, a lot of the teaching tools that help students perform the most "perfectly" in a single training session actu-ally have the weakest impact on long-term retention and improvement.

By aiming for perfect practice and avoiding failure, we make failure more likely once our students leave the classroom. Given how counter this statement runs to how many of us learned our own arts, I won't blame you for not believing me. So let's take a look at the science.

Motor Programs

When we talk about motor learning, it's important to be precise about the kinds of skills we're aiming to teach. The difference between per-forming a balance beam routine and winning a boxing match, for exam-ple, extends beyond the mechanical differences between a handstand and a punch.

Motor skills can be categorized into two broad groupings depending on the environment they're performed in: closed skills take place in an environment that is stable (i.e., one that is predictable, controlled, and maybe even static), which allows the performer to evaluate the conditions in advance and organize their movements without having to make sudden adjustments. Open skills are performed in a dynamic, un-predictable environment that forces the performer to adapt quickly to emergent conditions by reading the changes around them and responding on the fly.[1]

The balance beam is a stable environment; the boxing ring is not. All fighting skills are open skills. A punch is never thrown in isolation, against a static target—at least, not when it matters. Whether our ultimate application will be in a friendly sparring match, a martial arts competition, or a life-or-death fight against an earnest attacker, we need to be able to throw that punch against a moving, thinking target that does not want to be hit.

This context means that the motor skills we develop for fighting have a very strong cognitive component. Success depends not only on executing a physical movement well, but also on making the right decisions at the right time, and adapting that physical movement to the needs of the moment. When we talk about skill and performance in a fighting context, we're not looking at how well someone performs a given action in isolation (i.e., looking for the perfect punch, or lunge, or hip throw), but how well someone chooses the correct action and performs it in relationship to their opponent and environment (i.e., looking for the best punch that is possible right now).

So how does a person build that kind of skill? Not, "How do they drill it?" or "What curriculum do they follow?" but how, cognitively and biomechanically, does that kind of adaptability and capability get wired?

The best model I've found for this is the generalized motor program. Put simply, a motor program is a prestructured set of commands that allows the body to execute a complex action.[2] The human body is a complex mechanism with a ton of moving parts, and it's not feasible for us to consciously operate each one of those parts every time we need to move. If I want to throw a basic jab, for example, I've got to engage the muscles of my legs and hips to initiate the rotation and weight transfer, tighten my core to connect my hips to my shoulders, translate that hip rotation

---

1 Richard A. Schmidt, *Motor Learning and Performance: A Situation-Based Learning Approach*, 4th ed. (Champaign, IL: Human Kinetics, 2008), 8.

2 Schmidt, *Motor Learning and Performance*, 107.

into shoulder rotation, make a fist, and extend my striking arm toward my target, all while making tiny adjustments to my posture so that the motion doesn't throw me off balance.

There are dozens of muscles and a half-dozen joints involved in the action. If I had to consciously manage each of the contractions and extensions required for all of that motion to happen, it'd be impossible for me to throw a punch with the reaction speed necessary for it to be effective in a fight. The cognitive load of organizing all of that activity would also leave me no mental space for observing and analyzing my opponent's actions or planning my next action. A single punch might take as long as several seconds.

So instead, once I've learned the whole action, all of those commands get combined into a program labelled "Throw a Jab" and filed away in my long-term memory. Every time I want to throw that particular punch, I retrieve the program and run it, and my body does the thousand little things that need to happen to execute a good jab.

The most important thing here, for our purposes, is that the "Throw a Jab" program needs to be very versatile. If I had to build separate programs for "Throw a Jab at Someone As Tall As Me," "Throw a Jab at Someone Shorter than Me," "Throw a Jab at Someone Moving to the Left," "Throw a Jab at Someone Moving to the Right," "Throw a Jab Kinda Slow," and "Throw a Jab Really Fast," I'd have serious performance problems. For starters, I'd be completely stuck if I encountered a fighter taller than me, or one that moved toward me rather than to either side. I simply wouldn't have the program for that circumstance, and I'd freeze while my brain cycled through the programs I did have to find something that fit.

Even if I did have the right program, the freeze would still happen, just because of the sheer number of options I'd have to cycle through every time. There's a principle called Hick's Law that tells us that the relationship between response time and the number of stimulus-response alternatives (i.e., choices of what to do in response to a particular stimulus) is fixed and predictable. The more choices you have, the longer your response time will be, and that response time increases exponentially with every extra choice.[3] Too many options, and your response time becomes long enough that you may as well not respond at all. Your opponent will have already changed the conditions you're reacting to by the time you pick a response.

To get around these issues, our motor programs are generalized. They've got some features that are fixed, such as their sequence and fundamental timing structure (i.e., the order and rhythm of actions that defines a skill), and others that can be varied according to the needs of the moment, including speed, amplitude/size, direction, and even what limbs or muscles are used to perform the action.[4] I can throw a slow or fast, long or short jab with either arm, to any target, not because I have dozens of motor programs stored in my memory, but because my core "Throw a Jab" program is flexible enough to adapt to a range of conditions.

I don't judge my skill in throwing a jab by how well I execute the "Throw a Jab" program in a vacuum, but by how well I modify its variable components to suit the situation at hand—a process called parameterization.[5] If I'm really good, I can throw punches that I've never practiced on their own, just by reading the situation well and adapting on the fly. A well-executed generalized motor program doesn't just repeat things you've done before, but can generate completely new responses to an unusual stimulus. It's how we get those "Whoa, how'd they do that?" moments from top fighters, when someone with a lot of skill pulls off a completely new move and makes it work.

Blocked, Random, and Variable Practice

So if generalized motor programs are one of the keys to successful fighting, along with all of the observation and decision-making skills we need to apply the right program at the right moment, how do we successfully train them?

---

3 Schmidt, *Motor Learning and Performance*, 32.

4 Schmidt, *Motor Learning and Performance*, 125–127.

5 Schmidt, *Motor Learning and Performance*, 262.

A mainstay of almost all physical instruction, and certainly of martial arts training, is blocked practice. You pick a skill, and you drill it repeatedly until it's consistent and clean. Then you move on to the next skill. This approach makes coaching and group management very easy, because everyone is doing the same thing at the same time, and you can watch and give feedback effectively even with a big class.

It's also great for student and instructor morale. Repeating the same skill makes it easy to see incremental improvements over the course of a session, and it fits with our cultural understanding of how practice and hard work are supposed to look. Students can focus completely on perfecting their skill. They can manage their emotional and mental state to be as calm and centred as possible, pay attention to the internal and external feedback that helps them polish the details of the action they're performing, and refine the fine details that make what they're doing look and feel good.[6]

We can contrast this with random practice, where students practice a few skills in arbitrary order. They don't get to do the same thing twice in a row, and either work through a pattern that forces them to constantly switch from one skill to another, or interrupt repetitions of the same skill with breaks doing something entirely different.

It can be a chaotic, messy way to practice that makes it harder to deliver feedback or correction to a whole group at once, increases the odds of students running into each other or getting confused and losing their place in a drill, and offers very little of the satisfaction and sense of control of blocked practice. Students have to actively work to re-centre and focus themselves as they move from skill to skill, and may find it difficult to make incremental tweaks to their form between repetitions. Of course blocked practice is better, right?

In reality, blocked practice has been consistently shown to lead to better immediate performance during practice (i.e., students show more improvement over the course of a single session) than random practice, but substantially worse retention and transfer (i.e., students perform

---

6 Schmidt, *Motor Learning and Performance*, 257.

worse when they're asked to perform the same skills after an interval of a few minutes to a few days).

The students participating in random practice fail a lot more in training—how could they not? They're constantly having to remember what they were doing, to adapt to changing circumstances, and to try to apply feedback between non-consecutive repetitions. But they perform much better in follow-up tests. Failure in practice leads to better learning overall.

This phenomenon is called the contextual interference effect: conditions that lead to lower practice performance actually make students retain skill better, and so lead to more effective learning.[7] After it was first identified in 1979, follow-up studies of the contextual interference effect have tried to nail down what conditions it occurs under, what that tells us about motor learning in general, and how we learn to use generalized motor programs in particular.

One thing that quickly became apparent was that more difficult initial learning conditions (and thus higher error rates in practice) consistently led to greater retention rates and more success in follow-up tests. If a researcher made the random practice portion too easy, the contextual interference effect went away, and all of the subjects performed at the same lower level in follow-up tests.

For example, a 1990 review of ten motor learning studies found that the increase in retention was significantly higher for subjects who had to switch between different motor programs during their random practice (e.g., practising three different kinds of throws at a target, such as overhand, underhand, and sidearm), compared to those who varied their practice based on the same motor program (e.g., throwing underhand

---

7 This effect has been consistently demonstrated in both laboratory and non-laboratory conditions, across a range of activities from memorizing hand movement patterns to beanbag throws and badminton serves. For a review of early studies, see: Richard A. Magill and Kellie G. Hall, "A Review of the Contextual Interference Effect in Motor Skill Acquisition," *Human Movement Science* 9, no. 3–5 (1990): 241–289.

at three different target distances). The greater difficulty of having to change motor programs every repetition led to better retention.[8]

In another study, researchers had subjects reproduce three different keystroke patterns in response to on-screen cues. The subjects were broken into three different practice groups: blocked practice (thirty trials in a row of each pattern), random practice (blocks of fifteen trials of all three patterns, with no more than two trials of the same pattern in a row), and a guided random practice (random practice, but with a clear demonstration of how to type the pattern before every trial).

During the practice itself, the purely random group had an error rate two to three times that of the other two groups, which had nearly identical error rates. In retention tests, however, the pure random group had substantially lower error rates, and the guided group actually performed even worse than the blocked group, with an error rate about 1.5 times that of the pure random group.[9] The group that had to work the hardest to figure things out for themselves in practice performed best afterward, and trying to guide students toward more perfect execution completely eliminated the advantages of random practice.

This makes sense if we go back to our model of the generalized motor program and how it affects performance. Remember that skilled performance depends just as much on being able to choose the right program and adapt it to new circumstances, as it does on executing the basic program well. When you use blocked practice or offer a strong model for students to follow, they get plenty of practice executing the motor program, but they don't have to do a lot of work retrieving it from memory or adapting it to a new context. They choose one program at the start of each training block, pull it out of long-term memory, and then don't have to retrieve it again until the next block. Or they don't have to remember or retrieve anything at all because the model tells them what to do every time.

---

8 Magill and Hall, "Contextual Interference," 254–255.

9 Timothy D. Lee and others, "Modeled Timing Information during Random Practice Eliminates the Contextual Interference Effect," *Research Quarterly for Exercise and Sport* 68, no. 1 (1997): 102–104.

In random practice, on the other hand, students have to select and retrieve a motor program every time they move. Their memory and decision-making skills get just as much of a workout as their body does. Not only that, but the changes in their position, energy, and focus from repetition to repetition force them to adapt to a slightly different context every time they repeat an action.

All of this is especially important for highly cognitive open skills like those involved in fighting. In martial contexts, a constantly changing environment isn't just a neat extra challenge, but one of the primary features of a fight. If your students' training doesn't force them to adjust for change and think on their feet, it simply can't prepare them for the realities they'll face once they try to put their skills to use.

Random practice isn't the only example of how making the training stage more difficult and error-heavy leads to better learning outcomes. In my earlier discussion of the contextual interference effect, I mentioned how random practice could involve either a mix of different motor programs or variations on the same motor program. The latter of these is sometimes referred to as variable practice.

While it's not as good as random practice at producing pure retention (i.e., recall and ability to reproduce a skill in follow-up tests), it's incredibly useful for increasing parameterization ability. Researchers have tested the effects of variable practice in comparison with constant practice, where subjects only work on one version of a movement. For example, in a throwing distance experiment, the constant practice group was told to practise making a throw to a set distance (twenty, thirty, or forty metres). The variable practice group alternated between throwing to all three distances. Both groups made the same number of practice attempts.

As you might expect, the constant practice group had lower error rates during the practice itself. They were able to dial in their performance and hit their set target consistently by the end of a training session. The variable group messed up a lot more frequently in practice, as they constantly had to recalibrate their throw to switch distances. But when both groups were given a new distance to throw to (for example, thirty-five metres), the variable group always performed at least as well as the constant group, and usually outperformed them.[10]

By practising variations on the same motor program, the variable group was building a mental model, or schema, for how to parameterize that program. So they ended up with one model for performing the basic action ("throw this thing"), and another for adjusting that action to suit a range of circumstances ("adjust hand speed, throw angle, and release point, depending on the target distance"). When they had to do something new, they could lean on that schema and make the necessary adjustments much more easily.

The constant practice group, on the other hand, had refined their motor program but hadn't had to build a parameterization schema. When they transitioned to a new target in the follow-up test, they had to figure out how to adjust their parameters through trial and error. The resulting gap in performance was substantial, even for a closed skill like a distance toss to a fixed target. Parameterization still matters for those types of skills, but there's a lot more room to adapt to feedback when you're working in a constant environment. The target isn't going anywhere, and you can keep repeating the toss until you get it right (though getting it right in fewer repetitions shows that you're more skilled).

In an open skill context like fighting, you rarely—if ever—get to repeat a skill under the exact same conditions. Your target is moving and often also changing its speed. If it stops, it's going to stop somewhere slightly different than it did the last time. On top of all of that, you're moving too, and responding to whatever attacks and position changes your opponent is making.

Parameterization is absolutely vital to fighting. In the course of a three-minute boxing round, a fighter isn't throwing the same jab hundreds of times, but rather making hundreds of slight variations on their "Throw a Jab" generalized motor program. If they only ever practise one of those variations, they're going to look really great in practice, but will probably get their clock cleaned in the ring.

---

10 Schmidt, *Motor Learning and Performance*, 274.

What I'm driving at here is that the practice strategies that give us the best learning outcomes are also the ones that make for the messiest, most error-prone training. This holds true across pretty much the entire field of motor learning, but is the most important for the highly cognitive open skills we need to fight well. Fighting is chaotic, and even a refereed friendly sparring match is going to have a high level of variability and unpredictability. Strategies like variable practice and random practice train the mind and body to work together to adapt to a certain amount of chaos and make our students more likely to succeed when they face the real thing.

This is not to say that there's no room at all for blocked practice, constant practice, or the guidance of a strong model or demonstration. These tools are useful for helping students understand the basic techniques and parameters of their fighting style, and for building their confidence before we push them to adapt and improvise. They're the bread and butter of many beginner lessons and have a place at the start of every training journey.

Where things go wrong is when we get stuck in blocked or constant practice methods. The confidence they build is comforting, and the ability they give us to refine and polish can make for some gorgeous movement. Someone who's practised the exact same punch or fencing play ten thousand times is going to look spectacular when they perform it under the conditions they've practised in. They're likely to be a favourite student, too—someone their instructor pushes to the front of the line when others are watching, who passes form exams on the first try, and who gets the place of honour in public demonstrations.

Throw some chaos into the mix, though, and that star student is very likely to be outperformed by someone whose practice sessions are marred by a whole lot of mistakes, not-quite-right attempts, and experiments that only succeed half the time. It can be demoralizing to watch, and it might even feel like perfect practice has been cheated out of its due, but the truth is that the student with beautiful movement has been neglecting half of the skills they need for the task.

Choosing which tool to use for the job, tweaking it to fit, and putting it into play quickly is just as important as having the best possible tools. Good teachers understand this and work this skill into their training methods regardless of whether they frame it in terms of formal motor science research. For example, Maestro Sonny Umpad is known in the Filipino Martial Arts community for his innovative approach to flow, movement, and deception. Here's how one of his private students and official lineage holders, Maija Soderholm, sums up how he structured his training:

> Many Martial Arts to a greater or lesser extent have some kind of "flow training" as part of their system. Flowing with a partner builds sensitivity and generally acts as a segue between practicing static techniques and free sparring. . . The Visayan Style Corto Kadena and Larga Mano Eskrima of Sonny Umpad uses flow as its core training method (actually this was not so at the beginning of Sonny's teaching career, but certainly so for about the last decade) but unlike other martial arts, Sonny did not see it as a follow up to static drills and technique practice, he saw it as the foundation onto which all skills were mounted.

> He believed that it was more efficient to teach the movement and chaos first and insert everything else into it, than the other way around . . . The other key factor in his method was randomness, which was not just important but absolutely necessary for the flow to make sense.

> He believed that you can't learn about chaos if you know what is going to happen next. He said, "If I know what you are going to do and where you are going to be next, I can beat you no problem!" So the idea of setting this up in partner practice seemed ridiculous to him and held little value.

> He also disliked preset striking or blocking patterns. In his opinion preset patterns had inherent glitches or gaps that made them hard to insert into the chaos of an unchoreographed encounter. Default "Oh Shit" combinations could be useful, but

a fixation with patterns he believed was counter to learning to adapt in the moment.

He believed the biggest question to answer, bigger than: "What do I do when I get there?" (techniques, he believed were secondary to the movement) was: "How do I get to the right place, with time to do what I need to and get away clean?" (remembering of course that there is a very small margin of error when edged weapons come into play.) So that's what Random Flow training is for.[11]

Neither Soderholm nor Umpad uses the language of open skills, contextual interference, parameterization, or any of the other terms that we've been working with, but the principles are the same. You can't train for a constantly changing environment by controlling your practice conditions. Decision-making and adaptation beat pure technical execution. Fixed motor programs are not as useful as generalized ones that can be adapted on the fly to suit what's happening right now.

The specific training method you choose or the language you use to describe it aren't anywhere near as important as the conditions your methods create. Are your students simply refining a favourite technique until they can do it perfectly, or are they working out its parameters and limits against a range of targets and in a range of contexts? How hard are they working to understand when and how to take action? How often do they have to pull a new motor program from memory, or tweak the one they're using? How well does the environment they're training in reflect the one they're training for? How often are they screwing up?

The relationship between in-practice error and later success isn't an inverse one—someone who fails every time in practice isn't going to succeed every time in an earnest fight. But the training methods that give our students the best odds of success have a pretty high risk of in-practice failure built in. Students have to be allowed to fail, and fail often, for us to be able to even attempt better methods.

---

11 Maija Soderholm, "Random Flow and Why," *His Dark Side* (blog), March 8, 2011, accessed March 27, 2018, https://darkwingchun.wordpress.com/2011/03/08/random-flow-and-why-by-maija-soderholm.

And that means that we have to let go of the myth that perfect practice makes perfect. A student who "practises perfectly" by avoiding in-practice errors has optimized for performing really well in the practice environment. If that environment has in turn been controlled and structured to facilitate success, it's going to bear very little resemblance to the "real world" context that martial arts and self-defence training are supposed to prepare us for.

In his seminal book *Meditations on Violence: A Comparison of Martial Arts Training and Real World Violence*, author and teacher Rory Miller gives us an extreme example of how this can turn out. He describes a martial arts teacher who was an absolute master under very specific circumstances:

> If someone rushed him from at least two long paces away and flinched past their own point of balance, his techniques would work. Otherwise, not so well. They didn't work, generally, on the other instructors there, and he had brought his own students so that he could demonstrate successfully. I don't think this was conscious . . . I don't think for a second that he realized that he had taught his student to flinch in a certain way so that the techniques would work.[12]

The instructor's undoing wasn't lack of skill, dedication, or even knowledge, but a fear of failure. He chose not to acknowledge circumstances where his techniques wouldn't work (such as any case where someone was closer than two paces away), and eliminated them from his training repertoire. I'd bet that his senior students' success rate in practice was very close to 100 percent, for all the good it ultimately did them.

Now, most of us wouldn't over-manage our students' training environment to that extent. We recognize that different tactics are needed for different contexts, and that our opponent won't always obligingly give us the exact set-up we need to pull off our favourite technique. So we build a pool of tactics that cover a broader range of situations and add counters and counter-counters into our drilling.

---

12 Rory Miller, *Meditations on Violence: A Comparison of Martial Arts Training and Real World Violence* (Boston: YMAA Publication Center, 2008), 11–12.

And hey, maybe we mix up our training structure a little to shift away from the comfort of blocked practice and use random and variable practice to build up our students' capacity for recall and adaptation. Error rates go up a bit, but we know why that's happening, and we can tolerate it if it means that we're going to see fewer errors when it really counts. We can accept that guarding against the greater evil of failure under pressure requires letting in a bit of failure during training.

But maybe it all feels kind of inefficient, with only seven of every ten attempts our students make counting toward learning to do it right. Or worse, five or six out of ten. Surely it wouldn't be too bad to nudge that number upward just a bit? They only get so many hours of training in a week, after all, and students get demoralized when so much of their time is spent on things that don't work or matter.

If we view failure purely as a necessary evil, or an undesirable by-product of certain (admittedly good) teaching practices, it can still be difficult to accept how much of a given training session is spent watching our students get things wrong.

Failure and Problem-Solving

Luckily, failure is enormously valuable in itself. Mistakes provide just as much information and feedback as successes do, if not more. Physiologist N. I. Bernstein, who is best known for his work on the neurological basis of learning, frames things this way:

> The process of practice towards the achievement of new motor habits essentially consists in the gradual success of a search for optimal motor solutions to the appropriate problems. Because of this, practice, when properly undertaken, does not consist in repeating the means of solution of a motor problem time after time, but the process of solving this problem again and again.[13]

---

13 N. A. Bernstein, *The Co-ordination and Regulation of Movements* (Oxford, NY: Pergamon Press, 1967), 134.

Mistakes tell us which solutions don't work. They point us toward the holes in our reasoning and the flaws in our movement, and show us what needs to be fixed in order to solve our problem.

What happens when a student makes a mistake? In Bernstein's terms, they've tried an imperfect solution to the problem they're solving. Maybe they moved too early or too late, or they overshot their intended target position. Maybe they chose the wrong motor pattern and threw the wrong strike or block. Maybe they chose the right action at the right time but executed it with poor mechanics, or from a bad position.

The beauty of working in an adversarial context like fighting is that they'll know right away that they got it wrong, because their opponent will use that error against them. If your block is too weak or too late, you get hit. If you perform your parry with the wrong part of your blade, or at the wrong angle, you get hit. If you throw your strike poorly, at best you miss or hit with a disappointing amount of force; at worst, you get hit in return. Confirmation that you've made a mistake is immediate and unambiguous.

From a problem solving perspective, this is wonderful. Fighters don't have to wait months to see if an experiment of theirs has panned out, or if it will have unforeseen consequences. They either hit without being hit back, or they don't. In the martial arts world, long-term planning is measured in seconds or maybe minutes (if we're working over an entire match), not the days, months, or even years that are common in business and science. Every training mistake brings us closer to Bernstein's optimal solution.

One way to think about practice, then, is in terms of experiment design. Our training space isn't all that different from a research laboratory, in that we use it to study violence in a controlled environment that takes away some of the risks and challenges of field work. A scientist who's looking to solve a specific problem starts by isolating that problem and re-creating its conditions as precisely as possible in the lab.

They build a model of the tiny slice of reality that they're studying, and then measure, poke, prod, and interact with it in ways that teach them as much as possible about how it works. Our drills serve the same purpose. They isolate a particular interaction between fighters, or between fighter and environment, and let us poke and study it from as many angles as we want. And since this is fighting we're studying, the problem we're usually trying to solve is figuring out which techniques and tactics are successful in that particular interaction and which ones aren't.

For example, let's say that we want a wrestling student to learn how to perform a single-leg takedown from standing. We could have them watch a perfect demonstration multiple times and then talk them through the motion step by step. Or we could give them a quick demo so that they understand what they're trying to achieve, and then have them try the takedown against a partner who will respond naturally to whatever they do.

So what happens when they're left to experiment? Maybe the first time they drop too slowly, and their partner is able to counter with a sprawl. The second time, they drop at the wrong angle and run their face into their opponent's knee. The third time, they drop onto their rear knee instead of their lead knee, and don't have the forward momentum to complete the takedown. The fourth time, they time it right, angle it correctly, and drive off their lead knee to bring their opponent to the ground.

Four attempts; only one success. But each failure teaches them about a key component of the successful attempt. Over a span of less than a minute, they will have learned about the timing, angulation, and footwork needed to pull off a good takedown. Not only that, but they'll have learned what getting it wrong three different ways feels like, and what getting it right feels like.

Their simple experiment has turned up a lot of data. They can use that data to guide every future attempt and parameterize their motor program in order to get things right consistently. If they'd gotten everything right on the first go, or been laboriously talked through every attempt so that error was impossible, they'd miss out on both the problem-solving process and on gathering the information they need to calibrate on their own later.

One of the key uses of failure, then, is developing an internal sense of what effective and ineffective actions feel like, so that you can tell in the moment if you need to adjust what you're doing. Being able to quickly identify good and bad movement requires a lot of experience with both.

Heavy bags are good teachers precisely because they provide so much feedback on hit quality. Work on one long enough, and you can recognize a perfect strike by the sound it makes, and the feel of the bag's impact against your skin. The only way to get there, though, is to throw hundreds of imperfect strikes.

The more information we have on what doesn't work, the better we become at homing in on what does. The moment when everything falls into place and an action "clicks" is an incredibly powerful training incentive, and it only exists in contrast to all of the mistakes that preceded it. This is particularly true when getting things wrong is uncomfortable or painful and success feels good. Our students will gravitate toward the good feeling that success provides and measure it against the pain of failure.

Of course, without the right guidance, there's a risk in this as well: unpleasant feedback like pain is just as effective as instructor intervention at building a strong aversion to error. To really reap the learning benefits of failure, we need to teach our students how to think about their mistakes and understand how they happened, rather than just avoiding them because they feel bad. It takes discipline to get hit in the face and think, "Interesting. I wonder why that happened?" rather than, "Ow! I never want to feel that again!" This reflective attitude that views pain and failure as a teacher rather than a threat is also a key component of psychological resilience.

In fields like business and writing, it's become commonplace to recognize that the most successful people have failed spectacularly in the past, and that their willingness to learn from failure and face it again is a major component of their success. Bill Gates regularly gives inspirational talks about how many times Microsoft failed before it became a juggernaut. The startup world has embraced this idea so aggressively that there's an international conference devoted entirely to failure and what it can teach, called FailCon, that's hosted dozens of worldwide events since 2009. Its tagline is "Embrace your mistakes. Build your success."[14]

In 2008, bestselling author J. K. Rowling gave a widely quoted commencement address at Harvard that covered this idea at length:

> So why do I talk about the benefits of failure? Simply because failure meant a stripping away of the inessential. I stopped pretending to myself that I was anything other than what I was, and began to direct all my energy into finishing the only work that mattered to me. Had I really succeeded at anything else, I might never have found the determination to succeed in the one arena I believed I truly belonged. I was set free, because my greatest fear had been realised, and I was still alive, and I still had a daughter whom I adored, and I had an old typewriter and a big idea. And so rock bottom became the solid foundation on which I rebuilt my life.
>
> . . .
>
> Failure gave me an inner security that I had never attained by passing examinations. Failure taught me things about myself that I could have learned no other way. I discovered that I had a strong will, and more discipline than I had suspected; I also found out that I had friends whose value was truly above the price of rubies.
>
> The knowledge that you have emerged wiser and stronger from setbacks means that you are, ever after, secure in your ability to survive. You will never truly know yourself, or the strength of your relationships, until both have been tested by adversity. Such knowledge is a true gift, for all that it is painfully won, and it has been worth more than any qualification I ever earned.[15]

---

14 "About," Failcon, accessed Mar 28, 2018, http://thefailcon.com/about.html.

15 J. K. Rowling, "The Fringe Benefits of Failure, and the Importance of Imagination," *Harvard Magazine*, June 5, 2008, accessed Mar 28, 2018, https://harvardmagazine.com/2008/06/the-fringe-benefits-failure-the-importance-imagination.

Failure has an enormous ability to toughen us. It shows us who we are and what we are capable of under pressure. It provides a bedrock assurance of our own ability to survive. It builds resilience. Those who have never failed have no proof of their capability under the worst kind of pressure, and the fear that they might not make it through can be paralyzing. Uncertainty makes us freeze.

That paralysis is bad enough in a career or business context, where it might keep you from doing what you really love or from financial success. In a fight, it can be deadly. While recreational students who aren't familiar or comfortable with failure may simply choose not to spar or compete, a person placed in a self-defence situation who can't take action out of fear of failure is only going to get themselves hurt.

Even if our failure-averse student works up to stepping into the ring or fighting back against an attacker, they're still stuck with the problem of unfamiliarity. No good instructor would willingly send someone who's never been punched into a boxing match. We instinctively know that it would go very badly, as would sending someone who's never been thrown into a judo match, or asking someone who's never been shouted at to break up a bar fight. With no experience of what it's like to be on the sharp end of the techniques and circumstances they'll be facing, our hypothetical student is most likely going to freeze while their brain tries to sort through all of the new data flooding it under stress.

The same is true of students who don't know what it's like to screw up and have to keep going. If a fencer has been taught to expect a given technique to work every time they execute it, what's going to happen when they throw it in a match and it's countered in a way they've never seen? If a self-defence student has only practised disarming a compliant opponent, what's going to happen when they meet with resistance from an earnest attacker?

The fighter who's used to getting things wrong and figuring out how to survive anyway is always going to have an advantage over the one who hasn't been taught what to do when they mess up. The one who's avoided failure or responded to it by stopping the drill and resetting so that they can do it right is going to have a hell of a time recovering from that first misstep.

All too often, we let our students believe that a single mistake is deadly, when the truth is that it's a rare fight that hangs entirely on the first successful strike. In competition and sparring, taking a few hits from an opponent can give us vital information about their timing, tactics, and movement habits that may turn the tide of the match down the line. In an earnest fight, being able to eat a few nonlethal shots on the way in to a takedown or counter can make the difference between fighting back effectively and being overwhelmed. Even in truly deadly encounters where weapons are involved, survival often hinges on being able to get through the first hit and keep fighting anyway.

Most survivors of knife attacks get stabbed or cut at least once, and many of them are hit considerably more than that.[16] Over the last four years, I've assisted with in-service training for people working in dangerous professions where stabbing attempts are not uncommon. The first thing we teach them is how to recognize that they've been attacked with a knife. The reality is that you often don't see the weapon coming, and the first hit can feel more like an ineffectual punch than a potentially lethal wound. The clearest giveaway is multiple, rapid hits to the same target.

In training, we often don't let students react until they've been stabbed several times, because that's how things usually happen in real knife attacks. If getting hit is "failing," then they've failed three to five times before they can even register what's happening. We need to train them to use the information from that failure to guide their next actions ("That crappy punch has landed in the same place five times . . . Oh shit, I'm being stabbed! Time to hit them hard and create some distance!") and to keep fighting even if they've already been hit.

---

16 For example, a 2005 study of 158 stabbing survivors found a total of 663 stab and cut injuries across the victim pool. Average hit rates were 3.7 stabs/ cuts per male victim, and 6.4 stabs/cuts per female victim. Ulrike Schmidt and Stefan Pollak, "Sharp Force Injuries in Clinical Forensic Medicine—Findings in Victims and Perpetrators," *Forensic Science International* 159 (2006): 114–115.

One student survived a stabbing a few weeks after going through his in-service training. While attempting to restrain a suspected thief, he was stabbed multiple times in the face and neck before he was able to grab his own weapon and disable his attacker. When he spoke to one of the trainers I work with a couple of months after the incident, he confirmed that he only realised what was happening because of the way he'd been taught to respond to repetitive light "punches," and fought through just like he'd done in practice. If he hadn't learned to use the data from being hit to inform his actions or—worse—if he'd given up or frozen as soon as he realized he'd been stabbed, he would have died.

The story of his survival gives us a great model for how truly tough and resilient fighters behave. They are adaptable and can change tactics quickly to adjust to a changing situation (e.g., switching from trying to restrain someone to using a weapon against them); they can work through mistakes and use them to gather information and adapt tactics (e.g., noting the pattern of stab hits to identify that a weapon was present); they don't give up after the first failure; and they don't freeze under pressure.

Most importantly, they trust their own decisions and abilities. Our student didn't wait for external confirmation that his attacker had a weapon; he relied on his own experience, his internal sense of what was happening, and the problem-solving skills he'd developed in training to identify the threat and act decisively. He not only knew what to do, but also understood when and why to do it. These are the qualities that we need to nurture in all of our students, and they can be integrated with any body of techniques or training system in existence.

It starts with letting our students make mistakes. Mistakes happen naturally if we're building the cognitive and decision-making components of their skill set, along with the physical component. Mistakes teach students what getting hit feels like, what being surprised feels like, and what it's like to be off-balance and at a disadvantage in a fight. They give them the opportunity to push through and recover from those things. They teach students that they can survive even serious pain and harm, and that the smaller pains, like a punch to the nose, are not so bad. They teach them how to process information and make decisions without guidance, how to self-assess and self-correct, and how to keep growing in their solo practice and in a fight.

Not only are mistakes inevitable if we're training right, but they're also one of our most powerful teachers. If we want our students to fight well, and to be tough and resilient, we need to change our relationship to failure in training. We need to make room for mistakes to happen, and leverage those mistakes into learning opportunities. We need to let go of the notion of the perfect strike, or the perfect play, or the perfect action, and recognize that the teaching methods we use to achieve them may actually stunt our students' growth. We need to push them to change tactics quickly, parameterize their movements to adapt to new circumstances, and try new things that may or may not work.

So how does this look in practical terms? The thing about failure-averse training is that it's easy to structure and to manage. Heavily controlled environments are safe, and repetitive actions are easy to monitor and give feedback on. Issues are easy to spot because you just have to look out for the person who's not moving like everybody else, or who has deviated from the plan. Embracing failure means letting a little bit of chaos into the classroom, and that requires new strategies for keeping students safe and for maintaining discipline and our ability to coach effectively.

I've already suggested that we can approach drills as experiments rather than models of correct action. The rest of this book provides the framework for making those experiments as safe and useful as possible: policies and classroom strategies that create a functional and effective lab environment; a detailed breakdown of how to design and perform the most dangerous and complex type of experiment, the stress test; and a closer look at how to make sure that students with a range of backgrounds and learning styles get the most out of their training time. Let's get started.

Every failure—every mistake—has a cost. It might be large or small, but it's always there. In martial arts, the costs of failure are threefold: there's a physical cost that ranges from minor discomfort to serious injury or even death; a psychological cost ranging from a bruised ego to long-term trauma; and the social cost of being judged or excluded.

To integrate failure into a functioning classroom, we need to be able to address all three of these costs and either bring them within an acceptable range or eliminate them altogether. And to do that, we need to recognize that not all students bear those costs equally.

Understanding Risk

It's easiest to see with physical costs. If you put a 100-pound woman and a 250-pound man in the ring together, the woman will pay a much heavier price for every error. Whenever she gets hit, she's risking severe injury. It's possible for her to badly damage her opponent, sure, but he'll be able to brush off many more of her strikes than she can his. In a boxing match, he could get knocked out if her power generation and targeting were perfect, but otherwise he'd be fine. She, on the other hand, would be looking at a very high chance of concussion, and decent odds of a broken bone or three.

This disparity in risk is big enough that every boxing association has weight classes, and most instructors will only allow friendly sparring between opponents that mismatched under tightly controlled circumstances.

It's pretty universally understood that smaller, weaker fighters pay a heavier physical cost than larger, stronger ones in a mixed group.[1] But outside of the strict weight class boundaries of competition, it's not really necessary or practical to segregate students by size (and it can be actively counterproductive in contexts like self-defence, where very few real-world matchups are symmetrical).

So we need tools that allow students with dramatically different injury risk profiles to train together safely. This means addressing not only size disparities, but also pre-existing injuries and other health-related risk factors.

What about psychological costs? Most of us quite rightly don't worry too much about bruising egos, and many instructors see it as a benefit, rather than a cost, of training. What we absolutely do have to worry about is the risk of inflicting long-term psychological harm. It's been well established in psychiatry that anyone can be traumatized by witnessing or participating in a violent encounter.[2] For this reason, as much as to avoid bodily harm, we put hard limits on things like targeting and level of contact in order to separate in-class drilling and sparring from what most people consider "real violence."

Even then, though, a controlled, physically safe drill can still be psychologically risky for someone who has experienced serious trauma in the past. Conditions like post-traumatic stress disorder (PTSD) leave many people susceptible to intense, debilitating psychological reactions if they encounter a trigger.[3]

---

1 For more on the specific physiological differences between men and women and the degree to which they contribute to physical risk, see page 143.

2 For more on psychological trauma, including post-traumatic stress disorder and less severe trauma-related symptoms, see "Dealing with Psychological Trauma" on page 163.

3 In the context of trauma-related conditions, a "trigger" is any stimulus that reminds the subject of their trauma (consciously or unconsciously) and causes them to experience intrusive memories, flashbacks, or an intense and

While triggers can be anything that reminds a person of their trauma—including colours, smells, tastes, places, or phrases that are otherwise innocuous—and are thus very difficult to account for entirely, there are a lot of habitual actions that happen in fighting that are likely to be triggers for those who have experienced violence. Being grabbed. Being pinned. Having a hand placed across one's mouth or throat. Being struck, especially by someone who is shouting or visibly angry. If these come up in the course of training, they can be enormously upsetting to an unprepared student.

A student with trauma-related triggers is at greater risk for certain kinds of harm in the course of their training, just as a smaller or weaker student is at greater physical risk in a mixed group. That's not a personal shortcoming, but a reality of differing risk profiles that needs to be accounted for when managing the training environment.

Social costs can be the trickiest to figure out. At first glance, an environment that punishes failure by mocking or excluding those who don't perform to its standards seems like a meritocracy—if an unkind one. It's the same with communities where jokes about students' gender, ethnicity, sexual orientation, age, etc. fly around indiscriminately, and so target everyone equally. In both cases, the treatment itself may be equal, but it will impact different students differently depending on their risk profiles.

For example, stereotype threat is a well-documented phenomenon.[4] The way it works is pretty simple: when someone is targeted by a negative stereotype while they're performing a skill-based task, their per-

---

distressing emotional reaction. Glenn Schiraldi, *The Post-Traumatic Stress Disorder Sourcebook: A Guide to Healing, Recovery, and Growth*, 2nd ed. (New York: McGraw-Hill, 2016), 24.

4 The original study that identified stereotype threat has recently been called into question as part of the psychological field's so-called "replication crisis." Specifically, it's become clear that the study's claim that stereotype threat is solely responsible for performance differences between white and black students was not actually supported by the data. Despite the discrediting of this conclusion, many follow-up studies have confirmed that stereotype threat does exist, and is one of many factors that can affect performance, though the size of its impact varies.

formance drops. In sports, one of the most prevalent and enduring stereotypes is that women are less skilled and less well suited to sport than men. It's so pervasive, in fact, that multiple studies have confirmed that simply drawing attention to a woman's gender before a test of athletic skill is enough to trigger these negative associations and affect her performance across sports as diverse as soccer, golf, and tennis.[5]

This effect is worse in environments that also actively perpetuate negative stereotypes by dismissing women as weak, or joking about "hitting like a girl" or "throwing like a girl." If you make the same "girl" joke to a male and a female student, it's going to have different impacts on performance and learning ability as a result of stereotype threat.

Now this doesn't mean that it's impossible to acknowledge that men and women are different, or to draw any attention whatsoever to gender (or any other identity characteristic that tends to come with negative athletic stereotypes, such as homosexuality, or many ethnic, religious, and social backgrounds).

In field studies, the implicit stereotype threat of drawing attention to an identity has been countered by also invoking another, positive identity such as "team member."[6] In lay terms, passive negative stereotypes sting less if they're paired with a sense of belonging and social safety. On the other hand, actively singling people out for who they are in an overtly negative way that separates them from their peer group will make them perform worse.

Beyond performance dips as a result of stereotype threat, there's the more pressing issue of attrition when people consistently pay too high a social cost. Being targeted for harassment, mockery, or discrimination is just plain unpleasant, and few people are interested in spending their leisure time in an environment where they feel like outsiders. This same social exclusion can happen through more subtle means than overt bullying.

---

5 Sarah E. Martiny and others, "Dealing with Negative Stereotypes in Sports: The Role of Cognitive Anxiety When Multiple Identities Are Activated in Sensorimotor Tasks," *Journal of Sport & Exercise Physiology* 37 (2015): 380.

6 Martiny and others, "Dealing with Negative Stereotypes in Sports," 384–385.

In my time teaching, I've encountered two general categories that students fall into in terms of their training motivation and goals. I call them competitive learners and collaborative learners:

Competitive learners are primarily motivated by measuring their performance against that of their peers. They usually . . .

- need frequent opportunities to test themselves against peers both formally (e.g., tournaments or examinations) and informally (e.g., sparring);

- are comfortable in clear hierarchies, and use the goal-setting framework of advancing in rank or competition standings to guide their training.

- need a community that gives them opportunities for testing and challenge, and that provides motivation in the form of role models and close competitors;

- contribute to their community through performance (bringing home medals, representing their school at events, etc.);

- fear stagnation and loss of standing.

Collaborative learners are primarily motivated by a sense of belonging to a community that shares a goal or ethos. They usually . . .

- need to balance the drive toward technical or fitness progress with fun, social interaction, and the freedom to live a full life outside of training;

- find hierarchies threatening or demotivating, because they create an expectation of linear progress that doesn't match the student's own goals;

- need a community to provide social support, an emotional connection to their training, and the safety to try new things;

- contribute to their community through social acts (e.g., volunteering at events, cheering on peers, bringing food to share);

- fear exclusion and excessive pressure to perform.

The majority of martial arts spaces are designed to cater almost exclusively to competitive learners. Because many of the things that actively motivate competitive learners can trigger a fear of failure in collaborative learners, they're far more likely to stagnate or drop off in the early stages of their training. This has nothing to do with their drive or potential for success, and everything to do with their learning environment.

If performance is the only path to belonging, and if nonstandard progress or a lack of competitive drive is mocked or punished, they're not going to last long. They're not being pushed out for being female, or queer, or members of an ethnic minority, but rather for not having the same drives and learning needs as the dominant social group. The net effect is the same: those who don't feel like they belong don't stick around unless they are exceptional.

So we've now got a heuristic for students who are likely to pay the highest costs for failure in a fighting context: they're physically smaller or more vulnerable; they have a history of psychological trauma; and they have socially oriented learning styles and/or a history of being targeted by negative stereotypes about their suitability for fighting or athletic performance.

It's worth noting that this risk profile also sounds an awful lot like a description of the kind of student who is the most likely to benefit from martial arts training and has the greatest need for good self-defence skills.

If we want to take vulnerable people and make them stronger and more capable, we have to take care not to break them or drive them away in the process of causing that transformation. And that means making sure that our training structure and environment takes into account their higher risk profiles. We cannot eliminate all risk, and we shouldn't try to, but we need to be aware of the specific challenges that our most vulnerable students face, and plan accordingly.

So how do we recognize these varying risk profiles in a way that supports vulnerable students without making the training space sterile or needlessly artificial? One of my favourite frameworks for thinking about this is Rory Miller's oft-quoted progression for self-defence training:

> First, you must make an emotionally safe place to practice physically dangerous things. And then you must make a physically safe place to do emotionally dangerous things.[7]

This framing recognizes that physical and emotional danger are inherent to our training (we can treat social danger and psychological danger as sub-classes of emotional danger), that they both matter, and that they both need to be addressed for effective learning to happen. The order is also critical: if emotional safety isn't established first, then none of the other really important stuff can happen.

Most instructors are very good at the second half of the equation. We intuitively get that we need to manage the potential physical consequences of the scary stuff. Being hit is emotionally dangerous. It can be terrifying for people who've never experienced it or, worse, who've experienced it only in the context of interpersonal violence or abuse.

Hitting others is scary too. It's one of our biggest social taboos, and many of our students will come to class having never hit another human being and having been taught their whole lives that they should never, ever do so. Coming up against those ingrained boundaries can be extraordinarily difficult, and instructors often spend many, many hours carefully helping students renegotiate their relationship with violence so that they can be okay with hitting and being hit. Very often, our primary tool for doing this is reducing the perceived physical risk.

---

7 Rory Miller, "The Progression," *Chiron* (blog), February 10, 2014, accessed March 28, 2018, http://chirontraining.blogspot.ca/2014/02/the-progression.html.

We can use plastic or wooden weapon simulators; we can scale back force or speed; we can avoid or protect vulnerable targets like the eyes; we can add padding to bodies for impact arts, and flexibility to blades.

Along with managing legal liability, these precautions are designed to mitigate our students' fear of harm so that they can engage in higher levels of contact and more emotionally dangerous activities like sparring and stress testing.[8] Students who are scared of hurting others feel reassured that they probably won't actually harm their target, and can get comfortable with contact. Students who are scared of being hit can experience impact without debilitating pain or long-term consequences, and discover a context in which getting hit isn't the end of the world.

Even for students who aren't negotiating difficult psychological barriers, physical safety facilitates learning. It's pretty obvious that a student who's rightfully scared of having their arm broken in a drill isn't going to have the mental focus or learning capacity to absorb the lesson that drill is meant to teach (unless it happens to be "Having your arm broken is bad"). If they're preoccupied with their own safety, they can't learn. At best, they'll be distracted and will miss out on bits of critical instruction or be too tense to execute skills with flow and finesse. At worst, they'll panic and flinch, and injure themselves or their partner in the process.

Taking visible steps to mitigate physical risk helps to manage that fear and lets students focus all of their energy on learning and technical execution. Everybody wins, and the overwhelming majority of instructors have no difficulty understanding why or how this works.

Unfortunately, many of us get this while skipping entirely over the first step of Miller's progression: making an emotionally safe place. Padding and mats notwithstanding, a lot of what we do is still physically dangerous, and the only way to manage its risks is through self-control. Sword

---

8 The fact that these safety precautions make students more likely to engage in higher-risk behaviour means that they're not actually reducing overall physical risk (since not sparring at all is still safer than sparring with protection). What's important here is the effect they have on the students' perception of risk, and thus their willingness to participate in the full range of activities that go along with their training.

thrusts to the head need to be controlled to prevent brain injuries that few fencing helmets can mitigate. Joint locks can easily turn into breaks if they're taken too far. Some throws will break your partner's neck if they're completed at speed, and some targets—like knees and eyes—are so vulnerable that any action targeting them has to be reduced in power or retargeted to avoid crippling damage. When our students practise these techniques, they place an enormous amount of trust in their training partners, and being paired with someone who doesn't reward that trust can end horribly.

Bullying and harassment make it next to impossible for that level of trust to build between students, and can erode it where it's already been established. If a female student is worried about whether the guy she's partnered with is going to hit on her again, or "accidentally" grab her breast, she can't trust him. If an Asian student feels like he has to prove he's not a bookish stereotype or has to put up with constant shitty kung fu jokes, not only will he be affected by stereotype threat, but his relationship with his training partners is going to be compromised. If a queer student is anxious about how their classmates will react when their spouse comes to pick them up after class, or a transgender student is worrying they'll be called out for using the "wrong" bathroom or referred to with the wrong gender, they're stuck in a constant loop of having to assess whether they can trust their training partners for reasons that have nothing to do with their training.

The background noise of harassment and discrimination strips these students of the psychological safety they need to be able to learn, and they're just as vulnerable and distracted as the unpadded student worrying about getting a broken arm in an unsafe drill.

By explicitly prohibiting harassment, discrimination, and bullying in my school, I cut out that background noise. Codes of conduct and so-called "safe space" policies are often treated as inherently political (and absolutely can be deployed as political tools), but this doesn't have to be the case. A simple, clear, and enforceable code of conduct is just another piece of safety equipment that ensures that all of your students can train on an equal footing, with as little distraction as possible.

Creating psychological safety isn't about policing people's privately held opinions or beliefs, but about setting norms of conduct that make it easier for everybody to trust their training partners.

I've been told that anti-harassment policies introduce "distracting" politics into the neutral space of the training floor, but I'd argue instead that their existence is what creates neutrality in the first place. Nobody operates in a political vacuum, and spaces that are usually considered apolitical are just ones that reflect the political and social mores of the surrounding culture. If everyone coming into your space were coming from the same social background—same country, same neighbourhood, same socioeconomic class, same religious context, etc.—then you wouldn't need to explicitly lay out ground rules because everyone would have been raised with and would buy into the same rules already. "Don't be a dick" might suffice, because everyone would agree on what constitutes "being a dick."

In a pluralistic space, though, you can't assume that's the case. Being clear about what is and isn't acceptable puts everyone on the same footing. For example, the general political makeup of my school skews toward the left—as you'd expect in an urban community on Canada's west coast—but our student and instructor population runs the gamut from traditionally conservative Christians to polyamorous socialist atheists. We don't all agree on economic or social policy, or have the same perspective on current events, but we are all on the same page when it comes to how we treat each other because we're all following the same rules.

Without clear rules of conduct, students who were coming from further right than the leaders of the school would be forced to navigate the social assumptions and culture of an unfamiliar group, and would run the risk of being penalized for crossing lines they didn't even know existed. A code of conduct does just as much to protect them as it does anyone else.

Similarly, there's nothing weak or coddling about keeping that stuff off the floor. The argument that prohibiting slurs or sexual comments leaves students unprepared for encountering those things in the "real world" assumes that they're not otherwise exposed to them. That's impossible. A woman who needs to know how to deal with catcalling, or a Muslim needing to deal with Islamophobia, or a gay man needing to deal with homophobic abuse hears that stuff all the time. It's omnipresent, and excluding it from a place where they spend a couple of hours a week won't put a dent in their real-world exposure.[9] It does give them a break, though, and an opportunity to focus exclusively on their learning.

I've also found that prioritizing psychological safety dramatically increases the amount of physical risk that my students are willing to take on. I've known sparring environments where all bouts were extremely heavily regulated, fighters were so heavily padded that their movement was compromised, and people still got hurt regularly because they couldn't trust each other to exercise self-control, or take responsibility for each other's safety.

In my school, students routinely engage in unarmoured, controlled free play with steel weapons and walk away unscathed. Partners with weight differences of over a hundred pounds get into grappling matches that incorporate strikes, joint locks, and other nasty tactics, without anybody being harmed. The primary thing keeping my students safe is each other, and they trust that tool so absolutely that they can do away with many other precautions.

Psychological safety, like physical safety, is a basic cornerstone of running a functioning training space. If we establish it well, we give our students room to push themselves well beyond their initial limits. Far from making them weaker or less resilient, it gives them room to stretch their wings and test their true strength. Rules are so much less limiting than fear.

---

9 There's a legitimate argument to be made for deploying these kinds of personal, loaded, trigger terms in very specific training contexts, such as scenarios that simulate real-world targeted attacks or social conflicts. That's different from letting gay jokes casually fly in the middle of your workout, though.

Identifying Problems

Establishing psychological safety for all students is a multistep process: you need public-facing policies like a code of conduct that set expectations for students and communicate your school's rules of engagement to everyone who comes in the door; you need internal policies that govern how your instructors and staff interact with students and resolve disputes or rule violations; and finally, you need to cultivate a culture of trust and mutual responsibility that reinforces your values during training.

Before getting into how to structure governing documents, it's critical to establish what kinds of behaviour they'll be regulating. As instructors, we want to strike a balance between safety and needless encumbrance— you don't want your code of conduct to act like the overly heavy padding that gums up a fighter's ability to move. We need to make sure that any policy we lay down is practical and enforceable from our end.

For this reason, exhaustive lists of prohibited behaviours are generally a bad idea. It can feel productive to put together a big catalogue of the things you don't want students to do, but anything over a page long gets hard to remember and internalize. Worse, trying to be exhaustive can open up loopholes, as a dedicated harasser can look for small gaps in your carefully worded policy and find ways of making others miserable without technically breaking the rules. Instead, you need to build a more general framework that accounts for the categories of behaviour that are the most disruptive to your classes and leaves enough flexibility to address misconduct of varying severity.

That itemized list might still be a good starting point, if only because writing down concrete problem behaviours (that you've encountered in your own school already, seen elsewhere, or had reported to you) gives you a much clearer idea of what you're most concerned about, and what broad terms like "harassment" and "bullying" actually look like in practice.

> ### Exercise: Build a List of Problem Behaviours
>
> Think about what kinds of behaviour would prevent you from going back to a given group or space, or would take a group of students from being fun to work with to being a problem group. What makes you feel uncomfortable and unwelcome? What makes you angry when you see others doing it? What incidents or patterns have preceded a member's departure from a group you've been in? Be as specific as possible.
>
> Once you've got a good number of concrete examples, break them down into categories of behaviour that are roughly equal in severity.

When I write policy, I work with the following classification of problem behaviour:

- **Firing offences:** this is the big, scary stuff. It includes physical violence (whether that's an attack outside of training, or an obvious and one-sided escalation of force in sparring or drills); rape and other sexual assault; stalking; threats; and abuses of power by staff or senior students (e.g., harming or threatening subordinates they don't like, or demanding sexual favours in exchange for advancement or higher-quality instruction).

- **Red flags:** these are behaviours that single out an individual or group for targeted abuse, and are often the precursors to firing offences. These include verbal harassment (especially slurs or stereotypes and unwanted, offensive nicknames); hazing or pranks; sexual comments, harassment, and overt come-ons; and deliberate exclusion from group activities.

- **Background radiation:** this is the low-level behaviour that doesn't quite rise to the level of what many would call bullying or harassment, but which makes training more psy-

chologically costly for some students. It includes things like
the casual use of gendered pejoratives and homophobic
language (e.g., "pussy," "sissy," "like a girl"); routinely getting
trans or nonbinary students' pronouns wrong; treating female students as less serious or competent by default; using
drills and incidental contact as an excuse to let a hand linger
on an attractive training partner for too long; and comments
or jokes about what kinds of people belong—or don't—in the
community.

Every one of these categories of behaviour has a negative impact on the
training environment, but they look and feel different, and need to be
dealt with in different ways. Let's take a closer look at each of them to
work out some of these details.

The one positive feature of firing offences is that none of the behaviours
in this category are ambiguous. Once identified, they require immediate
and decisive action. Most instructors have no trouble seeing this type
of misconduct for what it is, and even schools with no official conduct
policies will take a zero-tolerance stance on many of these behaviours.
They're the most severe and dangerous, but also the easiest to spot and
build policy around.

Firing offences are best dealt with through discipline: you make it clear
that these behaviours are prohibited, set enforceable and appropriate
punishments for perpetrators, and crack down when you see something
or have it reported to you. At my school, the consequences of firing offences are severe. A perpetrator will be removed from the training space
as a matter of course, and will also receive a lifetime ban.

Firing offences are often also criminal offences and are so destructive
to the foundation of trust within a community that there's no compel-
ling reason to allow perpetrators to return.[10] Depending on the nature

---

10 While there is some overlap between criminal offences and firing offences,
it's important to remember that a training space is not a court of law, and that
a criminal conviction or legal standard of evidence shouldn't be necessary for
enforcing discipline. If you believe that a person poses a serious risk to the
safety of your group's members, you have the right to remove them.

of the offence and the wishes of the victim, it's also entirely possible that the police will have to be involved.

Cases this severe are generally rare and a well-managed space may go many years without seeing one. In the six years of Valkyrie WMAA's existence, I've never witnessed a firing offence. I have, however, told a potential student that they were not welcome in our classes after receiving credible reports of a firing offence that they had committed at another school in our area. The risks posed by these behaviours are high enough that they easily outweigh the cost of losing a single student or instructor.

Red flags are often less noticeable than firing offences and may be less severe in their immediate impact; however, even those that don't escalate to worse behaviour are enough to drive targeted individuals out of the school. For students who aren't targeted but who witness red flag behaviours, the training space can become a minefield where they have to actively avoid becoming targets, and must divide their focus between learning and self-preservation. Because of their potential for escalation and the degree to which they poison the community, red flags need to be dealt with as decisively as firing offences.

The first priority is still to interrupt the abusive behaviour and ensure the safety of any victims, and that generally means immediately removing the perpetrator from the space. An unrepentant perpetrator is likely to reoffend or even escalate to firing offences, so a lifetime ban might be in order, but there is also some potential for rehabilitation. If it's clear that someone who's previously engaged in bullying is genuinely repentant and has made a concrete effort to change their behaviour, and if the victim is willing to share a space with them, then they might be able to reintegrate into the community.

In the past two years, I've dealt with two red flag cases, both of which involved low-level sexual harassment. The first perpetrator started by treating our open sparring sessions like dating minglers, flirting with female students, asking them out on dates, and making comments to one student about her breasts. When this behaviour was brought to our attention, we sent him an email identifying the inappropriate behaviour and making it clear that we considered it sexual harassment, and thus a violation of our code of conduct. We told him that he was welcome to continue attending our events if he stopped this behaviour immediately, and that any future offences would get him banned. We also brought his behaviour to the attention of his instructor (he was an outside student who occasionally attended our events and had his own teacher at another organization). After a few months' absence, he apologized to us and to the women he had targeted and changed his behaviour dramatically. Since then he's been an attendee at our events without any problems.

In the second case, the perpetrator was a workshop attendee who used training drills to touch his female training partner inappropriately, and then spent the post-event social hour trying to ply her with alcohol and following her around the space. He likewise received an email restating our policy and identifying his behaviour as harassment.[11] In follow-up discussions of the incident, we also heard stories from women who'd encountered him at other events and confirmed that this was an ongoing pattern of behaviour. He didn't reply to the email and has not tried to make any amends. As a result of this and the follow-up information we received, he isn't welcome at any of our future events.

We had two similar incidents, two similar responses, and two very different outcomes that depended on the perpetrators' willingness to change.

Background radiation is the largest category of unacceptable behaviour and the toughest to define, but it's very important to recognize and address it. On its own, any one of the behaviours I've put in this category may only be worthy of an eye-roll or a slap on the wrist, but taken together, they can quickly turn your school into a space where certain people just never seem to show up or stick around, and where red flags and firing offences are increasingly likely.

---

11 When I've addressed red flags and firing offences, I've communicated with the perpetrators in writing as often as possible. This is especially important when setting conditions for a return to classes or banning someone from returning, as it creates a date-stamped paper trail for the decision. It'll be a lot easier to rely on written records than my memory of a verbal conversation in any future dispute.

Communities with a lot of background radiation often have high turn-over, or they have retention problems with students in targeted groups. It's the first thing to check for if you notice that your school doesn't seem to have a lot of women around, and something that needs to be kept in check if you want a healthy, diverse training community. This doesn't mean that your school needs to be squeaky clean and humourless, but that you do need to make sure that one person's idea of a good time doesn't ruin the training experience for everyone else.

Background radiation behaves a lot like its namesake: it's not really no-ticeable or appreciably harmful in small amounts, or for those who only come into occasional contact with it. If you're exposed to it in the long-term, though, it's a debilitating poison that lets much uglier things—like cancer—take root.

Background radiation is best managed with a combination of discipline and social engineering. Bad behaviour needs to be called out and ad-dressed in a visible manner, and repeat or willful offenders must face consequences. Focusing purely on negative behaviour is an exhausting and thankless task, however, and isn't enough to prevent recurring is-sues on its own. Instead, it's easiest to prevent bad behaviour from aris-ing in the first place by modelling its opposite. If instructors and senior students treat everyone with dignity and respect, you'll spend very little time on formal discipline.

When we were building Valkyrie WMAA, Courtney and I were very aware of the negative experiences many women have with martial arts. We'd both encountered major and minor sexual harassment, dismissal and belittling of our skills and accomplishments, and other gender-specific background radiation. To avoid replicating the same problems in our own space, we started building an environment where they were very unlikely to pop up.

We put two women in charge of the administration of the school and made sure that women always had a voice in crafting policy and build-ing the curriculum. We featured female instructors and students promi-nently in our promotional material and brought in female guest instruc-tors whenever possible. Our male head instructor made sure to treat all of the women around him with respect, and regularly stepped back from the spotlight when there were opportunities for a qualified woman to answer a question, demonstrate a technique, or represent the school publicly.

We all cut gendered pejoratives from our vocabulary and got in the habit of politely correcting each other when one snuck in. We celebrated traditionally "girly" things like glitter and fashion alongside serious skill development and challenging training. We made it clear in every action and word that women and femininity belonged in our space, and would be taken seriously regardless of how well they fit the stereotype of a serious martial artist. We also backed it up with a code of conduct that specifically prohibited sexual harassment and gender-based discrimination.

When we moved the school into its permanent space in 2015, women made up about 30 percent of our active student body. One year later, that number had risen to 47 percent. Today, the proportion of women has grown to just over 50 percent of our active student population, gendered background radiation is almost non-existent, and the two red flag incidents we've dealt with were both perpetrated by nonstudents.

There have been no firing offences, and we've developed an international reputation for being very welcoming to women while maintaining a martially sound mixed-gender facility. We've taken similar approaches to combating background radiation against gay, lesbian, and bisexual students; transgender and nonbinary students; people of colour; and students with low fitness levels and physical disabilities.

Identifying which behaviours we needed to address and what categories they belonged to has given us clarity and direction on how to build the space that we want.

Your list of problem behaviours may end up being different from what we chose to focus on, but the same process of identifying and classifying them will lay the groundwork for any policy development that follows.

Public-Facing Policy

When most of us think of formal behaviour policies, we begin with public-facing documents such as codes of conduct. So what does a code of conduct look like, and how does it work? Some instructors balk at actually publishing their policy for fear that it'll be overly restrictive or leave them open to accusations of misconduct if it's poorly or inconsistently enforced. A good policy does the opposite—it sets reasonable expectations within the student body and creates a framework for discipline that allows instructors to treat everyone fairly with a minimum of additional effort.

There's no good excuse for not having one, and it doesn't have to be complex or overly detailed. Most martial arts and self-defence schools are not large organizations. We have few staff, often maintain tight-knit communities where people know each other well, and don't often deal with big crowds of people all at once. All of this means that we can usually get away with keeping things very simple, and even the most detailed policies seldom go past a single page.

Exercise: Draft a Code of Conduct

Using your list of problem behaviours as a starting point, put together a single-page document that lays out your expectations for student and staff behaviour.

Start with positive examples: what do you want people to do when they're training with you? Lay out how you want them to treat the space, its equipment, and its other users. Finish with a summary of unacceptable behaviours and their consequences and an explanation of how to report violations or issues.

Any policy you write has to have the following features to be enforceable and effective:

- It must clearly identify who it applies to, and in what context. Does it cover just students? Students and staff? All attendees at an event or everyone on your school premises? Does it extend to conduct at outside events such as tournaments where your members represent the organization?

- It must include a way for people it covers to confirm that they've read and agree to abide by it. If you already require visitors to sign a waiver of liability, it's easy to add a line to the waiver that addresses this. An example from our waivers:

  > I further agree to strictly obey instructors and observe safety rules. I have read, and will abide by, the Valkyrie WMAA Training Space Rules.

  For large events where signups are quicker and less formal, you can also have a sign-in sheet next to a copy of the rules that just requires attendees to provide their name and signature as confirmation that they've read and agreed to the posted rules.

- It must clearly identify unacceptable behaviour, and should offer some non-exclusive examples of what that looks like. This is your opportunity to set expectations and clarify any ambiguous areas such as what kind of physical contact is or isn't normal in a training context. If you use terms like "discrimination" or "harassment," you should also clarify the scope of those terms, and what characteristics or groups are protected from discrimination. For example:

  > Anyone who engages in discriminatory or harassing behaviour will be removed from class and may also lose future training privileges. This includes—but is

not limited to—discrimination based on race, gender, gender identity, sexual orientation, ethnic or religious background, and ability; as well as verbal, physical, and sexual harassment.

- It must lay out clear consequences for unacceptable behaviour and should offer a range of responses based on severity (as in the example above). This makes you accountable to victims of misconduct by confirming how and to what extent they will be protected, and ensures that anyone who breaks the rules is treated fairly and has been informed of the consequences of doing so beforehand. The goal is to make enforcement and discipline straightforward and transparent, and reduce how much pushback you or your staff get when you address misconduct.

- It must include a clear chain of communication for reporting misconduct, and that chain must account for the power dynamics of your space. Who can students or staff talk to when things go wrong? How can they do this? Do you have a posted email address or feedback form? Is there an option for anonymous reporting? Does everything funnel through the instructor on duty, or are there alternative paths for filing complaints against staff or event organizers?

- It must be visible and accessible to everyone who needs to read it. Post it on the wall of the school. Link to it from your website or Facebook page. Print it on the back of your waivers.

The most important thing to remember is that a code of conduct is a living document. It can—and should—be revised periodically to make sure that it's doing what we need it to.[12] You're probably not going to get

---

12 This, in turn, means you'll probably need a mechanism for informing current students of updates to the rules. This might include re-posting them publicly and asking students to re-sign their waivers after a revision, or including language in the code of conduct and any signed forms that acknowledges that the rules are subject to change, and that students are

it perfect the first time, and any loopholes, omissions, and weaknesses will make themselves known only after you've put it into use.

I've updated our school rules three times in five years, cleaning out sections it turned out we didn't need, adding ones that were missing, and updating the language to clarify questions that came up over time. They've gotten much stronger over this period, and we've learned important lessons about how to communicate with our students and manage our community in the meantime. That growth has only been possible because we put a policy out there in the first place and allowed it to evolve with experience.

If you'd like to reap the benefits of some of that experience when putting together your own policy, start by reading those used by well-established schools and organizations. You'll want to choose something that you know has had the chance to be enforced and tested. Valkyrie WMAA's policy is posted publicly on our website.

I'd also recommend looking at the policies for large events such as PAX and Emerald City Comic Convention.[13] Gaming and geek conventions used to be notorious for sexual harassment of female attendees in particular and have come under substantial scrutiny in recent years. They've had to develop solid policies under pressure, and have had them tested in an environment that's not easy or straightforward to police. While not everything in them will apply to a small, private business like a martial arts school, they're a great example of policy building and testing and a good place to look for inspiration.

Internal Policy

Your code of conduct is essential to setting realistic expectations for students, staff, and the public, and laying the groundwork for rules enforcement. Internal policy is how you make sure that gets done fairly.

---

responsible for abiding by the most recent version.

13 For links to these policies, see page 242.

These policies are also going to vary a lot more than the public-facing material. Depending on how many staff you have; how frequently you deal with incidents; what levels of force, risk, and contact you use in classes; and how your school is structured, your internal policies may look completely different from those at the dojo down the block.

Exercise: Rough Out Your Internal Policies

Build the basic framework for your internal policies by answering the following key questions:

- How will misconduct be handled?

- How will personal relationships be handled?

- How and to what degree will staff be educated on interpersonal issues?

- What kinds of records will you keep?

Your answers will determine what kinds of documents you create. At minimum, keep a list of your detailed answers in a legible format. In time, these should be fleshed out into more formal policy documents that follow the same rules of clarity and enforceability that apply to your code of conduct.

Each of these questions addresses a different core area of management: discipline, interpersonal relationships, education, and documentation. A policy that addresses all four may not be completely airtight, but it will cover the major domains where issues usually crop up. Let's look more closely at each one.

How Will Misconduct Be Handled?

You've already defined your rules via a code of conduct; this is where you lay out consequences. Take a look at all three categories of offences—firing offences, red flags, and background radiation—and decide how to deal with each type. You'll want a range of possible responses, from expulsion and even criminal charges, right down to a quiet private warning or conversation. Your framework doesn't have to address every possible example of misbehaviour, but it should address each major category and have some procedures for tackling special cases.

Since discipline is where you're most likely to get complaints and pushback, it pays to be specific here. If you can show that an expelled student did something that falls under the definition of a firing offence, and that you have a standard punishment for those types of offences, it's a lot more difficult for them to accuse you of favouritism or unfairness.

Having punishments mapped out in advance also saves you and your staff from having to make judgement calls in the heat of the moment. Conflicts can be emotional and complicated, especially if senior or popular students—or staff—are involved, and it's much easier to navigate them with guidelines that were laid out at a calmer time. The table on page 49 is an example of a reference grid that lays out basic response guidelines for everyone involved in an incident that requires discipline.

Make sure to explicitly address staff and instructor misconduct as well. A public code of conduct binds everyone in an organization, including those in leadership roles, to the same rules of behaviour. However, the impact on the community is often greater when an instructor breaks those rules.

What would be red flag behaviour in a student or event attendee, such as verbal harassment or bullying, might be a firing offence if it comes from an instructor because of its disproportionate impact on the target and the classroom environment. Your disciplinary model needs to account for the power difference between instructors and students. We often hold our leaders to higher standards than other community members, and those standards—as well as the consequences for falling short of them—should be clearly laid out in advance.

	Examples	Immediate Response (any staff on scene)	Additional Follow-Up (management)
Firing Offences	Assault (physical or sexual); abuse of power by staff or senior students; stalking	• Remove perpetrator(s) from class • Provide any necessary medical care to victim(s) and get a written statement of what happened • Report incident to management	• Cancel perpetrator(s)'s membership and inform them in writing that they have been banned • Discuss possibility of pressing criminal charges with victim(s), if relevant • Review incident report and make adjustments to policies, procedures, and staff training, if necessary
Red Flags	Verbal and sexual harassment; hazing or pranks; bullying and deliberate exclusion	• Remove perpetrator(s) from class • Provide any necessary medical care to victim(s) and get a written statement of what happened • Report incident to management	• Based on the severity of the offence and perpetrator(s)'s prior conduct, suspend or permanently ban them and inform them in writing • If the ban is not permanent, work with staff and victim(s) to make a plan for reconciliation and re-integration of the perpetrator(s) • Review incident report and make adjustments to policies, procedures, and staff training, if necessary
Background Radiation	Casual use of slurs and/or stereotypes; inappropriate sexual comments and/or attention; mis-gendering	• Inform perpetrator(s) that their behaviour is inappropriate, and tell them how to correct the issue • Follow up with victim(s) and confirm that the behaviour has been addressed, and provide any immediate assistance required • Report incident to management	• Review perpetrator(s)'s actions and history, and determine if additional discipline is needed • For repeat offenders, escalate to a temporary suspension or permanent ban • Review incident report and make adjustments to policies, procedures, and staff training, if necessary

How Will Personal Relationships Be Handled?

Many small, adult-oriented schools feel more like extended families than professional environments. Even in more formal spaces, personal relationships (whether those are close friendships or romantic/sexual relationships) between staff and students are not uncommon. Instructors' spouses and partners will often join the class as students, and workplace romances aren't unheard of. These can be healthy, or they can be exploitive and harmful to the whole community.

You need to have clear expectations for how these relationships will be handled before they start: should staff members disclose all personal relationships with students? Should instructors teach their own partner, or do couples need to be separated in training?

Are public displays of affection between a staff member and student permitted during classes? What about between two staff members? Two students of different ranks? To what extent—if any—should couples modify their behaviour while at the school? Should certain kinds of relationships be banned outright?

You don't need hard and fast rules for every occasion, but you should have a good handle on the power dynamics and potential pitfalls involved.

You'll also need to think about cases where affection is not reciprocated—from either end. How will you deal with a teacher who pursues unwanted intimacy with a colleague or student? What about students who get a crush or decide that their instructor is their new best friend? These situations can be uncomfortable and even dangerous for the people involved and disruptive to the entire teaching environment.

Unhealthy relationships can be incredibly volatile and have the potential to sink an entire school if they're left to their own devices. Having a plan for dealing with relationship challenges when they first surface will save you a world of trouble down the road.

How, and to What Degree, Will Staff Be Educated on Social and Interpersonal Issues?

Alongside any conflicts that arise on the training floor, your students will bring with them a range of backgrounds and personal challenges. Many people with depression and anxiety use exercise as part of their treatment and as a coping strategy, and their mental health will affect their learning. Some people respond to trauma from violence in their past by taking up self-defence training.

How ready are you to teach students who face these kinds of mental health challenges? What about someone who comes to you for fitness or weight loss training and has a history of eating disorders? What about students who are transgender or nonbinary, especially if they're in the process of transitioning, or have been subject to discrimination and harassment elsewhere in your martial arts community?

We're physical instructors and coaches, not social workers, counsellors, or mental health specialists, and it's important to recognize the limits of our own expertise. At the same time, we need to be able to effectively teach a whole range of students, many of whom will be facing challenges that are well outside of our personal or professional experience. What's your plan for working with them?

What kinds of issues do you feel comfortable dealing with, and where do you need to "refer out" to a specialist? Do you have a basic, 101-level understanding of how PTSD triggers work and what kind of support to provide to someone who's triggered in class? Do you know enough about the social challenges faced by women, LGBT people, or ethnic and religious minorities in your community to be able to make them feel welcome?

If there are gaps in your knowledge, how can you fix them? Whether you prefer to read books, watch videos, take courses, or draw on the experience of people in your social circles, it's good to have an education plan set up in advance.

If you have multiple instructors at your school, this becomes especially important. Plan how you want to assess and fill knowledge gaps that leave your staff ill equipped to teach certain students, and get a good sense of staff strengths in advance. You're likely to have some teachers who are particularly good at working with trauma survivors, or who bond well with insecure beginners, or who have professional and personal backgrounds that make them better suited to taking on certain kinds of teaching challenges. Having that information down on paper gives you an internal referral network that will make it much easier to pair students in need with the right instructor for them.

What Kinds of Records Will You Keep?

If you get hit by a bus tomorrow, will anyone be able to reconstruct your methods and keep the school on its feet? What if someone decides to challenge a disciplinary decision you've made or the way you've handled a personal relationship, either in a public forum or a court of law? We're pretty accustomed to thinking about how to preserve our lesson plans and source texts for posterity, but we need to do the same thing with our administrative material.

One easy way to make sure you're keeping adequate documentation is to send a follow-up email after you've talked to a student or staff member about any matter of discipline. It creates a date-stamped record of the conversation and its contents that you can refer to if there's a conflict down the line, and it also reduces the odds of misunderstanding (or feigned misunderstanding) in the moment. You may want to keep additional records of more serious incidents (e.g., a copy of any police report you file or witness statement you provide) and first aid issues.

This is also a good time to check relevant workplace law for your area. Does your jurisdiction require that you document injuries, first aid incidents, or cases of harassment or discrimination that violate civil or human rights statutes? What about hiring/firing laws? If you have to let an instructor go due to inappropriate behaviour, do you have enough documentation to defend that choice in a labour dispute?

How exactly all of these questions get answered is going to be up to you, but it's critical that you ask them before a bad situation blows up in your face. Internal issues are always stressful—even when the infraction in question is relatively minor—and you don't want to have to come up with your plan of action in the heat of the moment. The more you've thought about how you want to approach common challenges in advance, the faster, smoother, and more consistent you'll be at handling them when they come up.

Policy writing isn't what we got into teaching for, and some of the questions you'll be asking yourself aren't easy or pleasant to think about, but it's essential preparation. Think of this stage as packing your bag for a long trip or choosing your everyday carry tools. It's a bit fiddly and time consuming, but it will save you a world of trouble down the road.

In a teaching context, policy is also the infrastructure that maintains your school environment. If you do it right, you'll cut out a substantial chunk of the stressors and distractions that keep your students from training at their best, and build the sense of safety and belonging they need to really challenge themselves.

Training Culture: Cultivating Self-Reliance

3

Policies are key to setting up a healthy training environment, but they're only the first piece of the puzzle. They let us set the ground rules for how our space will operate, clarify matters of discipline, and create a baseline level of trust within the student body. They're essential infrastructure that guarantees the opportunity for every student to push their limits and develop genuine strength, but they don't do anything to actually encourage or facilitate that pushing. For that, we need culture.

How we conduct ourselves and how we structure our classes reinforces the safety net that will help students thrive, and it also allows us to show them the path toward growth.

I'm going to talk very little about specific drills or class formats here, because those details vary so widely from school to school and from discipline to discipline. What I want to introduce instead is a set of principles that have been present in every good training environment I've ever seen, and some general teaching tactics that leverage those principles to great effect.

At the core of everything in this chapter is trust. It can take multiple forms, from the external trust that students place in their teachers (to keep them safe from serious harm; to teach them things of value; to wield their power responsibly) or their fellow students (to not hurt them deliberately; to share the space and teaching resources so that everyone can learn; to play by the rules), to the internal trust they must place in their own cognitive and physical capabilities in order to succeed.

Trust isn't the same thing as blind obedience or reckless self-confidence because it's rooted in a realistic assessment of the person or thing being trusted. It's active, not passive, and it must be built and maintained through practice.

We build our students' trust in us by effectively managing boundaries and consent; we build their trust in each other by teaching good partnership practices; and we build their trust in themselves by giving them the freedom to opt in and encouraging them to self-regulate.

Consent

Trust is integral to any healthy learning environment, but it's particularly important in martial arts and self-defence because of how central boundary setting and enforcement are to our practice.

In self-defence, this is obvious. One of the first things that almost every women's self-defence course addresses is how to assert yourself against creepy behaviour and low-level violations of personal space with a hard "No!" or "Stop!" When I teach how to deal with dangerous or erratic people, I explain how to draw clear lines in the sand such as, "If you touch me again, I'm leaving," or "Lower your voice, or I'm calling security," in order to assess their willingness to comply and their threat level. I talk about how predators often violate a target's boundaries in subtle ways before progressing to an assault. I teach my students that people who don't respect the boundaries we set, or who don't look for consent before touching us or otherwise crossing social boundaries, are probably dangerous.

In a martial arts context, boundary enforcement is less verbal, but it's still there. We don't tell an attacker that we'll hit them if they get too close, but we do strike the moment they step into range. We routinely put limits on how hard we'll hit each other, what targets we'll hit, and when a fight is considered "over," in order to keep our training partners safe. These limits are enforced by mutual consent. Breaking those rules can get a student kicked out of a competition or class, cost them a training partner, or earn them a stern talking to from their instructor.

Consent and clear boundaries keep our students safe during training, and they are also vital tools for keeping them safe in a real fight.

This means that letting students establish and enforce boundaries has to be integral to training. All too often, I see instructors letting the authority they have over their students blur the line between giving someone a much-needed nudge, and running roughshod over their boundaries and violating their consent.

This can show up in the context of "tests." A student will enter a training fight expecting a certain level of contact, only to face a sudden escalation when their partner draws a weapon, ramps up their speed or impact, or goes for a target that was previously considered out of bounds. The rationale for doing this varies, but it usually involves testing the targeted student's ability to adapt to changing circumstances, and is often justified as being more realistic, since "real fights don't have rules."

Setting aside whether that characterization of real-world violence is actually realistic,[1] springing a surprise like that on a student who hasn't consented to it can irreparably damage their trust. When any of us agree to a fight or training drill, we're coming to it with expectations of how and where we're likely to get hit, and we use those expectations to assess whether or not we want to play. That assessment can be critical to our safety.

For instance, I've got a history of traumatic brain injuries (three concussions on record, and another two suspected) that means I have to be careful about putting myself in situations where I might take a hard hit to the head. I still do it sometimes, but I need to go in prepared and limit my exposure to that specific kind of contact.

A self-defence student of mine had been assaulted by someone who pinned her down with an arm across her throat, and needed to be warned in advance if we were going to be working on chokes or other exercises that put pressure on the trachea. She opted in to some of those drills, and sat out others because she knew that they'd trigger serious psycho-

---

1 It's not. For a detailed discussion of the many kinds of violence and their implicit and explicit rules, see page 97.

logical symptoms that she didn't want to deal with right then. Another student has a bad knee and a very physically demanding job. Leg locks and kicks to the knee are okay some days, and on other days could take him out of work—and a paycheque—for weeks or even months.

If an instructor put any of us in a fight or drill with contact levels we'd agreed to and then changed the rules, they'd be putting us at risk of serious, maybe permanent, harm. Even if the worst didn't happen, they would be communicating to us that they don't care about our safety and that by training with them, we forfeit the right to make informed decisions about what injuries we're willing to risk and how much pain we're willing to suffer. Their actions would show us that they, not we, have final say over what happens to our bodies.

That kind of erosion of bodily autonomy makes it really hard to set effective boundaries, in training or otherwise. If you tell your students not to trust people who violate their boundaries in a conflict, but you set them up to have their boundaries violated in class, you're aligning yourself (or whoever you pit against them in a surprise attack drill) with the very predators they're supposed to distrust.

They'll end up with one of two choices: to take you at your word as an instructor and mentally categorize you as someone who cannot and should not be trusted; or to trust your behaviour over your words, and ignore boundary violations, since they can't be so bad if you do them. Neither response is healthy for the teacher-student relationship, and the second one could put them in serious danger if they're faced with a real-life predator. If you desensitize them to unacceptable behaviour in class, they'll let it slide elsewhere as well.

This means that our students must always have the opportunity to say no to any exercise or drill, and that their choice must be respected. Respect in this case requires not only allowing them to step out or sit and watch, but also treating that as a valid training choice. If we tease them about their reluctance, try to cajole them into changing their minds, or let other students bully them into participating, we're not really letting them set their own boundaries.

Surprise and escalation do have a place in martial arts and self-defence training, and I'm not arguing that you can't run drills or games similar to what I've described above. All you have to do is add consent. If your goal is to have students respond realistically to the introduction of a weapon, for example, you can set it up with an explanation of your goals and a summary of what might happen:

> *Today, I want to test your ability to react to someone pulling a knife in a fistfight. I know you can defend yourself in drills where you see the weapon coming, so it's time to ramp things up.*
>
> *We're going to play a game. You're going to do some sparring with a partner. Punches and kicks are both allowed, and you'll be hitting at about 60 percent of full power. At some point in the fight, your partner might pull a training knife out of their pocket and start stabbing you. If they do, you can escalate to elbows, knee strikes, throws, and locks. Keep the power level south of 80 percent, and stop the fight as soon as you hear anyone call, "Break!" You'll work with three partners in all, and any number of them may or may not pull a knife.*
>
> *If you're ready to play, grab a partner and head out onto the mats. If you'd rather sit this one out, you can have a seat on the bench and watch, or you can help me keep an eye on the fighters and make sure nobody goes off the mats or runs into a wall.*

This description lets your students know exactly what level of impact and risk they'll be dealing with, and allows them to make an informed decision about their participation. It also outlines a clear mechanism for signalling their consent (picking a partner and getting on the mats), and gives students who don't opt in a job to do (safety monitor) if they want to stay engaged with what's happening on the floor.

For drill participants, the element of surprise is still there, as they don't know when the escalation will happen or even who—if anyone—will introduce a weapon, and their psychological and physical capability will be tested effectively. They'll also go into the drill with clear knowledge of what might happen to their body, and trust will remain intact.

If they're risking an injury or a psychological trigger, they've made that decision for themselves.

Practising that kind of risk assessment will also serve everyone very well outside of training. If they get used to looking at a potential fight and deciding whether it's worth getting hit in the head, or kicked in the knee, or dealing with the psychological aftermath of a PTSD trigger, they'll be more likely to make good choices when challenged in the street or given the opportunity to either intervene physically in a violent situation, or hang back and call for backup.

The last and most important thing to remember about consent is that it's situational and not transferable. If a student agrees to a specific drill or level of contact today, that's all they've agreed to. You don't get to assume that they're okay with the same thing in a month's time, or with a dramatically different partner. If they're okay with you touching their body to make adjustments to their position or guide them through technical corrections, that doesn't necessarily mean you get to lay hands on them in a social context. You don't have to have a long conversation about consent every time you introduce a new drill, but a quick check-in is mandatory. Let them know what's about to happen, and let them opt in to the activity or contact.

> *In the next exercise, your partner will take mount and try to limit your breathing using their body weight. Your job will be to reverse the position and either get mount on them, or escape entirely. If you're ready to go, grab a partner, grab some floor space, and set up with one of you in mount.*

Or

> *Can I adjust your hip position here?*

If the kind of training you're doing requires occasional no-holds-barred, anything goes fights, ambushes, or surprise escalations, or otherwise fluid contexts where it's not practical to explain everything that's going to happen immediately beforehand, you can still manage boundaries appropriately. Set aside a time where that kind of training happens, and clearly separate it from the rest of your classes. Maybe it's a once-a-month workshop, or one hour of dedicated training a week, or a twenty-minute segment at the end of a specific regular class.

Be clear about what kind of training will be happening and what general level of contact students can expect (e.g., "In this class, we'll hit at up to 80 percent power to all body targets, including the groin and head. I recommend bringing a cup and a mouthguard"). If that's clearly communicated before anyone walks onto the training floor, then attending that class is also an expression of consent to everything up the highest level of force you allow there. This kind of blanket consent is best saved for specific high-intensity contexts that are carefully monitored and controlled, such as stress testing.

Exercise: Draft Some Consent Scripts

Walk through your teaching curriculum or a standard class and identify places where you need students to provide informed consent. Look for sensitive physical contact; sudden changes in intensity, contact, or targeting; and psychological triggers.

For each situation, write down an example of how you would ask students for their consent. This might be a direct "May I [do X]?" question, a summary of the exercise and a physical cue that students can use to show they're ready to participate, or a warning and opportunity for students to opt in to an entire class or program.

Find a couple of scripts that you feel comfortable with, and that fit naturally into your teaching style and class format.

Consent is the bedrock on which we build trust. It cuts down on injuries, can stop bullying situations or rivalries from spiralling out of hand, and reinforces the strength of the instructor-student relationship. If the way you approach your training reinforces the fact that your students are the ones with the ultimate right to decide what happens to their bodies, and who gets to touch or hit them, you'll be doing a lot more to empower them in the face of conflict than a million speeches about the value of saying no. Actions speak louder than words.

Good Partners

Just as students need to be able to trust us, they also need to be able to trust each other. I've already discussed what happens to physical and psychological safety when someone's being a bad partner, and it's pretty self-evident that students learn better if they're not distracted and afraid of the person they're training with. What might be less obvious is that students also learn far better if they are being a good training partner, and that good partnering is a skill set and not a personality trait.

Building that skill set requires that we train our students not just in the physical techniques that will help protect them and their partner from harm (e.g., how to strike with low power and speed without sacrificing mechanics; how to throw someone safely; how to breakfall or roll out of bad positions; how to break the impact of a mistargeted or mistimed strike), but also in the tactical mindset that will allow them to deploy those techniques consistently.

Most fighting drills have two clearly defined roles: one partner must correctly execute the technique they're learning; the other sets up the conditions under which that technique must be executed, or the stimulus it responds to.

Most martial arts have specific names for these roles. Traditional Japanese martial arts use *uke* for the partner creating the conditions, and *tori* for the partner trying to execute the technique. The historical Italian swordplay I've studied uses *agente* (or "agent") and *patiente* (or "patient"). Some styles use "attacker" and "defender," while others use "feeder" and "worker" or "player." There's no universally recognized pair of terms, and none of them are perfect. *Uke* and "feeder" can frame the partner setting the conditions as passive or lacking goals. *Patiente* and "defender" cause similar problems for the other partner.

In my own teaching, I normally just refer to everyone as "partners," and set up drills by describing what each side should be doing, and what their goals are. When calling out turns, I'll use references to the layout of the training space. So a drill might be introduced with this set-up:

> *If you're on the side by the orange wall, you're going to start with a one-two punch combination aimed at your partner's forehead. You should be trying to hit them, but not so hard you rock their head back if they don't evade. Grey wall side, you're going to avoid getting hit. You can block both punches, slip or bob-and-weave out of the way, or block one and slip the other—I don't really care, so long as you don't get hit.*

Whatever linguistic solution we arrive at, it's important to acknowledge that the way we frame these roles can dramatically affect how our students approach the drill and what they get out of it.

For the sake of that discussion, and for clarity whenever I'm explaining a drill or exercise in this book, I'll be using "feeder" for the partner creating the conditions of the drill, and "player" for the partner responding to those conditions and executing the assigned technique.

While a given fighting drill might frame the feeder and player as antagonists, it's important to reinforce the fact that the learning and partnered training process is fundamentally cooperative. Feeder and player often act in opposition to one another, but they must also share a number of core beliefs:

- That the overall goal of training is to learn, and to increase one's skill and capability

- That in an open skill environment, practising without a partner is incomplete, because it doesn't allow for a good simulation of the changing circumstances under which that skill will be performed, or the reality of dealing with the physical presence, psychological threat, and tactical complexity of interacting with another human being

- That each partner has an equally important role to play in the drill, and that their role exists in service to the goal of learning: the feeder sets the conditions under which a technique or set of techniques is executed, and the player adapts to those conditions and executes the technique(s)

- That every drill has a desired learning outcome, and that both partners are responsible for achieving it

- That every drill carries a level of physical and psychological risk, and that both partners are responsible for keeping that risk within acceptable parameters and mitigating injury whenever possible

Reminding our students of those shared beliefs and common goals is the first step to setting them up to be good partners. The next step is clarifying their individual roles, and setting them up to succeed as both the player and the feeder.

The feeder's job is often a thankless one. Many students think of them as the loser of the drill, or as a passive punching bag or striking pell whose role it is to get hit. Instructors often unconsciously reinforce this misunderstanding by describing the feeder as a weaker or less competent opponent ("So if your opponent isn't paying attention and gives you this opening, you'll be able to attack like this . . .," "If they make the mistake of changing guard, you can exploit it by . . .," "If they're trying to win through strength instead of skill, you can trick them by . . ."). It's a framework that can mess with learning in a whole host of ways.

There's an element of role-playing that happens in partnered work, and asking someone to step into the role of the "bad fighter" will affect their mindset and training. Sometimes, this means they'll give up far too easily. After all, they're being someone incompetent—not the good fighter they are or want to be—so they don't need to put all of their energy or skill into the drill.

Other times, the disconnect between how they see themselves and the role they're being placed in makes them feel bad about being on the losing side. Those students may respond by trying to "win" the drill and prove that they're not actually as stupid or incompetent as they've been set up to be.

Big fighters start hitting too hard or muscling through submissions that they should tap out of; fast fighters speed up outside the parameters of the drill; advanced fighters pull out techniques that are outside the scope of the exercise to allow them to defeat their partner. We've all seen this dynamic in action, and it's a frustrating waste of everyone's time.

To shortcut this problem, we've got to frame the role of feeder as an equal partner in the learning process, and not the loser of an imaginary fight being modelled inside the drill.

If they understand that their job is to provide the correct stimulus for their partner to respond to in practising a technique, it immediately gives them ownership of the exercise and a stake in its success. Language is the easiest way to do this. When describing a drill or exercise, you can give equal weight to what both player and feeder will be doing, and explain it from both perspectives:

> In this exercise, we'll be working on evading an incoming cut and moving to safety past your partner. So the player will start at striking distance, and the feeder will throw a diagonal cut to either one of the player's shoulders.

> The player will slip past the cut by moving in behind the blow, then throw a follow-up attack to the feeder's body and keep moving until they're behind them and out of range.

> The feeder's job is to give big, clean, forty-five-degree cuts. They can come from either side, but the cut needs to be clearly visible and needs to continue on a smooth plane, so that the player can predict its path and learn to move past it safely.

That final sentence lays out the conditions that the player needs in order to learn, and sets clear expectations for what the feeder should be focusing on.

Depending on the goal of a drill and its intended context, the actual be-haviour we expect from the feeder can vary a lot, and the cooperative nature of training certainly doesn't mean that they have to be compliant.

In fact, the feeder might well set their conditions by being a tough, non-compliant, pain in the ass. They might move slowly and strike at one-quarter of their normal power, or they might throw hard and fast shots equal to what they'd do in sparring. They might scream or swear or threaten, if they need to trigger a particular psychological response. They might provide a very limited set of stimuli (one attack, coming in along one line, with predictable timing), or have the freedom to surprise the player.

The feeder doesn't need to be kind, or gentle, or particularly helpful in the way we generally understand that term. They do need to prioritize their own safety and their partner's safety, as well as the learning out-come. How they get there is up to them, and up to us as instructors.

This focus on learning outcomes and conditions can dramatically change how the feeder mentally engages with an exercise, and what they're able to learn from a drill. They're not just attacking, or defend-ing, or resisting, or otherwise acting as an obstacle; they're actively set-ting up the learning environment for their partner.

That hands them an interesting tactical challenge: they need to recog-nize and create the conditions that a technique needs to succeed. What openings does their partner need to be able to see? What timing pattern or rhythm do they need to establish? Where do they need resistance to push against or exploit for momentum? What reaction or flinch do they need to trigger?

By learning how to provide those stimuli for a partner, the feeder will deepen their understanding of how to land the technique themselves, and how to defeat it if it's used against them. If a technique needs two or three conditions to be properly set up, taking one of those away can be enough to thwart it. As the feeder, they're in a unique position to explore the art of the set-up and file away what they learn for their turn to act as the player, or for their next fight.

This mindset allows both partners to learn actively. One of the biggest challenges for many students when they're the feeder is the assumption that they're just a tool for that portion of the exercise, and that their turn to learn anything will only come once they're the player. They switch off their brains for half of their training time, or get frustrated with the role of passive object and start acting out.

Giving them clear goals and their own problem to solve plugs them back into what's going on and shows them that they can basically double their training time by working just as hard as the feeder as they do as the player.

With newer students, these goals can be very explicit and can be a way of reinforcing the school's training culture and expectations. We know that learning works best when failure is part of the equation, which means that the feeder needs to make the conditions just challenging enough that the player succeeds most of the time, but not all of the time. To make this clear to students, I'll sometimes set a success rate target for a given drill. For example, I'll tell the feeder that I want them to facilitate a 75 percent success rate.[2] If their partner can pull off their technique roughly three times out of four, then the feeder is doing their job well. The player needs to work to set it up correctly and execute it cleanly, but isn't being overwhelmed by excessive resistance.

A concrete target also gives the feeder a goal in the drill that's a lot more interesting and specific than "get hit by the technique" or "get thrown." They'll have to focus on reading their partner's reactions and calibrating their force to what that person needs. It's a reasonably complex activity, and one that requires active engagement and practice. The player will

---

2 This number isn't entirely arbitrary. We've already talked about how "perfect practice" is terrible for retention and overall learning, and some researchers have quantified this. A 1995 study found that 100 percent success in practice led to 0 percent improvement. Retention increased linearly as success dropped all the way down to 50 percent, but most subjects became discouraged once their success rate dropped below 70 percent. Aiming for 75 percent success keeps demotivation at bay while introducing enough failure that students improve measurably from session to session. Andrew Somlyo, "Coaching in Theory and Practice" (lecture, Swordsquatch, Seattle, WA, September 9, 2017).

learn better because the resistance level of the drill is tailored to their experience and skill, and the feeder won't get bored or overly aggressive.

Laying out expectations for success rate—especially if they're significantly below 100 percent—also helps to normalize failure as part of the learning process. It's far easier for the player to accept that they're going to screw up sometimes if their instructor tells them up front that they expect to see a significant number of failures. It also creates a reasonably objective assessment tool for whether someone's being a good partner, and an easy reference point for giving feedback to the feeder as well as the player. You've now got access to statements like:

> *Hey, Paul, I noticed that Jess has pulled off that takedown four times in a row. Why don't you play with your resistance or footwork a little and make that harder for her? I want to see her nail just three of the next four attempts.*

Or

> *Sarah, I can see that Steve's not quite getting the timing on this lunge. Can you dial back the speed on your parries until he figures it out? Keep working in sets of five attempts, and you can speed up again once he's getting it four times a set.*

Focusing feedback on the feeder, rather than the player, has some additional benefits besides keeping the feeder engaged. It keeps the focus of the drill on helping the player find their own solution to a problem, rather than handing it to them.

Correcting the player is sometimes very much appropriate—if they're making a mechanical error that puts them or their partner in danger, if they're repeating a serious mistake that they don't seem to be aware of, if time is limited and you need to set them up for the next stage in the drill, etc.—but it's astonishing how much self-correction will happen on its own if you adjust the parameters of the drill a little and give the player room to figure things out. I have far more success making lessons stick when I tweak what the feeder is doing to elicit a better response from the player than I do just telling the player what to fix.

This fits with a broader motor learning concept of how our brains interpret feedback during learning. In class, there are always two kinds of feedback available: intrinsic feedback and extrinsic feedback.

Intrinsic feedback is the feedback that students get from their own bodies—what they see, feel, and hear while performing an action. Examples of intrinsic feedback include seeing the path of a strike or parry, feeling an impact (or lack thereof), or hearing the sound that a weapon makes when it strikes. Extrinsic feedback includes the verbal cues that we usually think of when we talk about "feedback" in a training context, as well as things like video replays and written scores.

Intrinsic feedback is always present and learning how to process and interpret it is a critical part of the learning process—especially since it's often the only feedback available in a sparring match or a violent encounter, and thus the only tool that students will have for adapting their approach under pressure. Extrinsic feedback is most useful for guiding that adaptation process, motivating the student, and reinforcing the things they get right so that they repeat and build on what works.

For these reasons, extrinsic feedback works best when it's positive and offered intermittently.[3] Constant extrinsic feedback loses its reinforcing ability, and students who get feedback after every repetition of a skill tend to do worse on retention tests.[4]

In fact, the best time to offer feedback is usually when students ask for it (i.e., when they've already had time to process the intrinsic feedback, find what's not working, and attempt a solution), and that very experienced students often do best with intrinsic feedback alone.[5]

Another way to think of good partnering practices, then, is as a way of setting the player up to get the best intrinsic feedback possible. If the feeder is doing their job well, the player gets everything they need from feeling their way through their own successes and failures inside a given

---

3 Schmidt, *Motor Learning and Performance*, 292.

4 Schmidt, *Motor Learning and Performance*, 292–293.

5 Schmidt, *Motor Learning and Performance*, 296–297.

drill. The instructor's role then becomes that of a facilitator: we tweak the parameters of the drill when we need the player to get slightly different feedback, and provide positive reinforcement when we see that they're headed in the right direction.

If the feeder gets stuck enough that they ask for help, or either partner needs clarification on how the drill works, we can absolutely step in with a bit of advice or a suggestion for how to tackle the problem, but our words shouldn't be the primary driver of learning. The partnership is what makes learning happen, and we're there to guide the process and give it more fuel, not to take control.

Making all of this work requires a pretty high level of engagement and investment from the feeder (which is great for cutting down on boredom and resulting shenanigans), and it also requires treating partnering as a distinct skill set that needs to be developed as a part of the training curriculum.

Students will need to learn how to read their partner for cues of frustration, confusion, and discouragement so that they can adjust their level of resistance appropriately; they'll need to read their movement and interpret their actions so that they can be where they're most useful for setting up or challenging the skill that's being drilled; and they'll need to know how to calibrate their physical resistance, force, targeting, distance, and timing to keep their partner safe, keep the success rate at the right level, and set up the conditions that the instructor wants.

They'll also need language for talking about these things. They'll need to understand what their job is as the feeder or the player and will need to know how and why to ask their partner or their instructor for feedback. We don't want students actively coaching each other, but there should be space for them to ask for a bit more or a bit less resistance, or to draw attention to a problem they're having. Being a good partner requires a full suite of physical, interpretive, and communication skills on both sides.

To really develop our students into effective training partners, we need to devote time to growing these skills, which can feel like taking space away from technical training in an already over-full curriculum. The upside is that all of these skills have applications outside of training, and are substantial assets in any fighting context.

Reading emotion and movement is critical to winning most fights, and is essential for dealing with deception (from either end), as well as de-escalating a threat or catching a sudden attack or escalation before it happens. The same knowledge of angles and positions that makes for a good set-up can be used to make blocks, counters, and feints work.

Calibration is essential to playing by the rules of any competition, or using proportional and appropriate force in a self-defence context. Being able to talk about the problem you're dealing with, ask for feedback, and speak up when a partner isn't giving you what you need lays the groundwork for effective on-the-fly coaching in sparring or between tournament rounds, and for boundary-setting and interpersonal communication in the early stages of self-defence or de-escalation.

The soft skills of partnership are also key soft skills of combat, and building them into training is a great way to sneak in reps of these higher level concepts even in simple, mechanical drills.

They also allow for greater complexity and risk in training itself by providing the psychological safety required to do physically dangerous things (by letting the player trust their partner to care for them and prioritize their learning), and the physical safety required to do psychologically dangerous things (by having the feeder calibrate their resistance and force appropriately). Good partners can play harder, and push each other further, than mediocre ones.

Self-Regulation

One of the keys to a good partnership is leaving room for observing and interpreting intrinsic feedback. This helps with skill development, as our students learn what good and bad technique feels, sounds, and looks like, and can more easily replicate what works. It's also important for their health and safety, as some of the most important pieces of intrinsic feedback are concerned with potential injury: pain, discomfort, and emotional distress.

These internal cues point to weaknesses and gaps in training, potential triggers for freezing under stress, and to things that might be going wrong in the drill itself. Getting familiar with them allows for self-regulation—a basic skill that is integral to long-term health and training, and one that's not always encouraged in students of martial arts and self-defence. Sure, pain and fatigue are occasional parts of any training regimen, and being able to push through discomfort and distress can be crucial in a competitive or self-defence context, but too many teaching environments recommend ignoring these signals as a matter of course.

Pain isn't just "weakness leaving the body" or whatever badass slogan is hung on the wall of your gym. It's a neurological signal from the body to the brain telling it that something is wrong.

Sometimes that "something" is a muscle or joint that's being used in new ways and will relax and feel better if you keep moving; sometimes that "something" is an injury that's going to cause serious damage if you don't stop immediately. In order to be able to tell the difference between these kinds of pain, and to safely bypass the pain that's actually just discomfort at something new, you have to pay attention to what's going on in your body. Ignoring all pain means that you can't tell the difference and are in danger of permanent harm if you push through the wrong thing.

I've found that one of the biggest challenges in teaching modern adults is that most of them don't pay much attention to their bodies at all. If you ask them to engage a specific muscle group, or to tell you what position their hips are in when they're throwing a punch, you'll often be met with confusion. They don't really know where their body is or what it's doing, and aren't used to turning their attention inward.

I've seen this many times with office workers, and until recently I'd always assumed that it was a symptom of sedentary jobs and lifestyles. This changed in 2016, when I was invited to help teach a group of new special municipal constables with our police department. They were all young, fit people who had passed a physical aptitude test as part of their recruitment. They had backgrounds in team sports, weightlifting, running, and other physical activities. Many of them also didn't really know how to move and were struggling with their physical training because of poor proprioception and an inability to improvise and adapt to new movement patterns. I was brought in to run an ongoing sixty-minute workout that would build the basic physical literacy, mobility, and spatial awareness they needed to be able to quickly acquire new technical skills and solve physical problems in the field.

I've since worked with five groups like this, and one of the biggest commonalities that emerged among students who were struggling was an almost complete lack of self-regulation. Not only did they not have a good idea of where their body was in space, but they didn't understand what it needed to keep working. They skipped water breaks. They held bodyweight lifts long enough to pull muscles or collapse from fatigue. They ran themselves hard enough during drills that they came back to training the next day too sore to move. If I told them to hold a position for thirty seconds and didn't count the time for them, they'd keep going well past the planned hold length.

Now these were police recruits, and they were accustomed to a very discipline-heavy training environment where group cohesion and conformity was necessarily prioritized over personal comfort. But it wasn't a coincidence that the students who were the worst at moving were also the least in tune with what their body was actually telling them—which was usually, "Stop!"

The same problem is endemic in many martial arts environments, where discipline and group cohesion are similarly prioritized, but for less clear reasons. Few—if any—of us are building an army. Modern martial arts training generally comes out of a desire for fitness, personal improvement, and physical mastery; self-defence practice is all about learning to improvise and adapt, and strict conformity is anathema to it. Sure, class discipline is important, but we don't have the same need for uniformity as a military or paramilitary force.

Treating our students like adults who can decide for themselves when they need to step out and take care of their needs costs very little and makes a big difference to morale and internal understanding.

In my classes, I let students take water breaks and rests as needed, so long as they don't disrupt teaching and are respectful of their training partners. This lets less-fit or injured students take care of themselves instead of being shamed into fatigue and dehydration, teaches everyone to pay attention to their own bodies and support their training correctly, and gives students having a rough day the option of scaling back a bit without stigma.

The same leeway is afforded to those facing emotional challenges (tears, frustration, anger issues, etc.). I acknowledge that stuff happens, and I trust students to recognize and care for their own needs with a quick check-in from instructors but no pressure to explain what's happening or "pull it together." This has the side-effect of teaching students that they have a responsibility to be a safe and present training partner, and that withdrawing (temporarily or otherwise) when they're not able to train safely is sometimes the smarter and more considerate choice.

Because so many fitness and fighting environments emphasize "toughing it out" and "pushing through," it can be difficult for students to actually take breaks or pull back. I've developed a number of strategies for modelling and encouraging self-regulatory behaviour in the classroom.

For instance, I start the majority of our workouts with a series of animal crawls and sprints. Before the first one, I'll remind students that they should pay attention to their bodies during these exercises, and that if they feel any sharp pain or intense fatigue, they should just stop and walk the rest of the distance across the space instead of continuing with the exercise.

I'll then make sure to do exactly that at least once during the workout. If the students see me choosing to take care of myself instead of forcing it, it normalizes that behaviour as something that even the most experienced and fit of us can do. Similarly, if I see someone grabbing a quick sip of water or scaling back an exercise that's aggravating an injury or otherwise too much for them, I'll praise them for it in front of the class.

Exercise: Build Self-Regulation Models

Take a look at your own training, and identify your self-regulation habits. How do you assess yourself for injury or overtraining? What support tools do you bring to a workout, from water and snacks to braces, wraps, ice, and other injury management tools? How do you make the call to stop or slow down? Ask your fellow instructors and training partners the same questions.

Once you've got a short list of reliable tools, figure out how to integrate them into your teaching. Which behaviours can you demonstrate naturally over the course of a typical class? Which ones need to be pointed out verbally and actively encouraged? When is a good time to explain your internal check-in process?

Make space for at least three self-regulation methods in your curriculum, and lay out how you're going to teach them.

Part of the reason we put so much emphasis on self-regulation at our school is because every member of our teaching team has paid the price for pushing through something they shouldn't have. Meniscus damage from walking around on a blown knee; shoulder arthritis from too many reps of the same aggressive fencing shot; traumatic brain injuries from continuing to fight after a minor concussion and getting a second one on top of it.

Our head instructor, David, used to be particularly bad at sitting things out when he was hurt. During a bout of bursitis a few years ago, he brought a wooden cane with him to class, and nicknamed it "Mr. Cranky." The rest of us were under strict orders to not let him work out or push himself too hard while he had the cane.

Over time, Mr. Cranky evolved into a universal symbol that an instructor was too injured or sick to be pushing themselves. It lives at the school now, and any one who's teaching while under the weather can pick it up. The cane is lighter than a sword, but still lets us demonstrate fencing actions if we need to, and it signals to our fellow instructors and students that we're not going to be at 100 percent that day.

Having Mr. Cranky around has done a great job of forcing the most reluctant of us—the teachers—to self-regulate. It's also made that self-regulation visible to the students and taught them that it's not only acceptable, but expected.

The benefits of increased self-regulation are obvious for students (and instructors) who habitually push themselves too far and end up overtraining or injuring themselves. But what does it do for students who are already prone to giving up? Doesn't letting them stop when it gets hard just encourage them to avoid challenge? Won't you get students who sit out the majority of class and bail at the first twinge of discomfort? Won't they just never try the hard or uncomfortable things in the first place?

My experience has been that this almost never happens, and it's because training is fun.

When you take self-punishment out of the equation, the only incentive for participation has to be positive. In compulsory training environments like police academies, military basic training, and high school gym classes, everyone has to be there, and non-participation is usually punished. Martial arts classes are voluntary, and the only reason anyone sets foot in the door of your school is because they want to. That same desire drives class participation. Only the most dedicated masochist will spend their money and limited leisure time on sitting unhappily at the side of a class they don't enjoy.

The overwhelming majority of students want to train and want to challenge themselves, or they wouldn't be there in the first place. By allowing them to self-regulate, you give them an autonomy over the terms of their participation that'll actually increase dedication and compliance over time.

If time out—whether it's for physical or emotional reasons—is a resource that's always available to them, simply knowing it's there is enough of a safety net to encourage a harder push. Students who rest too often or avoid stepping outside their comfort zone will find that they're progressing more slowly and having less fun than their peers. They're motivated to last a little longer, and push a little harder, because the reward is feeling better and enjoying themselves more.

To put this in behavioural science terms, we are trying to give them two particular kinds of motivation: the intrinsic motivation of enjoying the exercise for its own sake—including fun, excitement, and the satisfaction of facing down a challenge—and the autonomous extrinsic motivation of enjoying an exercise because it gives them something they value, such as health, empowerment, or a sense of control.

This autonomous extrinsic motivation is separate from what is sometimes called "controlled" extrinsic motivation, where the goal of the exercise is set by someone other than the student—whether that's a doctor prescribing exercise for weight loss, a coach who wants to see certain performance benchmarks, or peers who will include or exclude them from a group based on performance.[6]

A growing body of studies in the field of self-determination theory indicates that initial participation and long-term adherence to physical activity and exercise is best supported by intrinsic motivation, autonomous extrinsic motivation, and meeting basic psychological needs for autonomy and belonging or relatedness.[7]

In other words: students are most likely to show up and stick around if they have fun during training; if the training helps them grow in ways

---

6 Pedro J. Teixeira and others, "Exercise, Physical Activity, and Self-Determination Theory: A Systematic Review," *International Journal of Behavioral Nutrition and Physical Activity* 9, no. 78 (2012): 2–3.

7 Teixeira and others, "Exercise, Physical Activity, and Self-Determination Theory," 26–27. This 2011 review looks at 66 peer-reviewed studies in the field of self-determination theory, and draws some broad conclusions about which motivation tools are most effective for initial participation and long-term adherence to exercise programs.

they personally value; if they feel like they have some control over their training environment and structure; and if they feel like they are part of a community.

Self-regulation feeds most of these drives: it gives students a clear sense of control over what happens to their body; it offers the reward of fun and growth if they do choose to participate; and it promises them that they won't be excluded or punished if they need to rest or slow down.

There's also ample evidence to suggest that they won't miss out on much learning if they sit out an exercise or two, or take an extra water break. In fact, a 1995 study found that there isn't a measurable difference in skill improvement between a lesson that is 100 percent physical practice, and one that's 25 percent physical practice and 75 percent observation, so long as that observation is mentally active and engaged with the material.[8]

This doesn't mean that we should all be running to make our classes three-quarters lecture—boredom is a big factor in talking-heavy sessions, and there are benefits to physical practice beyond pure skill development—but it does mean that a student who sits out a single drill or a few minutes of sparring time isn't automatically taking a huge hit to their learning. The downsides to self-regulation are minimal, and the benefits to motivation and psychological well-being are substantial.

Opting In

Allowing for self-regulation and prioritizing consent is a lot easier if exercises are structured on an opt-in basis.

Most group classes rely on students opting out of things they find too challenging or risky. Everyone is shown one way of doing an exercise or drill, and it's up to those who can't do it to either step out of the lesson, or ask the instructor for accommodations and alternatives. Running classes this way is simple, and it exerts what looks like a positive peer

---

8 Andrew Somlyo, "Coaching in Theory and Practice" (lecture, Swordsquatch, Seattle, WA, September 9, 2017).

pressure on everyone to try the harder things first, and only ask for help if they really can't do it. Simple and effective, right?

This approach can work fine in heavily segregated classes, where students are grouped by narrowly defined ranks, and everyone in a given group is at the same level of development. Most martial arts classes, however, have a reasonable breadth of skill and physical ability even within ranks, and many of us run integrated classes that include beginners or near-beginners alongside very experienced peers.

Forcing less experienced and less capable students to opt out in mixed contexts has the effect of singling them out every time they struggle. And so they have to make a choice: do I keep going even though I can't really do this part? Do I tell my instructor (and show any senior students nearby) that I don't get it, again, and embarrass myself?

Neither choice is great for learning, and both exert a subtle social pressure that tells the student that they're not really good enough to be there. This pressure is particularly acute for collaborative learners, who need to feel like a valued part of the community in order to keep training. It's also a lot more likely to fall on female students.

The majority of men and boys who come to martial arts have grown up knowing that fighting is something that belongs to them. Roughhousing isn't always encouraged, but it is understood as something that boys do. They fight with their siblings, they scrap in the schoolyard, and even if they've never participated in a bar fight or a brawl at a hockey game or concert, they've seen one break out between other men. They may be punished for engaging in this kind of social violence, but it's still a part of their life experience, and the media they interact with—whether that's films, TV, books, or video games—confirms that men fight. They're also a lot more likely to take part in high-contact school sports such as football, rugby, wrestling, and hockey, many of which aren't offered to girls on a widespread level.[9]

---

9 In Canada, for example, 4 percent of women who participate in sports play hockey, compared to 23 percent of men; there are 2 women's tackle football leagues in the country, with a total of 13 teams at the amateur level, compared to 55 men's teams across professional, college, and junior leagues. Michelle

The message that most girls get is that fighting isn't for them. Not only is it unacceptable and unseemly, but it's fundamentally the province of men. Girls don't hit. They don't fight. When they touch someone, that contact is either caring or sexual—never violent. The sports available to them growing up can be very challenging, but they tend to be individual sports like figure skating or gymnastics, or team sports that actively discourage contact between players, like soccer and basketball.[10]

All of these background differences mean that your average man will enter a martial arts classroom with some experience in high-contact sports and with some experience of what it's like to hit and be hit. Your average woman won't, and her first challenge in training will be to acclimatize to an environment where she's expected to strike other people. She'll already feel uncomfortable and as if she needs to prove that she belongs, and asking for help becomes loaded with the baggage of "letting down the team" by confirming that many women struggle with violence.

If she routinely has to choose between saving face but not actually learning, or getting the help she needs at the cost of belonging or reputation, she's likely to take the unspoken third option and just leave. I've devoted an entire later chapter to overcoming the specific challenges that women face as they enter fighting environments (see "Hitting Girls and Other Taboos", beginning on page 129). For now, I'll just note that teaching practices like the opt-out model are more likely to put them in that uncomfortable position, and to contribute to the attrition of female students and beginners.

A better way to teach mixed-experience groups is to build workouts and technical exercises that scale up from basics, rather than scaling down from a more complex version. You can present a range of variants to

---

K. Brunette and Norman O'Reilly, *Women in Sport: Fuelling a Lifetime of Participation* (Toronto: Canadian Association for the Advancement of Women and Sport and Physical Activity, 2016), 13.

10 The 10 most popular sports among Canadian women are swimming, dance, soccer, ballet, gymnastics, skating, running, basketball, volleyball, and trampoline; 7 of these are solo sports, and the 3 team sports all prohibit contact between players. Brunette and O'Reilly, *Women in Sport*, 11.

your class, and let every student opt in to the variant that best fits their current experience and skill level.

> **Exercise: Convert Your Drills to an Opt-In Structure**
>
> For every skill that you teach, you've most likely already got a mental catalogue of easier and harder variants that you offer to students when they ask for help or need an extra challenge. Pick one of your core skills and write out all of these variants in order from easiest to hardest. Next, plan a lesson that presents all of them as equally valuable options and allows students some freedom to choose.
>
> Once you've found a lesson framework that you like, turn it into a general model that you can apply to all of your demonstrations and drills.

Let's take the example of a physical exercise and a technical drill to flesh out how we can use the opt-in model to teach different kinds of skills:

Physical Exercise: The L-Sit

I use gymnastic lifts regularly in my class workouts to help students develop strength and stability through their shoulders' full range of motion. The first one I teach is the L-sit. In this challenging exercise, the student sits, then puts their hands on the floor next to their hips and uses them to support their entire body weight. Their body pulls into a seated "L" shape, with their torso upright and their legs parallel to the ground and held straight out in front of them.[11]

The L-sit is difficult enough that most students won't be able to do it in this form until a good few months into their training. Instead of showing this version of the lift and then providing "easy" or "light" or (God for-

---

11 For photo references and a video walkthrough of the L-sit and its variants, see: http://boxwrestlefence.com/valkyriewmaa/valkyrie-fitness-bit-1-l-sit.

bid) "girly" alternatives to the "normal" version, I start from the simplest variant and work my way up. In order, I demonstrate:

1. A straight hold on high parallettes or chair backs with the same upper-body position, and with the legs relaxed and hanging straight down. This lets students get the correct arm position and engagement through the front of the torso (with the pectorals bearing down to lift and a tight core keeping the pelvis aligned below the shoulders).

2. The same hold, but with bent knees. I'll lift my legs until my thighs are parallel to the floor, and explain how this adds leverage and thigh engagement to the exercise.

3. The same hold, with the legs extended and held at a low angle (forty-five degrees from straight down, rather than the ninety degrees of a strict L-sit). I'll also demonstrate how students can increase the angle as they get more comfortable with the load.

4. A strict L-sit on the floor or on parallettes.

5. A strict L-sit on gymnastic rings, with an explanation of how this adds more challenge by forcing the shoulders to neutralize the movement of the rings.

I'll invite students to choose whichever variant they want, and try to hold it for 30 seconds.

I reiterate these variants regularly to normalize their place in our training routine, rather than only highlighting them when there are new or weaker students in the class. The key is to make them available to everyone and make it clear to students that they are equally valuable training tools.

For this reason, I'll also always refer to them by their titles or descriptions (e.g., "straight hold," "bent-knee L-sit") rather than using value distinctions that set one version as "normal" and others as "less advanced" or "more advanced". Along with keeping junior students from feeling singled out, this normalizes scaling the intensity of your training based on your needs on a given day—I've seen many high-performing students use these variants to train through an injury, or focus on a particular aspect of a skill they're working on. It dovetails seamlessly with the principle of self-regulation.

Technical Drill: Cut Evasion

Much like physical exercises, most tactical and technical drills scale in complexity or difficulty of execution, and it's very common to work a class through a progression from a simple version of a drill to its most complex and chaotic form. For example, I might have the following swordplay progression set up for a group learning how to evade cuts:

1. Feeder throws a descending, diagonal cut that aims to cut Player from their left shoulder to their right hip. Player evades this cut by stepping forward and toward Feeder's right side. Player holds their sword in a ready position, but doesn't actively involve it in the drill. Both students reset after each attack and response.

2. Feeder throws the same cut. Player evades as before, and moves their sword so that its blade crosses over the line of Feeder's sword. The point of Player's sword should be aimed over Feeder's left shoulder, and its edge should be aimed at Feeder's face. Both students reset after each attack and response.

3. Feeder throws the same cut. Player evades as before, and places their sword in the same position as in version #2. Player takes an additional step forward and past Feeder's right side, drawing their blade across Feeder's mask or throat as they do so. They continue moving forward until they are out of Feeder's striking range, turning to face Feeder as soon as they are able. Both students reset after each attack and response.

4. Feeder alternates between two descending, diagonal cuts. They may either aim from Player's left shoulder to right hip, or right shoulder to left hip. Player evades and cuts Feeder's throat or face, moving to the appropriate side depending on the direction of Feeder's attack. Both students reset after each attack and response.

5. Feeder moves continuously, alternating between the two cuts from version #4 however they like. Player evades and counterattacks appropriately, adding additional evasions or parrying with the sword to cover their retreat back out of range. The students do not reset after each attack, and instead flow continuously for two to three minutes.

If I'm working with a mixed group with a range of skill and experience levels, I'm not going to try to get the entire class to version #5. I may decide that version #3 is sufficient to get the day's learning objective across to junior students, set it as the "final" version, and leave a good chunk of time for working on it. Once everyone has worked through versions #1–3 and spent a bit of time on the last version, I'll demonstrate version #4 as an optional challenge variant that students can try if they're comfortable with version #3. If some students are doing well with version #4, I'll give them version #5 as another step up.

Aside from giving the more experienced students more material to engage them, this approach also puts the students who only made it to version #3 in a good social position. They've done all of the drills that were asked of them, and got to see a cool variant that they can try the next time. The harder drills become an enticement and a reward, rather than a standard to live up to.

Framing lessons this way reinforces the core values that I've set up in my classroom. Students are trusted to understand their needs and limitations and to choose the version of an exercise that's appropriate to them. I'll happily encourage students who I think could stand to challenge themselves more to try the next variant up, but I'll never castigate or publicly shame someone for doing things on "easy mode." In fact, in this framework, "easy mode" doesn't really exist—everyone's working on what they need at the moment, while keeping the class focused on a shared lesson.

There's a strong positive pressure to challenge yourself, because the harder skill variants and drills are generally cooler looking and more interesting to perform, and the social cost for failure is low. Students will still understand failure within the context of the drill (which usually means getting hit), but it remains a tactical and technical consideration that has no bearing on their social standing within the class.

Modelling Failure

If you're this far into a book about how useful failure is, I probably don't need to tell you that it's unhelpful to punish imperfection with public shaming and teasing. That said, cutting out overt bullying is only the first step to teaching students that it's okay to fail. One of the most common messages that many of us send—usually without intending to—is that only low-ranking students fail visibly.

Instructors never make mistakes in demonstrations (and if they do, these are studiously ignored or glossed over), and expect their senior students to be near-perfect in their execution of skills. Beginners are expected to ask questions, move awkwardly, make incorrect choices, and get hit, because they don't know better yet. For more advanced students, the learning process often changes from one of visible trial and error to a steady polishing and refinement of existing skills.

When a beginner learns a new technique, they're expected to struggle with it for a bit before they become proficient. When a more advanced student learns a new technique, they're expected to integrate it smoothly into what they already know, as an embellishment, extrapolation, or extra tactical option. It's adding complexity, rather than developing basic building blocks.

This model teaches students that advancement requires them to simply stop failing at some point—or at least never get caught in a visible mistake. Some will be pushed to more diligent study by this implicit prohibition, but many more will simply be paralyzed by fear of embarrassment. They'll know that being seen to fail means being seen as inferior and less valuable to their community.

To break this cycle, we need to demonstrate that failure is not only acceptable, but expected at every stage in the learning process. And the most powerful way to do that is to start at the top. We need to screw up sometimes: to attempt things that are just a little out of reach, to play and improvise and make the wrong choice, and to have a bad day or a brain fart and treat it as an ordinary thing and not a crack in the armour of our authority.

One of the best places to start modelling failure is in warm-ups and workouts. Many of my group classes include a gymnastic workout. It's a great way to build the physical capacity and range of motion that we need to stay healthy while swinging swords around or throwing each other to the mats, and it's also a venue where failure is pretty much inevitable. Almost every lift progression that I teach contains exercises that nobody in the class—including the instructors—can do.

Performing something like a straight-arm planche takes dedicated training specifically for that movement, and it can take months or years to work up to it. Since we're martial artists, not gymnasts, we're unlikely to ever put in the focused time or energy needed to get to a full planche. Working through the earlier stages of the progression toward it, though, gives us substantial gains in shoulder, chest, upper back, and core strength, all of which are essential to what we actually do.

Taking a group through an exercise progression like that also means that we're routinely trying exercises that are at the limits of our abilities, right alongside our students. We look stupid, we fall over, and we strain mightily with no discernible progress. I've fallen on my face in front of a class more times than I can count, and nobody thinks less of me for it. There's usually laughter, and our students learn that everyone fails sometimes—even the teachers.

Not only that, but it cements the drive to keep learning. If I'm failing, it's because I'm challenging myself to try new things and to expand my horizons. It shows my students that nobody should ever stop trying to improve, and that challenging yourself is valuable for its own sake, rather than something you do until you're good enough to stop learning.

It's easiest and least risky to do this kind of modelling with physical skills—balance tricks, feats of strength, and so on—because it doesn't cost us much in terms of ego. There's even greater value, though, in integrating mistakes into technical instruction.

We've all had a demo go not quite as planned, whether because our partner didn't move in the expected way, because we didn't quite nail our technique, or because we were momentarily distracted or a little off our game and botched the timing or the communication with our partner. It can be hard to let that go, and it's very easy to blame our partner for messing it up, especially if they're a student and not a fellow teacher.

So what happens if we acknowledge that we made a mistake? Or that we weren't prepared for the situation that we were presented with, rather than what we expected to happen? At worst, we say "Oops!," reset, and take the action again. Our students will know that it can go wrong, and won't immediately give up if they don't get it right on their first try. At best, we can talk about why it went wrong and give our students more insight into the contextual factors that set up the technique for success or prevent it from working.

Even better, we can thank our demo partner for hitting us (which is usually what happens when we fail). It's an opportunity to reinforce good feeder behaviour by rewarding them publicly for holding up their end of the drill—even if we couldn't pull ours off.

Responding graciously to our own failures gives us the opportunity to improvise and adapt, and to show our students how to adjust for error in real time. It's an essential skill that's difficult to train formally. Some of the best moments I've had teaching came from having to adapt on the fly to something that went sideways in a drill or a demo. If we're teaching with the right attitude, our own failure is a gift.

Exercise: Build In Failure

It's one thing to respond well when we accidentally screw up in class. It's another to set up the conditions for our own failures and make sure that there are regular opportunities for our students to see us fail.

Make a list of physical skills (e.g., feats of strength and flexibility), technical skills, and tactical responses that are relevant to the material you teach, and that lie at the very edge of your ability: things that you can pull off cleanly 50 percent of the time or less. Try to incorporate one of them into every class you teach.

When we fail in front of our students, we show them that failure has a place in the learning process of every fighter. We show them that our success and skill is the product of hard work and repeated failure, and not some divine gift or natural talent. We make it attainable.

We also humanize ourselves. An untouchable, perfect instructor inspires awe, but they rarely inspire trust, and trust is what we really need to push our students further. Many students will push their body past its limits or do things they're psychologically uncomfortable with out of fear and a desire to live up to instructors' expectations. What they can actually learn from those experiences is often limited.

But if they push themselves because they want to? And because they feel secure in the knowledge that failure won't leave them broken or cast out of the group? That's when the real magic happens.

Play

So how do we facilitate that kind of learning? If we've set up an environment in which trust, self-regulation, and agency are prioritized, and which has safeguards in place to limit the nastiest physical and psychological consequences of failure, what does our practice actually look like? It's one thing to understand that students need room to fail and adapt to failure, and to vary and parameterize their motor programs. It's another to create a way of doing so that's safe, engaging, and appropriate for a martial environment.

Luckily for us, nature has already sorted out one of the best tools for facilitating motor learning and tactical development, and that's play. It's the most basic learning tool for young mammals of all species, including our own. Playing, and play fighting in particular, creates a dynamic environment that favours the development of open skills and has specific parameters (including both constraints on behaviour and win/loss conditions) that need to be adapted to on the fly. It's also fun—and therefore intrinsically motivating—and comes with substantially lower physical and social stakes than earnest combat.

Bringing play into our training spaces is far less taxing on teaching resources than trying to build complex, variable drills from the ground up. It also has the benefit of feeling like a natural space in which to experiment and interact with failure. Whereas many students think of structured drills as tools for polishing and refining their skills—and so end up focusing on perfection and performance quality even when that's not the instructor's intent—play creates a different psychological space that leaves more room for imperfection.

It also lets us make space for blocked practice and other more rigid drilling styles that can be appropriate at early stages of learning a skill, or that serve as a psychological anchor for students who only feel secure when their training involves a certain amount of rote learning.

If I've got a half-hour block in which to teach a given skill, for example, I can easily set aside half of that time for structured drills that lay down the basic motor program, and the other half for playing games that force students to parameterize and vary that program.

These games can look like slow, controlled sparring; "tag" or a similar game with limited rules and simple win/changeover conditions; or drills that give each partner goals and limits to improvise within (e.g., "Tag your partner on the top of the head," "Land two cuts, with at least one being to the back of the body," or "Avoid getting hit, but without blocking or parrying").

Another way to think about integrating play into your practice is to return to the laboratory experiment metaphor from our first chapter. If we're trying to come up with a solution to a martial problem, there are a number of different approaches we can take to experiment design, all of which leave a lot of room for play:

- **Testing a hypothesis:** present a specific solution to the class, and then have students test its effectiveness under a variety of conditions (e.g., a parry-riposte response to an attack, a favourite strike combination, a specific feint and follow-up). What are its strengths and weaknesses? Its limitations? Are there ways to neutralize or counter it, and are there effective counters to those counters? This can be a great approach for HEMA and other arts that rely on the interpretation of recorded plays and forms.

- **Parameterization:** present a general model for performing an action, and then have students figure out how to apply it under a variety of conditions (e.g., a fencing lunge, a grappling throw or takedown, an unarmed strike). What are the prerequisites for setting it up? How can those be achieved if we vary the angle of attack, distance, speed, or target? To what extent can the body mechanics be modified without losing effectiveness or causing injury? This is a particularly useful approach for building a deep understanding of fundamental movements in your art.

- **Improvising solutions:** present a problem, and then have students figure out their own solutions to it (e.g., an attack from a specific guard, a series of cuts with pre-determined angles, a grappling hold or control position). What are the dangers or challenges the problem action poses? What opportunities does it provide? How can we adapt our existing skills and responses to deal with it? This is a great way to lay the tactical decision-making foundations for sparring, and can be part of the preparation for a competition.

Exercise: Make Room for Play

Take a look at your standard lesson plan. How much of your teaching time is devoted to blocked practice, and how much is devoted to more open drilling and sparring frameworks that integrate play? If play makes up less than half of your class time, look for opportunities to shift the balance.

Which drills are absolutely essential to getting familiar with a skill, and which ones just layer on complexity? Can you replace those with one of the "experimental" frameworks above? Can you condense material to leave room for sparring or game playing in the last ten to fifteen minutes of class?

Not every class needs to be identical, but try to aim for an average of at least 50 percent play or experimentation time over a semester or block of your curriculum.

For more examples of how to use play in a range of contexts, including paired drills, structured free play or sparring, and flow pattern work, see page 219.

Along with creating an easy framework for random and variable practice, play is also where it's easiest to model the soft skills that we're trying to develop. All of the principles of good partnership apply, and can be subtly emphasized with rules that push the feeder or player into specific behaviours. It's easy for students to self-regulate and opt in to what looks like fun, and you can model failure by demonstrating a turn of a game or playful drill, including your own improvisations, adaptations, and mistakes.

Play is also a low-stakes way of assessing how students are able to actually apply their skills before they progress to more formal exams and stress testing. Watching them play a game where they're focused on achieving a goal and not performing a skill tells us a lot more about their progress than observing their twentieth consecutive repetition of the same punch or lunge. Once they've developed a base level of comfort and competence in that context, they can be pushed harder in more antagonistic drills, or prepared for formal testing.

The strategies in this section prioritize a few specific principles: trust, self-regulation, and agency. By treating our students as full partners in their training and letting them set and maintain their own boundaries, we empower them and reduce the social costs associated with learning.

This approach makes any self-defence training we provide more effective, because the physical and decision-making skills we teach are built on a bedrock of personal autonomy. To defend yourself, you need to be convinced that you are worthy of defence and capable of making sound decisions on your own. That requires agency. The same goes for success in sparring, or any other high-stress context where you have to rely on your own skills and decisions to succeed, instead of the guidance of an instructor.

These tools are also excellent for preventing burnout in intermediate and advanced students. Whereas beginners might drop out because they're overpowered or overwhelmed, more experienced students drop off from stagnation and boredom. Letting them self-regulate and putting just as much focus on being a good partner as on "winning" a drill gives them concrete things to engage with even when their progress is stuck.

Modelling failure as a natural and acceptable part of training gets rid of the myth that students who have progressed beyond the lowest ranks are expected to stop making mistakes or struggling. You can't break through a training plateau without some ugly, messy failures. In a healthy training environment, that's just part of the process.

Stress Testing and Stress Inoculation

4

You don't really know how strong you are if you've never been tested. Our students feel this and can't be confident in their own skills without sufficient pressure and challenge. On the teaching end, we need tests to confirm that we are doing our job and that the skills we've taught them are sticking. If we're training students for competitive sport or for self-defence, we also need to be able to assess their abilities internally, before they face a tournament or a real-life encounter. Sooner or later, everyone must be tested.

Testing physical techniques is easy enough. We can use formal examinations, demos or performances, and sparring with an instructor or other specially chosen opponent. Testing psychological conditioning, though? That's trickier. Many of the physical skill tests we come up with have an inherent stress level built in, but it's not necessarily the same as the stress of the real thing. To get a really good look at a student's emotional capacity—their toughness, their resilience, and their ability to recover from failure—we need to put them under a good amount of stress that closely mirrors what they'll face outside the classroom.

When the pressure they're training for is that of high-level competition, it's entirely possible to replicate that with minimal risk to the participants (or, at least, no more risk than what they'd assume going into the competition itself). But what happens if the context they need to be able to thrive in is a life-or-death one? Whether it's the historical frame of a swordplay duel, or a modern self-defence situation against an attacker with lethal intent, the stakes are exponentially higher when we're training students for a situation that could kill them.

If you teach weapon arts, you're very likely to come up against this wall at some point, at least with your most dedicated students. If you teach self-defence, it's always there. It's one of the most difficult things that we do and one of the most important to get right. Stress testing is like tempering steel: do it correctly, and it will make your students even stronger and more competent; do it wrong, and you'll make them brittle and more likely to break under pressure.

To start with, it's important to understand the pedagogical role of stress testing. At its most straightforward, a stress test is exactly what it says on the tin: an examination of how well someone performs under psychological stress. If your goal is to administer a rank exam or simulate a level of threat that simply doesn't exist in the modern world (e.g., medieval longsword combat, or an early modern rapier duel), then that may be enough. If, however, you're using stress testing as a way of making sure that your students are prepared to face a real threat in the future, then the test needs to be part of something bigger. When it's used as a training tool, rather than an assessment tool, stress testing is actually the final step in a process called stress inoculation.

Stress inoculation began as a clinical technique to help psychotherapy clients deal with fear, anger, and phobias. Since the 1980s, its use has expanded to include the clinical treatment of many forms of anxiety and performance enhancement training for people working in high-pressure jobs such as pilots, firefighters, emergency room doctors, and police officers. Stress inoculation treatment has three phases:

- **Phase 1:** education/conceptualization. The subject learns about the stressors they will be facing and how they affect the body and mind. In a martial arts or self-defence context, topics might include the physiological and psychological effects of adrenaline and other stress hormones; violence dynamics; or the fight, flight, and freeze responses.

- **Phase 2:** skill acquisition and practice. The subject learns how to manage stress through psychological and physical interventions and gets a chance to practise these skills in a low-stress environment. In a martial arts or self-defence context, this might include mindfulness, visualization, and mental rehearsal exercises; techniques for breathing and finding moments to "rest" while under pressure; decision-making and problem-solving models that help shorten response time; or techniques for breaking out of a freeze state.

- **Phase 3:** application and follow-through. The subject gets the chance to practise their skills in a simulation of the real-world stressor environment.[1] This is our stress test. In a martial arts or self-defence context, this might be a simulation of a competition, a duel, an assault or surprise attack, or a fight against multiple assailants.

Since its migration from a controlled, clinical setting to the occupational training field, stress inoculation has remained a valuable tool for making people a lot more effective under stress. A 1996 meta-study that looked at the effects of training population, training setting, practice length, trainer experience, and group size on the outcomes of stress inoculation found that it continued to work under almost any circumstances.

In every case studied, a properly followed stress inoculation procedure was very effective at reducing performance anxiety (anxiety about how well the subject would perform), only slightly less effective at reducing state anxiety (anxiety about the event itself, including its possible outcomes and risks), and only slightly less effective than that at improving performance. The weakest of these effects, the performance effect, was still equal to or stronger than other established performance-enhancement techniques, such as mental practice and overlearning.[2]

---

1 Phase summaries taken from Terri Saunders and others, "The Effect of Stress Inoculation Training on Anxiety and Performance," *Journal of Occupational Health Psychology* 1, no. 2 (1996): 182–183.

2 The average effect sizes were: performance anxiety reduction $r=.509$, state anxiety reduction $r=.373$, performance enhancement $r=.296$, compared to performance enhancement from mental practice ($r=.255$) and overlearning

Stress inoculation has been adopted into a broad range of occupational fields with consistent effects and is definitely a tool worth considering for martial arts and self-defence along with the more traditional examination-style stress test.

I've been lucky enough to participate in stress inoculation and stress testing as it's used in modern police training. The Force Options Training Unit of the Vancouver Police Department has developed a reputation for providing some of the most effective and comprehensive training in the world, and it stress tests extensively. Since 2015, I've been a member of their role-player program, which uses live actors to simulate situations ranging from simple searches and arrests to de-escalations of mentally ill and distressed subjects; responses to domestic violence, gang violence, assaults with edged weapons and firearms; and acts of terrorism and mass violence.

We use stress testing as an examination tool to make sure that officers have the required decision-making capability and technical skill to take on additional, advanced roles such as that of a taser operator. More frequently, we use it as the final stage in a stress inoculation protocol that helps ensure that they can make split-second decisions to keep the public and their partner safe, regardless of the circumstances.

Hundreds of hours of active participation in the set-up, execution, and debriefing of stress testing scenarios has given me a lot of insight into how to make them work. My colleagues at Valkyrie WMAA and I have also designed effective stress tests and scenarios for teaching civilians in a range of contexts: from verbal de-escalation and intervention in low-risk physical encounters through defence against violent attacks with and without weapons, to mutual weapon combat.

(r=.298). Saunders and others, "The Effect of Stress Inoculation Training," 176–180. Overlearning is the practice of rehearsing or practising a newly acquired skill after initial proficiency has been achieved. In martial arts training, this might look like repeating a play or kata multiple times after you can perform it perfectly to commit it more strongly to memory.

Whether it's part of a stress inoculation protocol or a simple assessment, I've found that a successful stress test will always have the following four key features: relevance, realism, safety, and follow-up.

Relevance

Any test we devise has to be relevant to the type of violence that's being prepared for. That sounds obvious, but there's more to preparing someone for a physical assault than, well, physically assaulting them. We need to understand the context in which that assault is likely to take place and make sure that we tailor the goals and framing of our test to replicate not only how the assault happens, but why, where, when, and with whom it's most likely to happen.

A punch to the face means very different things on the training floor, in the boxing ring, outside a bar at 1 a.m., or in the middle of a romantic evening at home. The act is the same, but its psychological impact and likely consequences are dramatically different, as is the range of appropriate responses.

There are a number of ways to categorize the type of violence that we're dealing with, and all of them are useful for making sure that the test you come up with is relevant to the situation you want to simulate. I like to use the following heuristic:

- Is it play or earnest?

- Is it symmetrical or asymmetrical?

- Is it social or asocial?

Play versus Earnest

This first pairing is one of the primary ways of distinguishing between combat sports and self-defence. We're used to thinking of children roughhousing as an example of violent play (there's a reason the term "play fighting" exists), but adults also play at violence all the time. Sparring and competition are our two most common expressions of play violence. This doesn't mean that they aren't serious—or dangerous, as anyone who's watched more than five minutes of a mixed martial arts (MMA) event can tell you.

What makes violence into play are the constraints and compromises built into its structure that are designed to reduce the risk of catastrophic injury. Play violence is consensual, and it has clear boundaries: it will usually take place in a prescribed space (e.g., a boxing ring, MMA cage, or a less formal sparring area); limit the kinds of attacks you can throw, what they can target, or both (e.g., banning elbow strikes, or eye gouges, or hits to the back of the head or the groin); limit the length of the fight, or lay out conditions under which a fighter is deemed unfit to continue; and may modify the tools of violence to make them less lethal (e.g., replacing sharp blades with blunt simulators, or heavy clubs with padded sticks; or padding fists or bodies to reduce the effect of a strike).

All of these rules work together to keep the odds of serious injury or death below an agreed-upon threshold, and they rely on mutual consent and agreement to work. Everyone in a play fight has agreed to be there, and they've agreed to play by its rules.

To put it another way, play violence is a game. The violence isn't the primary goal, but the means to winning that game. And the fighters aren't primarily interested in harming their opponent, but in victory under their game's rules. In fact, actually wanting to hurt your opponent is often considered unsportsmanlike, and fighters who admit to enjoying or aiming for serious harm may find themselves short on invitations to future events.

In many cases, there's also a layer of abstraction added via a point system that shifts the focus even further from injury. You're not trying to beat the other person to a pulp, but to score more points than they can. It just so happens that points are earned by hitting them with a big stick, or kicking them in the chest.

Earnest violence, on the other hand, is explicitly about harming the opponent. Sure, you might stop at a certain point (not every bar brawl is a fight to the death, after all), but the goal is to injure or to cause pain. Special equipment doesn't make any appearances, and any weapons used have their full lethal potential. Your goal in an earnest fight is still to win, but winning looks like coming out with fewer injuries than your opponent, or hurting and humiliating them badly enough that they give up, rather than having more points or getting a better score from the judges.

Earnest violence can be consensual, but it often isn't. If one or more parties to the fight didn't get to choose whether to participate, it's definitely an earnest fight.

In most cases, the only play violence we're likely to want to stress test for is high-level competition. Earnest violence, on the other hand, belongs to self-defence scenarios, law enforcement, and warfare simulations. The tests we devise will take very different shapes depending on whether we're dealing with play or earnest violence.

In both cases, we need to make sure that we understand the goals of the encounter and its rules of engagement. What are the fighters aiming to do? Are they scoring points via specific strikes, submissions, or takedowns (play), or trying to deal enough damage to break their opponent's will to continue (earnest)? What are their highest-value targets? Are they targets that will earn them more points when struck (play), or targets that have the best odds of crippling or disabling their opponent (earnest)? Will the fight be externally assessed by judges, referees, or spectators (play); or internally assessed by a fighter's own sense that they have taken enough punishment and need to stop (earnest)?

All of these contextual elements arise naturally from the distinction between play and earnest combat and will dictate the format of your stress test.

Symmetrical versus Asymmetrical

Our second pairing describes one of the fundamental features of any violent encounter. When we talk about whether a fight is "fair," what we're really talking about is its symmetry. Are the size, strength, and skill level of the participants roughly equal? Do they both understand the rules, and are they both equally willing to abide by them? Are their intentions and goals equivalent, and are they aiming for the same targets? Are they armed, armoured, and positioned equally?

A mismatch in any of these areas will tilt the fight in favour of one side or another, and sometimes radically so. For this reason, the majority of play violence leans toward symmetrical violence. If the goal is a test of skill, then it makes sense to strip out any unrelated advantages that might allow one fighter to win against someone more skilled than them. Conversely, a lot of earnest violence skews toward asymmetrical fights. Any advantage that comes out of a mismatched pairing increases a fighter's odds of hurting their opponent without getting hurt themselves, and there's not a lot of incentive to fight fair.

This becomes even more the case when we throw criminal behaviour and mindset into the mix. Most violent criminals are actually pretty risk-averse. Sure, they engage in inherently risky behaviours like theft, assault, and murder, but they also work very hard to minimize their odds of getting caught or hurt in the course of getting what they want. This is why target selection matters so much, and why a lot of self-defence instruction emphasizes making oneself a less appealing target for violent crime. Criminals are looking to skew the odds as far in their favour as possible, and that means picking a target who is smaller, weaker, slower, and less-prepared than they are.

It also means putting themselves at a tactical advantage (through surprise, positioning, and choosing the location of the attack), and a mechanical advantage (by using a weapon). The "worst case" self-defence situations that many students want to learn to defend against are also often the most asymmetrical: a rapist immobilizing a much smaller victim; a gunman firing into a crowd of civilians; a surprise assault with a weapon against an unarmed target.

Symmetry is the reason why sparring is a poor training tool for most self-defence situations: you cannot effectively use a symmetrical practice model to prepare for asymmetrical real-life encounters. When designing a stress test, it's important to map out exactly how symmetrical or asymmetrical the target context is, and replicate as much of that as possible. That can mean everything from deliberately mismatching the size and skill level of fighters (to simulate someone picking on a "weaker" target); to arming only one side or the other; to stacking the terrain, timing, and lighting conditions in favour of one fighter.

Considering possible asymmetries can also help prepare for some of the most challenging competitive contexts: how might you simulate a boxing match against an opponent who's known to cheat, for example? Or an outdoor fight where one fighter is likely to end up with the sun in their eyes? By the same token, if you're preparing someone for a competition that's strictly controlled and likely to be very symmetrical, pitting them against a much larger or much smaller fighter isn't going to be very relevant.

Social versus Asocial

Our final pairing looks at the cultural and communicative context of violence, and is a common categorization in self-defence training. When we talk about whether violence is social or asocial, we're concerned with what it's ultimately trying to accomplish. If the small-scale goal of a fight is determined by whether it's play (scoring points) or earnest (hurting without being hurt), we still need to sort out what its large-scale goal is.

Why are the fighters scoring points? What does hurting someone else accomplish? What is the fight for, and who is going to decide whether it has served its purpose?

In social violence, the fight is a means of communication and of affecting your social environment. It's about showing off, establishing dominance, teaching someone a lesson, or determining who does and doesn't belong in a group or space. Sparring is social violence. So is combat sport and martial arts competition. So is a "monkey dance" between two drunk guys in a bar, or the fans of two opposing hockey teams.

In all of these cases, the violence is a way of figuring out who's on top. It's a performance, and that performance requires an audience. That's why social violence often occurs in public spaces: so that a win can be witnessed, and a loss can be mitigated by face-saving gestures or the intervention of a fighter's peers. Because it's primarily concerned with things other than pain and injury, it's often possible to prevent or stop social violence through verbal de-escalation or other social interventions.[3]

Asocial violence has different goals. It is predatory behaviour that exists outside of social status games and relationships. A predator either uses violence as a means to get something they want very badly (these people are sometimes referred to as resource predators, and include thieves, carjackers, and muggers), or simply enjoys the act of violence itself (these are process predators, and include sexual predators and serial killers).

Asocial violence doesn't want an audience, as anyone witnessing it would recognize that they were watching a crime being committed or a social more being violated, and would likely intervene or contact the authorities. It is also difficult to counter through social means, especially at higher levels of force. Capitulation can work for resource predators, as they're more interested in getting what they want than harming another person, but nothing short of fighting back or escaping the situation altogether will deter a process predator.

These contextual differences have to be accounted for in designing a stress test. Should it have an audience? What will that audience's role be: will they cheer the fighters on (social); evaluate them (social); or try to intervene (asocial)? And what will the "win condition" for the test be: collecting a set number of points or demonstrating sufficient dominance (social); defusing the conflict by any means possible, including non-violent ones (both); surviving and escaping the conflict, by disabling the attacker if necessary (asocial)?

---

3 There are types of social violence to which these tools don't apply very well. Rory Miller talks about the special cases of the Status Seeking Show, the Group Monkey Dance, and certain flavours of Educational Beatdown. While these kinds of violence are social from the perspective of the perpetrator, they are so asymmetric and brutal that they are effectively asocial attacks from the perspective of the victim, and need to be treated as such. Rory Miller, *Facing Violence: Preparing for the Unexpected* (Boston: YMAA Publication Center, 2011), 30–35.

Distinguishing between social and asocial violence helps you understand how a scenario should play out to be considered successful, and how the fighters should interact with the world around them.

> ### Exercise: Break Down the Violence You Work With
>
> Write down the events that you want to stress test. What are the most stressful and dangerous situations that your students need to be ready for to complete their training?
>
> Break down each one according to the above categories: is it play or earnest violence? Symmetrical or asymmetrical? Social or asocial? Think about how these features will affect the details of the test you run.

Let's take a few different situations that an instructor might want to stress test, and look at how these three categorizations let us quickly build a relevant test. We'll examine a competition sparring match, a fight against a cheater, a formal duel, and an attempted murder.

Competition Sparring Match: Play, Symmetrical, Social

A sparring competition is play fighting, and comes with rules that will regulate the length and terrain of the fight, allowed targets, and scoring conditions. It is symmetrical in mindset and intent—both fighters have the same goals, and are using the same general tools to achieve them. It is also symmetrical in physical means—both fighters will have matching weapons and armour, and are likely to be evenly matched in size, weight, experience level, and even gender.[4]

---

4 A common exception to this physical symmetry is the open HEMA tournament. With no restrictions on gender, experience level, or weight class, these tournaments shift sparring from a fully symmetrical contest to a partially asymmetrical one: goals, rules, and intentions are still evenly matched, but physical attributes may be dramatically mismatched, and these mismatches must be accounted for in training.

As a social fight, it's got an audience that expects to be impressed and entertained by what they see, and which may be quite vocal in supporting their favoured fighters. It also has a more specialized audience of referees and judges, who are looking for specific things (valid hits, rules violations, etc.), and whose sightlines, biases, and training will affect how they interpret what they see.

A test would need to include a field of combat and clear ruleset, an appropriate opponent, a casual audience of spectators, and a specialist audience of judges or referees well versed in the ruleset.

Success would require playing by the rules, consistently hitting an equally-matched opponent, dealing with the psychological pressure of an audience, and communicating effectively with the judges to make sure that they score your valid hits and award you discretionary points for style and execution.

Sorting Out a Cheater: Play, Asymmetrical, Social

There are times in training or competition when one party doesn't want to play by the rules. Maybe it's a competitor who has decided they need to cheat to win, or a student who delights in out-muscling and crushing their partners in drills that are meant to be friendly. A fight like this is still play. It has rules and boundaries, and one party's disregard for or violation of them is central to the encounter.

It is asymmetrical in intention, and may be asymmetrical in targeting or level of force. It is also social, and that social nature is part of what makes it so stressful and difficult to manage. The "victim" needs to control their misbehaving opponent without looking like an asshole, escalating the stakes beyond what the audience considers acceptable, or losing face.

A test would need to include a clear framework (competition, classroom drill, etc.) and ruleset or set of expectations, a non-compliant opponent intent on breaking the rules, and a relevant audience of judges, instructors, or fellow students.

Success would require identifying the source of the asymmetry and addressing it via a range of socially acceptable options: from using skill and tactics to deliver an unequivocal defeat without causing serious injury or escalating to an earnest fight, to using communication and social skills to expose the cheater and encourage outside intervention.

Formal Duel: Earnest, Symmetrical, Social

A duel raises the stakes substantially: while injury is possible in a sparring match or competition fight, it's a very likely outcome for at least one party in a duel. This is an earnest fight, in which the intent is to do noticeable harm. It's a symmetrical contest, where combatants will be evenly armed, and have equivalent intentions around targeting and intended outcome.

It's also very much a case of social violence. The point of a duel is to demonstrate your superiority to an audience of peers, and that includes superiority of skill (by hitting well without being hit back), social standing (by conducting yourself with dignity, honour, and style), and morals (by showing restraint and limiting danger to bystanders).

A test would require a weapon set-up or ruleset that triggers a fear response proportional to the expected level of injury for the loser, an appropriate opponent, a clear social framework that governs expected conduct and boundaries, and an audience with its sympathies divided between the combatants and a vested interest in enforcing the social expectations of the duel.

Success would require landing decisive hits against a determined opponent, facing the fear of serious injury with a cool head, winning the sympathies of the audience through showmanship and ethical conduct, and dealing with the pressures of a hostile audience that's cheering for one's opponent.

Attempted Murder: Earnest, Asymmetrical, Asocial

A targeted, deadly attack is one of the worst-case scenarios any of us prepare for. It is earnest, and carries with it a risk of death or grievous injury. It is asymmetrical in nearly every way, with the attacker having chosen the time, place, target, and weapons to give them as many advantages as possible. It is also asocial. It takes place away from prying eyes and cannot be de-escalated through social skill or conversation. The only way out is to tilt the odds against the attacker strongly enough that they are unwilling or unable to continue.

A test would require an unfavourable setting (e.g., low lighting conditions, a narrow hallway or corner, unstable footing), and a genuinely threatening armed opponent with the element of surprise. It might also include bystanders or passers-by, if intervention is allowed as a possibility.

Success would require responding to the initial assault in a way that would prevent or reduce injury if it were real and then either disabling the attacker, disengaging and escaping, or triggering a successful intervention.

Realism

Understanding what kind of violence we want to simulate and what elements characterize that violence lets us build a test that's actually relevant to our students. If we get the pieces right, we can be reasonably sure that we'll be testing skills and decisions that are as similar as possible to the ones that our student will need to face the real thing. The next part of our job is selling them on it. For a test to be valid, and for a lesson to stick, our student has to believe that what they're facing is real.

But what does "real" mean in a simulation context? If we're simulating attempted murder, we can't do it by pitting our students against live weapons and an opponent with genuinely murderous intent. That would be grossly negligent at minimum, and would probably count as actual attempted murder of the very-much-illegal variety.

So what is real enough? A plastic knife? A blunt piece of steel? An electrified training tool like a Shocknife? And how hard should the attacker really try to hit their target? Do they go full speed, full power? Is 90 percent of that sufficient? 75 percent? To answer these questions, we need to first understand what makes simulations effective teaching tools from a biological and psychological perspective.

The key element of every stress test is, well, stress. When a human is exposed to stress, their body is flooded with a cocktail of neurotransmitters, hormones, and steroids. The most important of these are adrenaline and noradrenaline (also known as epinephrine and norepinephrine), acetylcholine, and cortisol. These chemicals trigger rapid changes in the autonomic nervous system, and set the body up for a fight, flight, or freeze response.[5]

Which responses are available depends on a host of factors, from psychological makeup and prior hormone levels to the specific nature and proximity of the threat. In very general terms, we differentiate between two broad categories of threat response: active (fight or flight), and passive (freeze).

In an active response, adrenaline stimulates the sympathetic nervous system to dilate the pupils, increase heart rate and blood pressure, suppress digestive function, increase respiratory function, and increase muscle tone, while cortisol dumps sugar into your bloodstream to fuel activity. You get faster, stronger, and less sensitive to pain and fatigue, while also losing some of your perception (including effects like tunnel vision and auditory exclusion) and fine motor control.

A brief freeze can be part of this active response by putting a temporary brake on action by lowering your blood pressure, and allowing the brain to orient toward the threat and prepare an appropriate response. In a passive response, this freeze either stretches on too long and stops you from taking effective action, or is accompanied by a big drop in blood pressure and near-total unresponsiveness (a state known as tonic im-

---

5 Fight/flight/freeze is the most common formulation for the body's physical reactions to stress, and is the one I use in my own teaching. Other models include fight/flight/posture/submit (made popular in Lt. Col. Dave Grossman's *On Killing: The Psychological Cost of Learning to Kill in War and Society*) and fight/flight/tend/befriend (which appears most prominently in evolutionary psychology research on how women and men respond differently to stress).

mobility, which can allow for survival in extreme cases where more active responses have failed).[6]

Stress testing requires triggering these reactions. We need our students
to understand how their motor performance is affected by adrenaline
and what they're physically able to do in the middle of an active response. Can they chain together complex series of techniques? How is
their targeting? Their power generation? Their footwork and movement?
Their memory and decision-making capacity? We also need them to be
able to flip quickly from a short freeze to a fight or flight reaction and
avoid the potentially lethal consequences of an inappropriate passive
response. We can only explore these reactions and improve them if the
initial stress response is triggered. No hormone cocktail, no stress test.

Luckily for us, the brain isn't particularly good at differentiating between simulated and real threats. In a study of medical residents, researchers found no difference between their stress level after a real-life
emergency and after a relevant high-pressure simulation.[7] The real-life
emergencies took place in an emergency room and included shock, respiratory failure, and heart attacks in real patients. The simulations were
conducted in a mock emergency room with a training mannequin that
could be programmed to mimic the physiological signs of heart attack
and pulmonary edema, and respond to the actions of the residents.[8]

The mannequins the researchers used are very sophisticated in their
ability to mimic human physiological processes, but they don't look
particularly lifelike. The SimMan model used in these simulations has
obviously synthetic skin, hard plastic hair, a permanently open, lipless

---

6 Karin Roelofs, "Freeze for Action: Neurobiological Mechanisms in Animal
and Human Freezing," *Philosophical Transactions of the Royal Society B* 372,
no. 1718 (2017): 2–4.

7 Roger Daglius Dias and Augusto Scalabrini Neto, "Stress Levels During
Emergency Care: A Comparison between Reality and Simulated Scenarios,"
Journal of Critical Care 33 (2016): 8–10. Stress levels were measured in both
physiological terms (blood pressure, heart rate, and salivary analysis of stress
markers) and psychological terms (rating on the State-Trait Anxiety Inventory
Score).

8 Dias and Neto, "Stress Levels During Emergency Care," 9.

mouth, and eyes with no irises or pupils.[9] It doesn't look enough like a real human to confuse you even for a second, but residents still responded to its physical distress like they would to a real person's suffering.

I've seen similar effects in simulated violence settings. Students have responded the same way to a rubber knife, or a hammer coming down on a plastic hand splattered in fake blood, as they would to the real thing, as long as the person holding the weapon treated it as if it was real. The key to realism in a stress test isn't creating perfect reproductions of items or even people, but having a situation play out realistically. Response and interaction are key; everything else is set dressing.

There are some limits to this—put your actors in so much padding that they don't move like normal humans, give them wobbly, poorly made rubber weapons, and put them in an empty, padded training hall while telling everyone it's a treacherous, rocky hill covered in blackberry bushes, and you'll rapidly tip the whole thing over into farce. Extreme cases aside, you can push elements like equipment pretty far as long as the humans in your stress test behave as they would in the real thing.

A plastic knife is plenty scary if it's in the hand of a screaming man who is so enraged he can't string together a coherent sentence and who is charging at you from across the room. Fake blood or even just a red ink splotch on a shirt more than does the job if the person wearing it is crying and shaking and curling up around the pain of the wound.

Students will regularly see past padded armour and full-face helmets if the body language and vocalizations of the actor fit with those of a regular person. Similarly, if they hit that padded person and that person responds to the strike as an unarmoured opponent would, the hit feels real even if it does no actual damage to the target.

My favourite example of this effect happened at an event where I was teaching an introductory workshop on stress testing to a group of about fifteen students. Because stress tests were the topic, we spent a lot of time on the bones of what we were doing: what kind of violence we want-

---

9 "SimMan," Laerdal, accessed Jan 31, 2018, https://www.laerdal.com/ca/doc/86/SimMan#/Info.

ed to simulate, how we would manage safety, what kind of response we wanted to elicit in a partner, etc. Nobody was under any illusion that what we were doing was "real," and we spent as much time discussing the mechanics of simulations as running them.

About halfway through, I wanted to introduce verbal aggression and yelling into a simple simulation of a monkey dance (earnest, social, symmetrical violence). The students were uncomfortable with using their voices and needed some guidance and a clear example. So I spent a solid five minutes talking about the dynamics of yelling in a testing environment.

I discussed what language to use, whether it matters if you get repetitive or say something ridiculous, and the psychological barriers we have to overcome in order to be able to scream obscenities at someone we care about in training. Then I grabbed an assistant and demonstrated the same simulation we'd just been playing with, but with added verbal interaction.

My (large, male) assistant started shoving me backward toward a wall while yelling insults and threatening to beat me up. I backed up and loudly begged him to stop and leave me alone. We didn't get very far before a handful of students jumped in and restrained my assistant.

Everyone in the class knew it wasn't real. We'd explicitly framed our demonstration as a demonstration, and it came at the end of a lesson that repeatedly acknowledged that what were doing was "fake." It didn't matter. A good third of the class was so emotionally engaged by what was happening that they actively intervened on my behalf. They felt pretty silly a moment later when they realized what had happened, but they also learned a very good lesson about the effectiveness of a little bit of acting and emotional engagement. As long as the feelings look real, people will believe.

If you've set up a scenario that's relevant to the skills you want to test and prepared your actors to behave in ways that are realistic for the context, there are a few extra things you can do to ramp up stress without necessarily compromising safety.

The volume of participants' voices and the language your actors use is an immensely powerful lever. Are they attacking in disciplined silence, or screaming at the top of their lungs? Are they making threats against the student? Or insulting them? How personal are they getting? Targeted language can be an enormous contributor to the stress of a combat scenario, and should also be managed carefully, as it's the most likely thing to hit on trauma-related triggers or push the stress level above what is safe.

Playing with lighting levels or space constraints can also change things considerably. Putting your students in places where they can't see all of what's going on (either because it's dark, or because part of the scenario is happening around a corner or behind a door) will increase stress. So will anything else that creates uncertainty, including giving the attacker the element of surprise. Think of the strategies that horror movies use to increase dread or set up jump scares, and you'll be on the right track.

Exercise: Set Stress Targets

Take another look at the situations you want to stress test. How stressed should a student be in each situation? Rank their expected response on a scale from one to ten, where one is the discomfort of meeting a stranger, and ten is the sheer terror of fighting for your life against overwhelming force.

Brainstorm how to achieve each stress level. Plan how to manipulate the environment (including lighting levels and terrain), feeder behaviour (including verbal and physical cues), and stakes (is your student protecting someone else? Is there an audience? Is time a factor?) to hit the number you've set.

The only caveat when you're adding stressors is that you're trying to approximate the stress of a real situation, not see how high you can crank your students' blood pressure in three seconds. If things need to be very,

very scary to approximate the genuine threat level of what you're simulating (like our "attempted murder" example from the previous section),
then you can lay it on more. If you just need to push students to where
they're anxious and uncomfortable, or briefly catch them by surprise,
stop there. Realism is about matching the level of stress of the simulation to the level of stress in the real event—no more or less.

Safety

So we've established that the primary goal of a stress test is to induce a
reasonably high level of stress in the student. I've also mentioned how
the physiological effect of the hormone cocktail that's released under
stress will likely include an increase in their power and speed, and a decrease in their sensitivity to pain and their fine motor control. And since
this is a martial arts or self-defence context, they'll be in that stress test
with one or more live partners and not an inert mannequin.

Short of a competition or a real-life violent encounter, a stress test is
likely to be the most physically and psychologically risky space our students will enter, and it needs to be treated as such.

If you've got good policies in place and are prioritizing self-regulation,
consent, and good partnership practices in your classes, then there's a
solid foundation in place for making your stress testing as safe as possible. If you don't feel like your students or coaches have a solid grasp of
those tools, you really shouldn't be running stress tests. The chapters of
this book are laid out in order from most to least essential, and skipping
ahead to the "cool stuff" here is only going to put you and your students
at unnecessary risk. Lay the groundwork first; then you can start pushing people's physical and psychological limits.

With those foundations in mind, there are still a number of safety concerns that are specific to stress testing. Let's return to the maxim of
creating psychological safety for physically dangerous situations, and
physical safety for psychologically dangerous situations. More than any
other thing we do, stress testing has the potential to combine both kinds
of risk. While the player in the drill is primarily being subjected to the

psychological risk created by stress, its effects on their body and ability to control their actions (and especially the force and speed with which they react) can make the situation very physically risky for the feeder.

This means that we need to address both kinds of danger, from two very different angles, to make sure that everyone comes out as intact as possible. In a stress test—regardless of its length or intensity—we have to manage the physical and psychological safety of each participant individually, as well as that of the entire environment. This breaks down as follows:

Physical Safety

- The player should perceive a substantial threat without actually being at risk of serious injury, which means controlling the feeder's power generation, targeting, speed, tool use, and level of adrenalization

- The feeder should be able to safely withstand the impact of any attack an adrenalized player throws at them, which usually requires personal protective equipment, environment modifications such as mats and other padded surfaces, and training in techniques like breakfalls

- All participants should be fully aware of the physical risks involved, and should have the freedom to call a halt at any time

- The space in which the stress test occurs should be made safe enough for the participants (including the removal or modification of potentially dangerous items and surfaces), and should be separated from the rest of the training space by clear boundaries

- The stress test should be supervised by one or more facilitators with complete knowledge of its goals and constraints, with a clear view of the field of play and all participants, and the authority to call a halt at any time

Psychological Safety

- The player should completely trust the facilitator to manage the situation appropriately, and should be able to debrief with and seek comfort from people other than the feeder

- The feeder should have as complete knowledge as possible of what will happen in the stress test before it starts, as well as the opportunity to rest quietly and debrief away from the player after it ends

- All participants should have the opportunity to discuss triggers and psychological concerns with the facilitator before the test, and should have the freedom to call a halt at any time

- The facilitator should take any triggers or past trauma into account when setting up the scenario and directing the feeder's actions and words, and should manage the overall level of psychological arousal very carefully

- Any audience or witnesses to the stress test should be fully briefed on its goals and constraints, and should be prevented from providing feedback or commentary unless explicitly instructed to by the facilitator

- The stress test should have clear start and end points, and designated time for preparation and debriefing/follow-up

These specific considerations can be boiled down to a few core principles: manage the level of force and potential injury in the stress test; manage the emotional arousal of the participants; and create clear physical and psychological boundaries.

> ### Exercise: Make It Safer
>
> For each of your planned stress tests, list the biggest dangers to your participants. Make sure to consider the physical arena of the test, the equipment and weapons present, the techniques that are likely to be used, and the emotional state of all participants.
>
> For each danger, come up with a one-sentence plan for mitigating it. Make sure that your solutions are balanced between boundary-setting, emotional management, and force and impact control. If you find yourself relying on safety equipment to address the majority of the dangers you list, revisit the structure of your stress test.

Let's work through these principles in more detail, starting with boundary-setting.

Boundary-Setting

The stress test needs to have very clear constraints on its scope: who is and is not involved? Where can they go? What can they do? Are there any actions or levels of contact that are prohibited? It must also have clear start and end points, so that the stress doesn't continue beyond the moment when the teaching goals have been achieved, and so that the physically dangerous bit is as brief as possible.

If I'm trying to work a student through surviving a surprise assault with a knife, for example, do we cut things off only once they've gotten away, checked themselves for injuries, and called the police; or can we break once they've fought back hard enough to create room to escape and started running away? If they get the attacker pinned and start delivering disabling blows, how many do I let land before it's "good enough"? Where things end depends on the problem we're trying to solve and the specific stressors we're dealing with, and it has to be balanced against the risk of physical or psychological injury if we let the test go on for too long.

The test also needs a safety cut-out for when any of its boundaries are breached, and this cut-out (a safe word or phrase, a physical signal like a tap, or both) must be available to all participants. Finally, it needs very clearly defined roles that do not change. The feeder remains the feeder for the duration of the experience, and doesn't suddenly switch to teaching or comforting the player the moment the scenario ends. The person facilitating and supervising the stress test is never involved in its events, and is the keeper of the test—they dictate when it starts, when it ends, and guides all of the participants through any follow-up.

If these boundaries are clearly laid out and rigorously enforced, they create a bubble in which very scary things can happen in relative safety. Entering this bubble must always be voluntary, and it must be very clear when that transition has happened. I use clear verbal commands like "Begin scenario!" and also demarcate a physical space that counts as "in" (e.g., "Everyone who is on these mats is a participant in this exercise. Folks on the wooden floor are not involved."). You can spring all kinds of surprises on people inside the bubble, but entering it (or going into "scenario mode") can never be a surprise.

There should also be a clear transition back into the regular world. Debriefings are essential to helping students understand what happened to them, what they did, and why they did it, and they also help bring them back out of the mental space of the scenario. At minimum, there should be a few minutes after the stress test to discuss what happened, and a bit of quiet space available for students to cool down in whatever way works for them. The feeder and player should get the time they need to transition out of their respective roles, and to re-establish their usual relationship—especially after a highly asymmetric and scary scenario like an attempted murder. They may need some time apart, or a chance to talk, or the opportunity for hugs or other positive physical contact.

For students who aren't yet familiar with the stress testing process, I run more hands-on aftercare, with a detailed discussion of the physical and psychological aftermath of an adrenaline dump, and some specific tools for managing it. I'll usually set aside thirty minutes to an hour for this process, and encourage students to take their time coming back to a level place before they leave the school and attempt to drive home or do anything else that requires them to be calm and focused.

Managing Emotional Arousal

This cool-down process fits nicely into our next principle of managing emotional arousal, which has to happen on a group and individual level.

We know that the player is going to get adrenalized, because that's the point of the exercise. The feeder is going to be fighting against a heavily adrenalized human, which is stressful in its own right. They may also be doing things like screaming, swearing, and otherwise conveying intense emotion, which is very likely to bleed over into their own emotional state.

We established in the "Realism" section that the mind isn't very good at distinguishing between simulation and reality, so long as the simulation behaves like the real thing. This is true not only for the test subject, but also for every other participant in the simulation. If we create a stressful situation, it stresses everyone—not just the player. This means that you'll have at least two adrenalized people on your hands, and may have many more if you're running multiple drills at once, or if you're adding bystanders, witnesses, and an audience to your test.

The facilitator has to monitor the emotional state of everyone in the group, and needs to actively manage how ramped up they get. The higher the level of emotional arousal, the less ability participants have to manage fine motor skills and high levels of cognitive processing.[10] A very heavily adrenalized person is probably going to struggle to keep their targeting precise and moderate their force output, and will not be able to make complex decisions easily. If both the player and the feeder are in this state, it becomes a lot more difficult to manage safety.

There are a few tools that can reliably reduce the feeder's level of emotional arousal. The first is personal protective equipment. If they are padded or armoured to a level where they are reasonably certain that

---

10 Schmidt, *Motor Learning and Performance,* 41–42.

they will not suffer catastrophic injury even if the player attacks with full force, their sense of threat in the situation will diminish.

Training makes an even bigger difference here: if the feeder knows how to fall safely, how to move with joint locks and other immobilizations to reduce their risk of injury, how to take a punch, and when to call a halt or tap out, they'll also be buffered by their confidence in their own abilities. For this reason, I prefer to use senior students and coaches as feeders in very high-pressure tests. When I partner less experienced students with each other for stress testing, I work at lower levels of physical risk and intensity.

Information is also a very powerful tool for the feeder. If they have a detailed picture of how the test will go, what they will and will not be subjected to, and what safeguards are in place to protect them, their anxiety will drop and take their overall emotional arousal with it. If the feeder is at a lower level of emotional arousal than the player, they'll be better able to control their targeting, intensity, and force output (and so protect the player from harm), and they'll respond quickly to unexpected developments and safety issues (protecting both themselves and the player).

Preparation, cool-down time, and overall timing are the best tools for managing the player and controlling group emotional arousal.

How you prime the participants before an exercise makes a huge difference to how adrenalized they get. If the player goes in cold, knowing only that something will happen to them, their uncertainty and anxiety will increase their emotional arousal dramatically. If they have a rough picture of what to expect, that will drop a little. Give them a precise idea of the shape and parameters of the drill, and it'll drop further still.

Similarly, how much time you give them to recover between tests or repetitions of a drill will govern how much their emotional state levels off before jumping back in. You can keep the stress level very high by not giving them a chance to rest beyond a quick physical recovery (getting their breath back, maybe taking a quick sip of water), or you can bring down a too-adrenalized group by pausing to discuss what's happening for a few minutes or going through a simple breathing or meditation exercise.

If we're prioritizing safety, our goal should be to get the player to the level of emotional arousal that fits the parameters of the test—whether that's the anxiety of a performance, rank exam, or tournament, or the near-panic of a sudden attack—keep them there only as long as we need to accomplish the test's goals, and then bring them down to a normal level before sending them out the door and back into the real world.

There is an art to fine-tuning the arousal levels of an entire group, and it can take time to build the sensitivity to others' emotional states that you need to catch subtle shifts as they happen. You can manage things on a broader level just by varying how much you prepare (or don't prepare) each participant, how long you let the stress continue, and how much support you provide in the aftermath. Monitor each test or group, make note of what changes have what effects, and build your expertise from there.

Partner Skills

Handling boundaries and emotional arousal levels takes care of a lot of the risk of physical injury. If the space and timing are controlled and nobody gets more adrenalized than necessary, we can keep unplanned surprises to a minimum, and make sure as many people as possible have the physical and mental faculties they need to stay in control. The principles of good partnership laid out in the previous chapter are the next piece of the puzzle. If the feeder is focused on facilitating the player's learning and not on winning the fight, then they'll do a much better job of keeping everyone safe.

This doesn't necessarily mean that the feeder must lose every time. If the player freezes, or takes an action that dramatically worsens their position, then the feeder may need to get the upper hand in order to help the player learn from their error. What it means is that the feeder cannot let their adrenaline and ego get the better of them, and cannot use the framework of the test to crush the player.

If the test simulates a symmetrical encounter such as a tournament match or duel, then it's the feeder's job to make sure things stay symmetrical, even if they see opportunities to cheat or overpower the player. If it's meant to be asymmetrical, then it's very likely that a certain level of compliance is required on the feeder's part.

At the highest levels of self-defence practice, for example, the feeder is likely to be playing the role of a stronger, larger, better-armed attacker with lethal intent. To get out alive, the player can't fight fair. They'll need to gouge eyes, crush throats, break joints, hit lethal and disabling targets, and do plenty of other things that would be outlawed in a sporting match.

To keep the feeder alive, most of those actions will have to happen at reduced force, either by being delivered at lower speed and intensity, or by being delivered through padding or armour. And because they're not actually lethal or debilitating, the feeder is going to have to do a bit of acting, and respond to them as if they were real.

If the feeder blows off the player's attacks, then one of two dangerous things will happen: either the player will escalate until the feeder reacts—even if that means hurting them for real—or the player will become convinced that their techniques don't work, and will believe that they are helpless in a "real" fight. If the feeder does their job well, both participants will stay safe and the player will learn the right lessons.

Safety Equipment

Equipment is the last piece of this puzzle, and it varies the most from situation to situation. When any item is added to the test space, whether it's an obvious weapon like a knife, sword, or firearm, or a piece of set dressing like furniture or costuming, we need to assume that someone might decide to use it as a weapon.

They might pick it up and use it to stab or bludgeon their partner, choke or restrain them with it, or push or drop them onto it. Everything in the space—including the walls, floor, and anything the participants happen to have in their pockets—is a potential weapon.

With that in mind, we need to ask two questions about everything in the test space:

- Does this need to be here?

- Am I comfortable with the test participants using it as a weapon?

The first question is a great way to identify and remove unnecessary hazards. You can have participants empty their pockets, you can tidy away clutter, and you can move aside large obstacles like training dummies or storage racks.

The second question helps us make the stuff that's left safe to use. If there's a corner of wall sticking out into the test space, how do I feel about somebody being run into it at full speed? If that thought makes me queasy, I can either move the test to an area without pesky corners, or pad the corner enough that I'm comfortable with the amount of damage it might do to a participant.

There are companies that produce foam replicas of common household furniture—from tables and chairs to refrigerators, dressers, and lamps—so that they can be included in realistic scenarios without becoming deadly weapons. If you're throwing a knife into the mix, consider what material you're comfortable having your participants stabbed with. Does it need to be steel or another rigid material? Or is rubber or nylon a better choice?

Once you've got your weapons sorted, it's time to look at armour. What do the feeder and the player need to wear to protect them from death or serious injury when they make contact with the weapons in the space? If they're going to be falling on concrete or running into brick walls, then knee and elbow pads might be essential. If they're on mats in a room with padded walls, falling and running into obstacles is less of an issue, and they might be able to forego pads. Are blows to the head likely? Even a little likely? Then a padded helmet is probably a good idea. If they're going to be stabbed or struck repeatedly in the torso, chest and kidney padding might make sense as well.

There's a tradeoff with armour, always. More padding means less mo-bility, a narrower field of vision (especially with helmets), and a bit less realism. Armour also doesn't protect against some of the worst potential injuries. No helmet can prevent a concussion, and arm and leg armour won't stop most joint injuries. I generally use the minimum amount of armour that will protect the feeder from the biggest risks in a test, and pair it with a carefully managed environment, feeders who are experi-enced with falling and mitigating damage from strikes and joint locks, and enough emotional regulation that nobody is too adrenalized to stop or think. You'll need to find your own comfort zone.

Do keep in mind, however, that armour is only a very small piece of the safety puzzle. There's a reason it's at the end of this section—if you're managing all of the other elements of the test well, including boundar-ies, emotional arousal, and partnership behaviour, then armour is just one final safeguard against injury, rather than the only thing standing between your students and crippling damage.

Follow-Up

The final piece of an effective stress test is follow-up. How we debrief and discuss what happened is an integral part of managing the test as a learning experience. Every scenario I did with the police training unit was followed by three simple questions, and I've used those same ques-tions to frame my debriefings for martial arts and self-defence stress tests ever since:

What did you see? What did you do? Why did you do it?

How exactly the test subject answers them can vary a lot. Some students will answer each question individually, working through the whole test in pieces as they pick out relevant details. Most will pull them into a narrative that walks through the whole experience from start to finish. Some will give a blow-by-blow account, while others work in broad strokes and focus on the most important moments of the encounter. In all cases, answering these questions starts to build vital self-evaluation and communication skills.

For students preparing for a competitive environment like a tournament, this format lays the foundations of tactical analysis. They have to break down their opponent's actions ("What did you see?"), recall their own reactions ("What did you do?"), and draw connections between the stimulus the opponent provided, and the response they chose ("Why did you do it?").

Both the details they identify and how they discuss their own choices provide fertile ground for a tactical discussion. Not only will they tell you what their thought process was during the fight, but the things they highlight or leave out will tell you how their perception works under stress, and how capable they are of recognizing openings, threats, and opportunities for action.

Most importantly, forcing them to actually talk through what happened pushes them to think deliberately about their actions in a fight, and to consider them in relation to their opponent and environment. Doing this in the immediate aftermath of the fight, when they are still under the effects of adrenaline, can be a very important skill for learning how to analyze and adapt their strategies in a multi-round tournament or during breaks in the middle of a match.

For students who are training for self-defence, the questions become even more critical. self-defence, after all, isn't a fighting style, but a legal concept. It's a legal defence—or justification—for harming another person, and it may well need to be argued in court. Even without the formality of a courtroom, anyone who acts in self-defence needs to be able to explain their actions to a police officer or other emergency personnel on scene, to a local authority figure like a boss or bouncer, to friends or loved ones who ask what happened, and to themselves.

These same three questions let them practise doing that. They start with the attacker's actions, or the situation that required intervention. "What did you see?" gets us body language and other pre-assault cues, the social and power dynamics at play, the physical behaviour of the threat, and any weapons or other tools that were present. "What did you do?" situates the student in response to that, and provides a narrative of the actions they took to escape, de-escalate, or control the threat.

"Why did you do it?" is the critical piece that adds their mindset (Were they afraid for their life? Did they have a plan? Did they consider the proportionality of their actions or level of force?) and their understanding of the likely consequences of the threat's behaviour (did the threat have the means, opportunity, and intent to cause serious harm?).

Taken together, these three questions build a narrative that can explain why an act of violence was in fact an act of self-defence.[11] If students can successfully answer them in the still-adrenalized aftermath of a stress test, then they will be better prepared to do the same if they have to speak to the police after a real encounter.

The answers you get to these questions may also help explain unexpected outcomes and help you evaluate your test design. If the player responded to a stimulus in a way that looked wildly inappropriate during the test, but their answer to "What did you see?" makes it clear that the threat looked very different from their perspective than from yours, that's valuable data. If their discussion of their thought process points to past experiences that they factored into their choices, that's something to take into account when training that student in the future. Three simple questions provide invaluable data for improving our tests.

Whether you use questions like these or a different discussion format, the immediate debriefing should be quick. It's effectively an extension of the test, in that it forces the student to do some important thinking while they are still stressed. They won't be in a mental state where complex discussions or detailed lectures are going to stick in their minds, so if you want to get into a longer technical discussion of how they fought,

---

11 If you're not familiar with the legal context of self-defence or some of the terms I'm using here, like pre-assault cues or the means/opportunity/intent framework, you need to do some more reading and preparation before running self-defence stress tests—or teaching self-defence, full stop. Those fundamentals are well outside the scope of this book, but there are some great resources available for improving your understanding of self-defence as a domain. Rory Miller and Lawrence A. Kane's *Scaling Force: Dynamic Decision-Making under Threat of Violence* has a nice, quick primer on the core legal concepts at play (pages 34–43), and Miller's *Facing Violence* includes a longer discussion of the principles of articulation and the violence dynamics that underpin a lot of decision-making in these situations.

or work through their actions and decision-making in more detail, it's best to save that for a longer follow-up in the next class or during a separately scheduled lesson.

Any follow-up on the day of the test is best left for emotional cool-downs and check-ins to make sure everyone is physically and psychologically intact after a stressful, potentially dangerous experience. I prefer to do a quick one-on-one debrief with each stress test participant immediately after the test that includes little more than the three key questions and one or two observations from the facilitator. If a group of students have all gone through stress testing together, I'll also have a group discussion at the end that allows me to assess and manage group emotions, and lets me get across general information more efficiently.

I always make sure my students are uninjured and as calm and lucid as possible before they leave my space, and will tell them to take a little extra care of themselves for the next forty-eight hours. At minimum, they should be asked to report any injuries or issues that they discover once the adrenaline has completely worn off. Pain from muscle pulls or contusions can take a good while to show up, and it's important for us to have as complete a picture as possible of what happened to our students during the test.

Long-term follow-up can be as minimal or as in-depth as your students need it to be. How exactly you tie the test to the bigger picture of the students' learning is going to depend a lot on how much time you have available (for instance, a workshop is going to have very different follow-up options from an ongoing class). Good follow-up will look for updates on the students' physical and psychological well-being, will pull lessons from what happened during the test for improving future training, and will give students the opportunity to reflect on their experience and what they learned about themselves over the course of the test.

This can be as simple as keeping an informal communication channel open after the fact, whether that's an email address where you can be reached or opportunities to chat before or after class. Because stress testing is such an intense process, it can take time for students to get their heads around what happened, what they've learned about their own responses to pressure, and how they'd like to adjust their training or push their development after the fact. If you can leave room for them to do that and come back to you for feedback or advice, they'll get a lot more out of the experience.

Exercise: Build a Follow-Up Template

Write a script for your post-test debriefings. What questions will you ask your students? What information do you want each of them to leave with? What information or feedback do you need to get from them?

Make a list of possible cool-down activities for after the debriefing. These can include guided breathing or meditation, group discussions, heavy bag work or other physical activity, and any other tool you find useful for returning a group to emotional equilibrium.

When planning a stress test, you can use this list as a "menu" from which you can choose activities appropriate to the group and time constraints of a given test.

A good stress test can take any number of shapes, from higher-pressure partnered drills or sparring matches, to mini-scenarios or "sprites" that force the player to respond to a surprise action with minimal context, to full-fledged scenarios that simulate an entire encounter from start to finish. Over time, you'll identify the kinds of tests that suit your needs best and figure out how to build them on the fly when needed.

Anything you build is likely to do the job if you prioritize the principles of relevance, realism, safety, and follow-up. If you're building a new test, it's always a good idea to try it out first with fellow instructors or senior students you trust. If you're still not sure where to start, you can flip forward to this book's appendices for more resources. See page 235 for a drill progression that you can use to introduce your students to stress testing, and page 243 for additional reading on this topic.

No matter how you do it, safe, effective stress testing is an essential tool for assessing your students' readiness for greater challenges and building their self-confidence. The greatest sense of agency comes from realizing that you can get the job done—that your training and practice have translated into a capacity to affect the world around you and to take action under pressure.

A good stress test is one of the best methods for instilling that confidence, and for making sure that it comes from a realistic assessment and not a fantasy. It lays the foundation for honest toughness and true resilience. If your students know that they can make their skills work for them when they are surprised, scared, and uncomfortable, they'll move through the world differently than they did before they were tested.

Hitting Girls and Other Taboos

5

While I've already talked a bit about teaching women, it's a topic that deserves its own chapter because of how often it comes up in our field. I've seen a lot of well-intentioned initiatives in both the martial arts and self-defence communities to cater more directly to women. I've also seen many of them crash and burn—or just kind of fizzle—when the women who participated came up against common misconceptions about how they were supposed to learn.

When it comes to training women to fight, there are as many dangerous myths floating around as there are good ideas. In my time as a female athlete, student, and teacher, three misconceptions in particular have stuck out as the most common, pervasive, and unhelpful. Too many people believe one or more of the following:

- That men should never hit women, in training or otherwise

- That women need to be met with overwhelming force to show them what a "real" fight feels like

- That women and men need to be trained in exactly the same way, and be treated the same way at all times

Every one of these beliefs may seem reasonable at first glance, but a bit more scrutiny shows that they're not just wrong, but actively harmful to women's training—and often to the entire training environment.

Before we take a closer look, it's worth mentioning that this chapter will deal with the gender dynamics of the classroom in rather binary and general terms. Every student's experience is unique, and their relationship to the social conditioning directed at their gender (or perceived gender) can vary dramatically from that of their peers. Women are not all the same, and many people who aren't women—especially nonbinary people and smaller, weaker men—are also negatively affected by these myths.

The goal of this chapter isn't to draw stark boundaries between groups of students, or to use stereotypes and generalizations to force them into narrowly defined boxes. Instead, I'd like to examine the training dynamics that these misconceptions create, and demonstrate some ways of countering their negative effects. The solutions presented here should create a better training environment for everyone, even as the experience of female students is our primary focus.

Hitting Girls

The fear of hurting one's training partner isn't gender-specific, but the way it manifests in the classroom often breaks down along gendered lines. I've mentioned already that being unaccustomed to hitting or being hit puts women at a disadvantage when they start learning to fight. Before they can really start applying many techniques, they have to overcome the social conditioning that tells them that hitting is bad.

I can't count the number of times I've had to speak to a student about her habit of pulling hits to avoid making contact. Some students get their timing and angle exactly right, aim for the right target, and then stop just short of a completed strike. Or their distance is good, but their targeting is off and they are trying to hit a spot three inches to the side of their partner's head.

Many women will have this problem regardless of who their partner is. It doesn't matter whether the partner is bigger or smaller, or what their gender is. It's as if there's a force field around them that deflects or stops any incoming blow at the last second. It's a problem for both the feeder and the player in any drill, and will definitely slow down the student's learning if she doesn't get a handle on it pretty quickly.

Luckily, it's usually a small-scale, individual problem. After all, not all women have this conditioning, and those who've had the opportunity to participate in rougher sports or who grew up roughhousing with siblings are usually just fine with hitting their partners and may even relish the rare opportunity to play with violence. Even if an overwhelming majority of women struggle to make contact with their partners, they're still a minority of the student body.

The average proportion of women in martial arts spaces hovers between 20 and 30 percent.[1] In a class of twenty, you might get four or five students who are women, and three or four of them will have this problem. They will struggle, and anyone partnered with them for a drill will get less out of it, but they'll also rotate to another partner soon enough. Over the course of a class, everyone will get a chance to work with a few partners who provide appropriate resistance, and the only people who suffer in the long term are the non-hitters themselves.

It's when you look at the other students in the class that it becomes a systemic issue. Where young women are simply taught not to hit (or kick, or bite, or express any kind of violence, no matter the context), young men are given more leeway to express themselves through playful violence—unless the target is female. "Girls shouldn't hit"; "Boys shouldn't hit girls." That same conditioning makes its way into our training spaces.

I very rarely have to convince male students to hit each other. Usually, my efforts go toward teaching them how to properly control their blows and enthusiasm to fit the needs of a drill. Hitting me, though? Or throwing a female drilling partner in wrestling? Aiming a punch at her face?

1 Reliable large-scale statistics are hard to come by, but Statistics Canada's 2005 and 2010 census reports on sport have men making up 72 percent (*Sport Participation in Canada* 2005, Table 6) and 83 percent (*Sport Participation* 2010, Table 8) of Canadians who participated in martial arts in 2005 and 2010. This matches my and my colleagues' anecdotal experiences, where schools that have gender parity or near-parity are dramatically outnumbered by those that have few or no women, and co-ed schools where female students are the majority are almost unheard-of.

All of a sudden that force field springs up, and it's often a lot more powerful than the one generated by women who don't like hitting.

The following quotes from a 2013 study on men's views on hitting women in practice are all taken from male martial artists participating in co-ed classes or events, and are reflective of the attitudes I've encountered in my own training:

> I know that I shouldn't [avoid hitting women during martial arts practice] but as we grow up that's how we're designed to act . . . It's part of the programming from when you're a kid. Being gentlemanly, that kind of thing.

> —

> I feel really uncomfortable that I could hurt a woman in that way, even if she's asking me to do it I feel really uncomfortable, you know, physically uncomfortable with doing that.

> —

> Nico: It's just not in me, man, to hit a woman, it's like I know I won't be able to do it even if I wanted to, like my hands just won't do it.

> Alex: But your hands hit Steve fine.

> Nico: I can do that 'cause he's a man. I can't hit Beth 'cause she's a woman, I can't do it.[2]

The men speaking here aren't sexist jerks who think women are weak or unworthy of respect. They're genuinely—and reasonably—concerned about injuring a smaller partner, and dealing with some deep-seated cultural programming around gender and violence.

---

2 Alex Channon, "'Do You Hit Girls?' Some Striking Moments in the Career of a Male Martial Artist," in *Fighting Scholars: Habitus and Ethnographies of Martial Arts and Combat Sports*, ed. Raúl Sánchez García and Dale C. Spencer, (New York: Anthem Press, 2013), 101–103.

They're probably decent guys. And just like our female student with a force-field problem, their training is suffering in these match-ups. If they aren't sure that they can effectively calibrate force without undermining their technique, they're either going to have to sit out that drill iteration, and so deprive themselves and their partners of a chunk of training time; or else fudge the technique and start internalizing bad mechanics, timing, and distance.

The impact on their partner, however, is going to be even worse. Let's take a simple boxing drill and explore what happens in more detail:

1. Feeder throws a jab-cross combination aimed at Player's forehead.

2. Player parries both strikes with their hands. If a parry fails, Feeder's fist should just make contact with Player's forehead.

3. Feeder and Player switch roles after each set of strikes and parries.

Now say we've got two students, Tim and Amy, doing the drill. When Amy is feeder, she aims right for the forehead, and taps Tim a few times when he misses his parry. She even messes up her calibration once, and hits him harder than intended. Amy apologizes, Tim has a bit of a sore face for a few minutes, and the lesson goes on. When they switch roles, Tim is really worried about hitting Amy (especially since she just whacked him in the face, and he knows it hurts), so he fudges his distance and throws his punches to the space a couple of inches in front of her forehead. He's still aiming carefully, so it looks like the same attack, but he knows she won't get hit if she misses a parry.

Amy's training is now compromised no matter what happens. If she screws up a parry, there's no touch to let her know that she's gotten it wrong. Her hand will make contact with Tim's fist (since a bad parry that touches but doesn't stop the strike is a lot more likely at this range than a complete miss), and she won't get hit in the face. From her perspective, the parry worked.

Even if she really does make good parries every single time, she's still in trouble. Timing a defence correctly requires a good understanding of distance, and Tim is ruining her ability to perceive it correctly. His striking distance isn't what he's actually showing her, but Amy doesn't know that. She's training to defeat a strike that isn't intended to land and her sense of distance and timing are going to be subtly off as a result.

These issues show up in all striking drills where the attacker changes their target to avoid causing injury; in swordplay drills where they change the angle of their cut or the line of attack (usually by switching from targeting the body to targeting the sword); and in free play or sparring where they stop their hits an inch or two from the target. If enough of Amy's drilling partners behave like this, she'll never learn how to defend against a genuine attack. This could be very bad news for her once it comes time to test for a higher rank, or compete, or work with a new training partner who doesn't behave this way.

At worst, she'll get hurt because she hasn't developed the skills to prevent someone from striking her in earnest; at best, she'll fail to defend against a bunch of attacks that she thinks she knows how to stop, and her self-esteem and sense of her own abilities will be shaken.

And that's purely in a martial arts context. If Amy's in a self-defence class and her partners won't really hit her (or try to), she could be in mortal danger. She doesn't know whether her techniques work against a noncompliant opponent, but she's likely to believe that they do. The first time she tests them in earnest should be in a training space where failure is a learning tool, and not in a genuinely threatening situation where failure will get her seriously injured or killed.

This scenario may seem improbable, but let's go back to that ratio of men to women in martial arts. Our hypothetical four or five women out of twenty students won't be training exclusively with guys who don't want to hit them, but the majority of their drilling time may well look like this. It's more than enough to build some very bad habits and provide them with bad data on how well their training is working.

That doesn't take culture and peer pressure into account either. If most of the men a woman drills with don't really hit her, then those that do are going to seem like an aberration. They're more likely to get told off for hitting too hard than all of the other students are for going too soft, especially if the majority of the class believes that hitting women is wrong (or just feels slightly uncomfortable about it).

If the instructor is among those uncomfortable men, then his views are going to have an outsized impact. Even if he never verbalizes his hesitation—and he may not, especially if he recognizes that it's not acceptable and is doing his best to ignore it—it's going to be visible every time he demonstrates with a female partner. The students watching may not realize that he's stopping short of proper hits, but they will copy his actions as precisely as they can, including the targeting quirks and angles of movement that allow him to just avoid hitting students that he doesn't want to strike.

Students routinely reproduce and exaggerate their instructors' movement patterns and body mechanics—to the point where you can often tell who trains with whom just by looking at how they walk or stand. They take on our unrecognized errors and cheats as a natural part of their own movement, and they'll take on our psychological stances as well.

In an average male-dominated martial arts class with an instructor who's hesitant about hitting women, it's very easy to develop a culture where women getting hit at standard levels of force just never really happens. There's no overt sexism or ill intent required on anyone's part to create an environment where women consistently get lower-quality training and are put in danger as a result.

I'm not suggesting that a 200-plus-pound tower of muscle should be hauling off at full force on a partner half his size and weight. Control is a vital element of all martial training—whether it's unarmed or weapon based. But control doesn't mean not hitting, and it certainly doesn't mean cheating your techniques to prevent any risk to your partner.

Drilling with control means throwing an attack with intention to hit, with clear aim for the correct target, with enough power to provide resistance and challenge, and with enough restraint that it makes contact without causing injury. It's a skill that we practise like any other, and every fighter should start working on it as early as possible.

One of my favourite exercises for doing this is a very simple evasion drill. I use this regularly with new students, and as a check-in with ongoing ones:

1. Feeder and Player stand facing each other, an arm's length apart.

2. Feeder reaches out and hits Player on the side of the head or face with an open hand. They should make solid contact, and hit hard enough for the impact to be unpleasant, but not hard enough to move Player's head. They should avoid targeting Player's ear.

3. Feeder throws a handful of strikes like this, alternating which hand they hit with. Player allows each hit to land.

4. Once Feeder has landed a few hits with no reaction from Player, Player starts evading the incoming blows. They may use footwork, distance changes, level changes, slips, and any other techniques in their arsenal to avoid being hit.

5. Every few strikes, Player doesn't evade and lets the hit land. This will keep Feeder honest in their targeting and level of force.

6. Once Feeder is aiming all of their strikes true and Player has gotten a decent workout evading them, Feeder and Player switch roles.

The great thing about this drill is that it's easy to frame it as a movement exercise for the player, while actually using it to train the feeder to hit appropriately.

I usually have students change partners frequently so that everyone has to work with a range of bodies and genders. With a new group, this lets me quickly spot the students who have difficulty hitting others, and to address that hesitancy before it has a chance to screw up everyone's training.

That diagnostic quality is why this exercise targets the head and face, rather than a "safer" target like the shoulder. Hitting someone in the face is much harder, psychologically, than hitting almost any other target. If someone doesn't like hitting, they can sometimes push past that discomfort with targets they perceive as being less sensitive or vulnerable, but still miss deliberately once they're really worried about hurting someone. A diagnostic exercise that relies on friendlier targets is likely to throw up false negative results for these kinds of students.

It's also very easy to tell at a glance that someone is deliberately missing the head. They'll either be swinging way over the top or stopping short of the nose, and both of these actions are easy to spot even across a crowded room. Open-hand shots are unlikely to cause damage, and they're loud when they connect well. That auditory feedback is important for students to assess the quality of their own hits, and I've even been able to use the overall volume in a class to judge whether a group is getting their calibration right.

Because this exercise is primarily concerned with addressing social dynamics, it needs to be framed just right. To set the tone, I prefer to pair with a larger male partner for the demonstration. I'll put him in the role of feeder and make sure that at least one of his hits lands with a solid "slap" sound. Seeing a woman get hit in the face or head can be a real shock for some students, and it's good to get that out of the way early. Contextualizing that hit is very important: the feeder does it without any big lead-up or emotion, the same way that they perform any other drill action.

It also helps to have me be the one doing the explaining, explicitly telling him to throw the shot, and treating it as ordinary and expected when it comes in. We'll keep the tone of the drill light and often laugh or joke during the demonstration to make it very clear that we're hitting each other in a spirit of play and learning, and to show that the hit has no impact on our relationship.

If you want to leverage this gender dynamic and don't have any female instructors, it's a great drill to hand over to a couple of students to demo instead, as it's all about tone-setting and partner behaviour and not technique. The visual effect of a male instructor telling a female student he's going to hit her in the head and then doing it is a little different, although that set-up can also work if it's handled well. The important part is to show the hit as an emotionally and socially neutral action.

If you see students struggling to hit, this exercise also gives you a framework for addressing it as a group issue. When I'm in my own classroom, which has an informal, low-pressure, cooperative atmosphere, I'll give a brief talk on consent and the responsibility we have to our training partners. I'll remind the students that every person on the mats that day has consented to being hit and made their peace with the fact that it's going to happen—and that it might hurt.

I'll also remind them that their job as the feeder is to give their partner a realistic stimulus to respond to. That if they really want to keep them safe from harm, they're going to have to focus on the long-term outcome of their training, and on preparing their partner for the competition, sparring match, or self-defence situations they're going to face down the line. I'll turn it into a bit of a joke about hitting people for their own good, while acknowledging the truth that lies at the root of that line. A little bit of pain and fear in practice is what they've chosen in exchange for far less pain and fear when it really matters.

When I'm working for the police department, in a discipline-oriented, competitive, high-pressure environment, I'll turn that pressure onto the feeders who won't hit. They might be the reason the whole group has to do push-ups, or the exercise runs longer, and they may well get a public dressing-down from one of the senior officers about how they're letting their training partners down and setting them up for injury or death because they can't get over their hang-ups.

The delivery can be tailored to the group, but the message is the same. Hitting each other is essential to training, and our responsibility to keep our partner safe includes both controlling our level of power and giving them an honest threat to counter.

Another good place to reinforce this practice is at the start of any sparring or higher-contact drill. I often have my students do the following calibration before an exercise begins:

1. Feeder hits Player a few times at the level of force that they intend to use.

2. Player gives Feeder feedback on their level of force. Something like, "That was a bit hard, can you scale it back a little?" or "I barely felt that. You can go harder."

3. Feeder recalibrates and throws a few more hits, Player gives feedback, and so on until both are satisfied.

4. Feeder and Player switch roles.

The first couple of times, this can take a minute or two, especially if the exercise or attack being thrown is new to either student. With practice, it doesn't take more than two or three quick shots and a "Yep, that works!" to get everything dialed in.

Making this a regular habit gives students ample opportunity to practise calibrating their force appropriately to their partner and the context they're working in. It also provides some key psychological lifelines: a student who gets hit too hard has a framework in which they're not only allowed to speak up, but expected to do so. They won't feel stuck between disrupting the class by stopping a drill cold, or toughing out a potential injury for the sake of getting along with their partner.

Just as importantly, the students doing the hitting can feel confident that their partner is okay with what they're doing. They don't just have the implied consent to be hit that comes with sharing a training environment, but explicit consent to be hit in a way that's been negotiated and clearly established.

I like to model this behaviour in sparring and drilling or demos with senior students as well. If it's normalized as something that everyone does, rather than a special consideration for certain students, nobody gets singled out and the habit becomes ingrained. Everyone's control and calibration improve, and students who are afraid of harming others build confidence in their ability to hit appropriately.

One might argue that letting students self-calibrate this way—especially with feedback from their partner and not an instructor—provides an easy out for timid students to avoid realistic force by asking their partners to go easy on them.

How are women supposed to learn if we make their partners restrain themselves? And how are those partners supposed to discover what they're really capable of if they always have to hold back? If you've read the earlier sections on opting in and stress testing, you'll already have an idea of how I'd answer those questions. But this is an objection that's often explicitly tied to gender, and it's worth digging into it a bit more.

Force and Realism

There's a very specific way in which we link force and realism in our imaginations when we talk about violence. The assumption I've come across in dozens of venues—from online HEMA forums, to self-defence debates in person and on social media, to blog posts and articles written by martial arts practitioners—is that the highest possible level of force is also the most realistic.

That it's not a "real" swordfight unless the fighters are swinging their weapons like clubs, with enough force to split an unarmoured opponent's skull. That a "real" unarmed sparring match is one that ends in blood and missing teeth. That a "real" self-defence situation is one that puts the target in the worst place humanly possible—blindfolded, tied down, pinned, and overpowered by someone with twice their muscle mass and a weapon—and anything less asymmetrical is also less realistic. We associate brutality and injury with realism.

This framework ignores the fact that violence comes in many forms and has a broad range of goals, many of which have little to do with causing catastrophic injury. The category breakdown in the "Relevance" section of the previous chapter (page 97) is not only a useful tool for building training scenarios, but also a way of thinking about violence that acknowledges its variety.

A rules-bound sparring match is just as real as a murderous assault, which in turn is just as real as low-level sexual harassment in the workplace, which is just as real as a first-blood duel. The consequences of these types of violence are different, and they feel different in the moment, but one is no less real than the others.

But maybe that's not what you mean when you say "realistic." Sure, we know that violence comes in different levels of intensity and with different sets of goals and so on. But it's still important to see if our students can handle the really bad stuff, right? What value does their training have if it can't handle the highest level of danger that's out there? How can they be truly safe, and truly fearless, if they can't handle the worst the world can throw at them? In order for them to have a realistic sense of their capabilities, those capabilities need to be pushed to their limits.

This is doubly true for women, the logic goes, because they are smaller and weaker and less socially conditioned for violence, and far more likely to be the targets of asymmetrical attacks. They don't start out big and tough like a lot of the men they train with, so we need to check how they measure up and whether they've managed to bridge the gap between themselves and their stronger classmates. I've heard more than once that pushing them to the limit is for their own good; that we can't have them thinking they are more capable than they actually are, or they'll end up in real danger. Sometimes the mindset involved is even less charitable than that—it's about showing women their place and making it clear to them that they're not really capable, that they couldn't really take down a man.

Whatever the motivation behind this need to stress test women at their absolute limit, it's a common idea. One of the most prevalent arguments for disallowing sex-segregated tournaments in HEMA competition is that it allows women to avoid the "real" test of fighting someone much larger, stronger, and more aggressive than them. There's a similar push to have female MMA fighters compete against men in order to see how capable they "really" are. In self-defence, it shows up in criticisms of teaching methods that are too gentle for the students, where "too gentle" encompasses genuinely bad teaching (e.g., having students train exclusively on a compliant, inert target) but also anything short of having a much larger attacker actively try to kill them.

When this kind of stress test is structured well and takes place in a well-designed environment with allowances for its inherent asymmetry, it can be a perfectly valid tool. Most often, though, what we actually see is either a mismatched sporting contest or an informal test where a male partner escalates a drill or sparring game, or sets up a "Show me what you've learned" encounter. In the majority of these cases, the woman loses the fight. Far from proving that she's not ready for "real" conflict, however, all that these situations demonstrate is that the people administering the test don't understand how violence works. They harm under the guise of teaching, and bring their students no closer to understanding their actual capabilities.

Let's look at the two most common versions of this phenomenon to get a better sense of how it manifests: the mixed-gender sport fight, and the all-out self-defence scenario.

Mixed-Gender Sport Fights

Sex segregation and weight-class divisions are the two most enduring ways of dividing athletes in combat sports, and they both exist for the same reason: to balance out inherent asymmetries in body composition and ability to generate power and to make each match as much a pure contest of skill as possible.

It's easy to see that someone who weighs 230 pounds is going to be able to generate more force with their strikes than someone who weighs 130 pounds, and that pitting them against each other is inherently asymmetrical in terms of physical risk. It's also pretty clear that the 230-pound fighter has a good chance of defeating their opponent through sheer mass and power, regardless of whether they're more skilled.

Separating by sex is a bit more controversial, but has just as much of a foundation in physical capacity to generate force.[3] A man and woman with about the same body mass index (BMI, a factor of height and weight) and fitness level will carry substantially different amounts of muscle. In general, men have around 1.5 times as much fat-free muscle mass as women their size, and about the same difference in skeletal muscle mass.[4]

The difference is almost entirely hormonal, and is so dramatic that transgender athletes who have undergone hormone replacement therapy as part of their transition have reported obvious and substantial changes in their physical capacity as part of that process.[5] Not every woman is weaker than every man, but two fighters of different genders in the same weight class are almost certainly going to be badly mismatched

---

3 I'm speaking here strictly of sex segregation as it's fairly applied in a modern sporting context, where men and women often compete in separate divisions. Women have long been kept out of combat sports and martial arts for social reasons (e.g., that it's unseemly for women to fight, or that they don't have the psychological capacity for it), and that's a whole other conversation.

4 R. S. Lindle and others, "Age and Gender Comparisons of Muscle Strength in 654 Women and Men Aged 20–93 Yr," *Journal of Applied Physiology* 83, no. 5 (1997): 1583; T. Abe, C. F. Kearns, and T. Fukunaga, "Sex Differences in Whole Body Skeletal Muscle Mass Measured by Magnetic Resonance Imaging and its Distribution in Young Japanese Adults," *British Journal of Sports Medicine* 37, no. 5 (2003): Table 1.

5 For a firsthand account of the impact of transitioning from male to female on athletic capacity, see Joanna Harper, "Do Transgender Athletes Have an Edge? I Sure Don't," *The Washington Post*, April 1, 2015, accessed June 27, 2018, https://www.washingtonpost.com/opinions/do-transgender-athletes-have-an-edge-i-sure-dont/2015/04/01/ccacb1da-c68e-11e4-b2a1-bed1aaea2816_story.html. Harper is the author of the first performance study of transgender athletes, which concluded that 8 competitive long-distance runners who had transitioned from male to female maintained the same level of competitive success after their transition. In other words, any physical advantage they may have had before transition was entirely mitigated by hormone therapy, and gender transition gave them no competitive advantage. Joanna Harper, "Race Times for Transgender Athletes," *Journal of Sporting Cultures and Identities* 6, no. 1 (2015): 1–9.

in strength and power generation capacity. Pitting a man and woman of the same weight against each other in a sporting match that is meant to be symmetrical thus introduces a substantial asymmetry of muscle mass.

This might be fine, except that the rules of most combat sports are designed with the expectation of symmetry. They disallow debilitating strikes to vulnerable targets such as eyes and the back of the head, small joint manipulations, and other nasty little tools that bypass size and mass differences to cause damage no matter how big the target is. Weapon arts regulate equipment to keep differences in armament from tipping the balance in favour of one fighter or the other, and ban sharp points, sharp edges, and other modifications that would let a weapon do additional damage.

If fighters are evenly matched in physical attributes, then resorting to "dirty trick" techniques and more dangerous weapons is cheating. If one fighter is substantially smaller or weaker, though, those are often the only reliable tools for overcoming a big power differential. A contest that bases its rules and win conditions on the assumption of an even match-up is going to be slanted in favour of the more powerful fighter once an asymmetry is introduced.

Sporting competitions use symmetry to try to isolate skill as the deciding factor in the outcome of a match. If we introduce physical asymmetry by having women and men fight each other, the rules and safety practices need to be adjusted to acknowledge the imbalance of physical attributes that now exists. It's entirely possible to have a great mixed-gender fight, but it's a lot more difficult for it to be a pure contest of skill if you just stick to the rules and weight class parameters that we use for single-gender combat sports.

Putting a woman in that situation and expecting her to win by skill alone isn't fair. She doesn't just need to be better than her opponent to win; she has to be better by a large enough margin to overcome the 1.5-fold muscle mass difference between her and an equal-sized man and all of the advantages that bestows on him. Sure, she might win, but she has to be extraordinary to do so. The bar for "good enough" is set far higher for her than her opponent.

Having these kinds of contests is fine, but basing our assessment of a woman's basic competence on them is unfair, and treating them as if they are fair fights does a disservice to both participants in such a match.

Self-Defence Scenarios

In self-defence training, these kinds of tests have far fewer official rules. They usually happen during informal sparring or roughhousing. The set-up is simple: either friendly play gets a little intense and escalates enough to get both fighters adrenalized, or a man applies a challenging technique to a woman and tells her to prove herself by fighting him off. Here's a description of how these encounters often play out, from a conversation I was part of on whether women could handle "real" stress testing:

> I don't think most women can handle any "real training" like that. Case in point, a friend's fiance a few years back (now his ex-wife) was big into MMA and such, did full speed sparring and everything. Bachelor and bachelorette parties come around [. . .] men have some wrestling matches, she wants to join in. Both had a couple drinks, but neither were drunk. Big guy vs smaller girl, overpowers and pins her under him fairly quickly and she breaks. Crying, incoherent, no longer fighting. (Mitigating factor, had a bad sexual assault in her background, but still. . .). If an otherwise tough and trained girl breaks in a realistic "training" bout, what does the average girl do? And don't excuse the couple drinks, it's a perfectly realistic situation.[6]

There are a few factors that make this specific situation extra challenging for the woman (alcohol, as well as the history of sexual assault), but the framing is very familiar. A friendly tussle ends with a woman pinned

---

6 Adam Bohnstengel, February 10, 2017, comment on Ken Renaud Dietiker, "We say this all the time. Unrealistic attacks lead to useless defense," Facebook, February 10, 2017, https://www.facebook.com/krdietiker/ posts/10211570976885476?comment_id=10211572813051379.

and powerless, maybe crying, and definitely convinced that she's got no real chance in a serious fight. Not only that, but the participants and onlookers are convinced that "it's a perfectly realistic situation," and that the outcome accurately reflects what would happen to the woman if her life were really in danger. It might—but only because this experience has trained her to expect to lose.

The piece that's missing from our speaker's assessment of the situation's realism is an acknowledgement of the unspoken rules of this game. If we apply our "Relevance" framework, this situation is play violence, social violence, and asymmetrical.

A tussle between friends isn't concerned with causing serious injury—and actually has avoiding major injuries as a primary goal, since most friendships are seriously strained by an unexpected broken nose or dislocated shoulder. Its goals are definitely social. The fighters are showing off for an audience, and might also be jockeying for social status by proving which of them is a better fighter (this is especially true if the man involved has put his ego on the line and doesn't want to be seen being beaten by "a girl"). It's also got a built-in asymmetry because of the size and strength disparities that affect sporting contests, and that asymmetry is probably magnified here without official limits like weight classes.

So we've got a woman facing a much larger man in a fight where she's not allowed to cause any serious harm or use techniques that look like she's fighting dirty. A woman who is being constrained not by formal rules, but by social pressure, to avoid harming the friend, family member, or romantic partner that she's fighting.

If it's a standard wrestling match where she's got to avoid a pin or a submission, she's dealing with a substantial mass disadvantage. A much larger man doesn't have to be more skilled to win—he just has to get a top position and let gravity do its work. You can't fight when you can't breathe, and someone 1.5 times to twice your body weight sitting on your ribcage will take the wind out of anyone.

If there's a technique being applied that's "realistic" for self-defence, she's probably dealing with a choke, being pinned and struck, or grabbed and pulled from behind. All of those situations require a high level of force in response. When I address them in my teaching, I encourage elbow strikes to the face and throat, driving thumbs into eyes, breaking joints, biting, and slamming the attacker's head into a wall or a floor. All of these are techniques that either bypass size and strength differences by targeting weak points in the body, or use the attacker's size and power against them to cause catastrophic damage. They're also completely off limits in a play fight.

Take those away, and you're left with techniques that pit strength against strength, mass against mass. It's almost impossible for the woman to win, not because she lacks skill or mental fortitude, but because she's making the completely rational choice to protect someone she cares about from life-changing injury, or to protect her relationship with them by avoiding a level of pain and damage that would be considered unfair by them and the audience. Most likely, she'll either lose, or win but lose a friend (or multiple friends) in the process. It's a trap.

There are valid ways of testing the limits of a woman's skill and psychological conditioning—just as there are for any student. If you want to genuinely stress test your students, there's a whole framework for doing so safely that's been laid out in the previous chapter. And yes, it involves acting, and "letting her win" when she's done the right thing (unless you want your feeders getting their eyes gouged and knees broken for real). What it doesn't involve is subjecting her to overwhelming physical force in situations where she cannot use the best tools for the job.

Most women will be physically outmatched by most men. They have to fight dirty and "cheat" to win. Any honest test has to allow for them to fight in a way that accounts for that physical reality, and any test that doesn't—that puts them in an asymmetrical fight without any tools to level the playing field—is no more realistic than letting them beat up an inert dummy.

If we treat it like it's real and fair, all we do is mislead our students about their own capabilities, and undermine their hard-won confidence. It's one of the quickest paths to demolishing a woman's faith in herself and trust in her instructors, and it's all the more insidious because it's often disguised as an opportunity to prove the opposite.

When Equal Isn't Equal

The issues raised above bring us to a larger problem in martial arts instruction: the fact that many of our students have very different bodies and physical capabilities and are often shortchanged by a one-size-fits-all training approach.

If I'm coaching two fighters through a mismatched fight like the ones described earlier, I'm not going to teach them both the same techniques or the same execution of those techniques. A big man wrestling someone who is much smaller or who has a physical disability is going to have different goals and tactics available to him than his opponent does, and coaching both of them the same way would be ridiculous.

This makes perfect sense when we look at a single obviously asymmetrical match, but many instructors lose focus on the issue when they're dealing with groups. It's partly a matter of logistics. We can't really take a highly individualized approach to every student's training when we've got an hour and a half, a single instructor, and twenty students. That's what private coaching is for, and group lessons will always involve some amount of generalization. That alone isn't a problem.

What can be a problem is how we generalize, and whose needs or experiences get prioritized in the classroom. There's a common refrain that pops up whenever gender differences are discussed in the martial arts community that goes something like this:

> *I'm an egalitarian. I don't care of you're a man or a woman—I treat everyone the same. Having women's only classes, women's tournaments, or any of that other segregated stuff is sexist. Women don't need anyone to give them special treatment, and trying to cater your teaching to them is dishonest pandering that just makes them feel like they don't belong. I'd rather respect them and teach them the same way I teach anyone else.*

I've encountered this a lot from people who are working in good faith and who have hit on the fairly straightforward conclusion that singling out any specific group and catering directly to their needs extends them a special privilege. Equality would be better served by treating everyone the same way, they argue. Equality = equal treatment.

This solution makes a whole lot of sense on paper. The only problem is that, in every case where I've heard a male instructor make the argument, "I treat all of my students the same way," what they mean in practical terms is, "I treat all of my students the way I treat other men."

We've already established that, broadly speaking, men and women differ in how they find motivation in a training environment, how they're socialized with regard to violence, and how their bodies work. From there, we can build two rough profiles of your typical male and female martial arts students:

Men usually . . .

- have high upper-body strength, moderate endurance, and about 1.5 times as much overall muscle mass as similarly sized women;

- have broader shoulders than hips, a flat chest, and a relatively high centre of gravity;

- warm up and get adrenalized quickly;

- are motivated strongly by competition;

- start with some familiarity with play violence and contact sports;

- are moderately comfortable hitting men, and uncomfortable hitting women;

- prefer not to show emotion under stress.

Women usually . . .

- have high lower-body strength, high endurance, and about two-thirds the muscle mass of similarly sized men;

- have hips equal to or wider than their shoulders, a protruding chest, and a low centre of gravity;

- take a while to warm up and get adrenalized;

- are motivated strongly by cooperation and belonging;

- start with little or no familiarity with play violence and contact sports;

- are uncomfortable hitting anyone;

- express their emotions to relieve stress.

Of course, some students don't fit into either box, or only tick some of the points in the category one would expect them to belong to. This model, like others in this book, is a quick heuristic for understanding the needs of groups of students, rather than a prescription for individuals. It's also important to note that neither set of characteristics is inherently better or worse than the other, and that these lists leave out the things that the two groups have in common, like a mutual love of their martial art, a desire for self-improvement, or the ability to learn and to fight well.

The differences are significant, though, and they have an impact on everything from biomechanics and movement patterns, to social and emotional dynamics, to basic logistics like the timing and duration of warm-ups.

And the thing about both martial arts and self-defence is that the vast majority of instructors are men. Not only that, but most instructors in our field didn't start with much formal training in how to teach, and even big schools usually begin life as small, backyard practice groups. This means that the majority of instructors start out teaching what works best for them and then adjust their training methods as they gain experience.

Your typical class that's run by a man is likely to have a lot of features that favour how men move, think, and learn:

- movement patterns and cues optimized for humans with broad shoulders, flat chests, and high centres of gravity

- a preference for techniques that capitalize on upper-body strength and early explosiveness

- brief warm-ups that aren't too intense

- formal external competition as a major goal for most students and informal internal competition as a motivator for progress

- a culture that expects some casual roughhousing, emphasizes emotional control and discipline, and frowns upon emotional outbursts like tears and giggling

In fact, this model is common enough that you might be thinking that I've just described a typical martial arts class, and not a specific, gendered subset of them.

A class with these features is likely going to work really well for most men. It'll still attract those women whose desire to train or love of the art overrides any mismatch between their learning needs and the class design. All but the most unusual of them, however, will have to actively modify how they learn in order to thrive.

They'll either put in extra work to build up their upper-body strength, have a non-standard fighting style that's a better fit for their body type, or just be less good at executing the school's preferred techniques. They'll subconsciously adapt their own movement to mimic that of fighters with larger shoulders, flatter chests, and higher centres of gravity—even if it causes them chronic pain or increases their risk of injury. They'll come in early or go running before class to get warmed up properly, push themselves harder during warm-ups and drills to get the burn they need to fight their best, or spend their training time at a lower performance level than they're capable of.

They'll learn to find value, motivation, and joy in competition, or be discouraged by what feels like an unkind or unsupportive environment. They'll suppress their nervous giggles when they're confused by a drill, and learn to hold back their tears until they can cry in the bathroom, or resign themselves to not being taken seriously in stressful situations.

And so we end up with an instructor who treats everyone equally, but with unequal results. Men who come to class find an environment that's optimized for their needs and learning style. Women have to spend a chunk of every lesson adapting to an environment that doesn't favour how they move, learn, and socialize.

Many will struggle to do as well as their male peers, and will never advance to leadership positions or high ranks. Others will burn out trying to adapt, or find that a few environmental factors are just insurmountably ill-fitted to their needs, and drop out. A few will thrive, whether through luck and predisposition (e.g., they happen to be stronger, broader-shouldered, flatter-chested, more competitive, and less emotive than most other women), or sheer force of will.

Through no direct effort or malice on the instructor's part, you've got a classroom where women have to work twice as hard just to keep up and are substantially more likely to struggle or drop out.

This is the reality I see in a lot of schools that are run by men who "treat everyone equally." There are often a good number of female students at the beginner level, because training is fun and initially attracts all kinds of people. At higher levels, the number of women drops precipitously, with many either remaining "beginners" for far longer than average, or leaving once they plateau and burn out. There are few female role models (senior students and instructors), and very, very few—if any—women in decision-making or management roles. Those that do lead and excel are anomalies, and are often "one of the guys" in temperament and fighting style.

And most of the men running these schools see the problem. They see that women are dropping out at high rates, or not coming through the door in the same numbers to begin with. They feel the lack of women at higher levels, but don't see anyone who's ready to be elevated to a role model position. They want to increase female participation and retention, and they want their school to be welcoming to everyone. They're not jerks: they don't hate women, and they certainly aren't deliberately driving them away. They just happen to have created an environment that makes it difficult for the great majority of women to do well.

This isn't an unfixable problem by any means, nor does it require abandoning the ideal of egalitarianism. If we shift our understanding of "treating everybody equally" to mean "treating everyone with equal respect and giving them equal opportunities to succeed," instead of "treating everyone as if they are the same," things fall into place rather quickly.

The policies and teaching approaches I've outlined elsewhere in this book are all based on that new definition of equality. They prioritize consent, personal agency, self-motivation, and equal protection from harassment and unsafe behaviour. From here, all we really need to add is a model for understanding and accommodating the training needs of students who are different from us so that they aren't fighting an uphill battle just to learn.

Whether you're a male instructor looking to do a better job of teaching women and nonbinary students, a female instructor aiming to better teach students of other genders, or you're addressing the needs of a group that's separated from you not by gender but by age, fitness level, or any other defining feature, you can use the same general process to figure out what they need.[7]

---

7 I find this to be a great way to get my head around building beginner programming, for example. Beginners are separated from the experienced fighters who train them by so many things—including physical capability and fitness, academic knowledge, and familiarity and comfort with violence and physical contact—that it's often helpful to treat them as a distinct population for this sort of exercise.

Exercise: Build a Model of Your "Default" Student

Imagine the kind of person who would walk into your school, immediately feel comfortable, progress through your classes at an average rate without accommodations or adjustments, and reach the highest level available to them through simple dedication and hard work.

If you struggle to come up with an imaginary person, sub-stitute yourself—after all, you've found success training the way that you do, and it's a good bet that your methods work well for you and people like you.

Once you've got a person in mind, build as detailed a profile of them as you can, taking into account their physiology, psychology, and social habits.

To get a real handle on what your typical student is like, you can work through the answers to the following questions:

- **What is this person's body like?** How is it shaped? Are they tall or short? Heavyset and powerful or light and flexible? Do they carry most of their muscle in their shoulders or their legs? What kinds of movement patterns are easy for them? Which ones are hard for them? Where do they need to be strong?

- **What motivates them?** Do they need the pressure of compe-tition to thrive? Do they need social contact and communi-ty? What are their training goals? What is their definition of "fun"? What scares them or causes them to shut down?

- **What is their relationship to violence?** Are they comfortable with moving people around and hitting them from the get-go, or do they need to be eased into higher levels of contact? How do they respond to asymmetrical matchups (e.g., be-ing paired with a much larger or smaller training partner, or someone of a different gender or dramatically different age)? Do they view sparring as a fun learning game, a test of mettle, or a dangerous experience that's best avoided?

- **How do they manage emotions?** How do they express themselves when they're distressed or frustrated—do they cry or laugh, lash out physically, shut up and withdraw, or try to talk through what's happening? Do they seek comfort from others or handle things privately? What embarrasses them?

- **What does their life look like outside the school?** How regularly can they attend classes? Do they have time to cross-train or attend special events? Do they have a lot of family responsibilities, like child care? How stable is their financial and housing situation? Where does training fall on their overall list of priorities?

These questions are not exhaustive, and you'll probably come up with some of your own. Once you've got a detailed idea of your typical student, it's time to turn your attention outward.

Exercise: Build a Model of Your "Target" Student

Come up with a representative student from the group that you're trying to serve better by answering the same questions as you did for your "default" student.

Aim to build just as complete a picture of their physiology, psychology, and social habits.

You may find that you don't know the answers to some questions, or that you don't have complete confidence in the answers you come up with. This will almost certainly happen if you're thinking about people who are not much like you, and who are not particularly well represented at your school.

Rather than hoping your guesses are good enough, talk to someone who is a member of that group. Better yet, talk to a whole lot of them. Once you've got a list of questions you want to ask, it's not difficult to turn them into a survey you can hand out to people in your social circle or make available to a larger audience online.[8] You don't need scientific rigour, but you do want to build as accurate a picture as you can with the resources you have available.

You can repeat these exercises for as many groups as you'd like. Once you have clear profiles built for both the people you currently teach and for the students you'd like to attract in the future, you can effectively assess who your training space is optimized for.

Exercise: Figure Out Who Your School Caters To

Take a closer look at your training methods. To what extent does the structure of your training fit the needs of your default student? How about your target group of non-default students? What are the overlaps between the two groups? Where do they differ, and who is currently prioritized in cases where their needs don't match?

You may find that your school caters almost exclusively to a single group, that it's evenly-balanced in all but a few areas, or that it's somewhere in between.

The easiest way to assess your training environment is with a parallel set of questions. Compare your answer to each of these with the attributes of your default and target students:

---

8 For a free and simple-to-use tool for doing this, I recommend Google Forms (part of the app suite for Google Drive). You can build an online questionnaire that you can either post publicly or share with selected participants via a link. It's also got pretty solid tools for analyzing your results, and it makes it easy to spot trends and consolidate answers.

- **What are its physical expectations?** Do you include strength training and conditioning in your practice? If so, what muscle groups and types of fitness does it prioritize? If not, what kinds of cross-training do you expect from your students? Does your body of technique favour any particular body type? Look at factors like flexibility, upper-body strength, lower-body strength, and height.

- **How does it motivate students?** What tools do you use to drive development? Are there opportunities to compete? Is there a rank structure or another system of concrete rewards? How important is social interaction and community? What opportunities are there for students to volunteer or otherwise contribute and feel valued? Are all of these opportunities skill-dependent?

- **How does it handle contact?** Is sparring and high-contact drilling a major part of training? How are students introduced to higher-contact training? Can they opt out or watch, or is it an "everybody fights" situation? Are classes and competitions segregated by weight class, gender, or age? What do stress tests look like, and how are students prepared for them?

- **How does it regulate emotional expression?** To what degree is discipline a priority, and how does that extend to emotional expression? What is considered an acceptable response to frustration or pain? How do instructors respond to inappropriate outbursts from upset students? What support is available for students who are having an extreme emotional reaction?

- **What are its lifestyle expectations?** What's the minimum class commitment you expect from students? How much extracurricular time are they expected to put in, including cross-training, volunteering, and events? How much flexibility is there in your hours and fee structure? Is financial aid available? Is it possible for students to bring their children to class or to an event?

- **Who are its role models?** What do the people in authority look like? How do they fight and train? How do they participate in the life of the school—are they teachers, competitors, administrators, or a mix? How do they express themselves? Do they all fit a narrow mould, or is there diversity in who makes it to the top?

How you act on what you've learned will depend a lot on how specialized your school currently is, what resources you have available (especially time, space, and energy), and how much you want things to change. If it turns out that you only need to make a few tweaks here and there to make your school more welcoming, then the problem may be very easy to solve. If, on the other hand, the group that you want to attract would currently have a very difficult time fitting in at your school, you need to make some hard choices.

If you have the time and energy to make a major change, an overhaul of your teaching methods and training culture could be worthwhile. You can shift from a school that heavily prioritizes students from one group to one with a more flexible and diverse teaching approach.

You could prioritize a mix of techniques that rely on a variety of physical strengths, teach movement skills that are ergonomically sound for a range of body types, and expand your understanding of correct form to include variations based on physiology. You could tweak your class structure to accommodate people who warm up at different rates (for instance, you might vary when sparring or evaluations happen, sometimes putting them early in the class period to capitalize on students being "fresh," and sometimes putting them at the end when those who warm up slower are just hitting peak performance).

You could encourage both competitive motivation (e.g., participation in external competitions, internal mini-tournaments, and the occasional friendly rivalry) and cooperative motivation (e.g., mutual verbal support, process-oriented drills and games that emphasize the shared experience of learning together, collaborative research projects, and regular social time). You could re-adjust your expectations around emotional expression and create an atmosphere where laughter is welcome so long as it doesn't interrupt the actual lesson, and tears can happen in private or on the shoulder of a friend, depending on what a student needs most.

This approach requires a lot of work up front and a willingness to step outside your own comfort zone to create an environment that isn't tailored specifically to your own learning needs (or those of people most like you). The payoff is a diverse training space that can accommodate a range of bodies and learning styles in a single, coherent community.

If you don't have the time and energy to redo how you run your whole school, or you just plain like the way things are and don't want to give up a culture and training environment that works for you, then spinning off a dedicated program may be the better choice.

If you want to add women to a male-dominated school, you could encourage some of your members to run a women's study group or class (it may only meet once or twice a month, or be entirely informal, depending on available resources). You could add women's categories to tournaments, or run women's-only tournaments. If there aren't enough women at your school to build something from scratch, you could bring in guest instructors for occasional woman-centric workshops and teaching weekends.

Some women will continue attending your main classes, of course, and some of them will do quite well. Adjacent women-specific programming will provide a better learning environment for those women for whom your usual way of doing things isn't a good fit. It may also act as an alternative means of entry into your main classes by giving female beginners a chance to get comfortable in a space tailored for them, and build up the confidence and skills that will allow them to do well in a range of environments.

This approach tends to be less disruptive and time-consuming at the start, but it does run the risk of creating cliques or social stratification if students from different program streams don't interact much. It also forces trans and nonbinary students to publicly choose which gendered activities they participate in, and may require public inclusion statements or extra safeguards against harassment to mitigate the social risks these students will be taking.

It's also possible to start out with a segregated stream for "non-default" students, and then move to an integrated model over time. Or you can use occasional focused events like tournaments or workshops aimed at a single group to enrich an otherwise integrated program.

No matter which path you choose, you'll need to be ready to do a lot of tweaking and polishing on the fly. Whether you're changing up how your whole program is run or just adding a new teaching stream, it will take time to discover all of the strengths and weaknesses of your new approach.

As you gain more students from the target group, you'll also get to know them and their learning styles much better. You may discover that your picture of their needs shifts over time, or that they bring strengths to the space that you hadn't accounted for, and that you can now make use of. Just as you periodically reassess your curriculum to make sure the material you teach is relevant and up-to-date, you'll need to check in on your school's structure and culture to make sure that it's serving your students' needs as the community grows and evolves.

Far from coddling women or "going easy" on them, shifting the training environment to acknowledge their needs and bodies can be a powerful foundation for building strength. Sure, forcing women to put up or shut up in a male-centred environment will make some of them tougher, but it will cause far more to simply drop out or never walk in the door in the first place. It's impossible to learn anything from your training if you stop attending.

Catering to women as they actually are (both physically and socially) actively builds resilience by teaching them to find the strength in their own bodies and ways of learning. If—for example—we show female students how to leverage their existing physical power instead of trying to make them mimic male patterns of movement and power generation, they'll progress faster and have a lot more confidence in their abilities.

Conversely, trying to force them into a mould that was built for fighters who are shaped very differently and process emotion very differently will only reinforce the idea that women are lesser—that their bodies and minds are the wrong shape for fighting well, and that they can only progress by becoming less like themselves.

A training space that embraces a range of bodies and learning modes teaches everyone, implicitly, that their own body has worth and power and can be made stronger through a process of refining what's already there, not discarding it and replacing it with something better. It also teaches students to see each other's inherent strengths, and to respect the capabilities of those who look nothing like themselves.

While this chapter has tackled three distinct myths about teaching women, I hope it's apparent that the solutions I present to them form a coherent approach. Making women stronger begins with understanding their perspective. How does having a woman's body and a woman's social conditioning and experience of the world affect how one approaches combat?

To teach effectively, we need to engage with that perspective. We need to:

- Look at our physical techniques and expectations and assess their suitability for a range of bodies, not just ones exactly like ours.

- Find where social conditioning gets in the way of training for students of all genders, and address those glitches in a way that recognizes where they come from and why they hold power.

- Allow for emotional and social expression that's comfortable and useful for all students, so that there are appropriate pressure valves for finding calm and safety in what is often a stressful environment.

- Apply stress and pressure in ways that are fair, realistic, and effective, and that don't drive the cost of failure too high for more vulnerable students.

If we can do all of that, then gender differences often recede into the background. Dealing with them the same way we deal with any other difference—in size, experience level, psychological background, learning style, or age—turns them into just one of many factors that are completely normal to adjust for in training.

Women aren't a particularly special case in martial arts. There's nothing that makes them more or less suited to fighting, just things that make some training environments a poor fit. Addressing those environmental issues goes a lot further toward creating parity in the classroom than any special event or pink re-branding of the school gear, and it often has the side effect of creating a better training environment for everyone.

Dealing with Psychological Trauma

6

No conversation about building more resilient fighters is complete without addressing the specific challenges that come with psychological trauma and recovery.[1] Every one of us will encounter students who come to martial arts or self-defence training in response to having dealt with physical or sexual violence.

Becoming stronger is part of the narrative of recovery in our culture, and many survivors have a very practical desire to avoid being victimized and to address what they see as gaps in their knowledge or capability. The combination of genuine skill and less tangible qualities like empowerment make martial arts and self-defence very attractive spaces for a lot of survivors of violence. There's also the simple fact that anyone can experience trauma in their lives, and a student who came to you for entirely different reasons might suddenly find their training entangled with their recovery. In our field, it's a matter of when, and not if, we'll end up teaching someone who is recovering from trauma.

Getting that right is difficult. It requires a good working understanding of what trauma is and what it does to our minds and bodies. It requires a very clear idea of what a physical instructor's role should be in the recovery process, and how the boundaries of the teacher-student relationship become particularly important with vulnerable students. It

---

1 The word "trauma" can refer both to physical and psychological injury. In this chapter, I'm primarily interested in the effects of psychological trauma and how they modify a student's relationship to their training environment. From here onward, I'll be using "trauma" to mean psychological trauma unless I state otherwise.

also means engaging with the complicated social context of trauma—including the roles of stigma and shame—and looking at the whole school environment and its potential impact on our students' recovery.

What Is Trauma?

When I bring up the term "trauma" in a training context, most people's minds jump immediately to triggers, flashbacks, and other symptoms of PTSD and related medical diagnoses. That's how I framed it earlier in this book, and it's the most common association for many of us. Understanding these conditions is important, but it also puts the cart before the horse.

To engage meaningfully with the aftermath of trauma and to understand what recovery looks like, we first need to understand what we mean when we talk about trauma itself. What qualifies as a traumatic event? What does a healthy recovery look like? Is there a single model of recovery? How do disorders such as PTSD fit into the recovery trajectory, and what are their expected outcomes? Once we can answer these questions, it becomes a lot easier to understand where trauma and recovery intersect with training.

In casual conversation, we might use the word "trauma" to refer to any especially distressing event. In professional usage among psychiatrists, counsellors, and other mental health professionals, it has a much narrower definition. Since PTSD was added to the third edition of the Diagnostic and Statistical Manual of Mental Disorders (DSM) in 1980, diagnosticians have worked to identify what kinds of events qualify as traumatic enough to trigger a strong adverse reaction.[2]

The earliest definition identified a traumatic event as "a recognizable stressor that would evoke significant symptoms in almost everyone [and was] outside the range of normal human experience."[3] Later revisions

---

2 The DSM is the primary tool used by North American psychiatrists to classify and diagnose mental illnesses. The most recent edition (the 5th edition or DSM-5) was published in 2013.

3 Chris R. Brewin, *Post-Traumatic Stress Disorder: Malady or Myth?* (New

became more precise in their phrasing, and the current edition of the DSM specifies "actual or threatened death, serious injury, or sexual violence."[4]

Some clinicians working in trauma recovery break down traumatic events further into three general categories: intentional human actions, which are deliberate, malicious acts such as physical and sexual assault, torture, abuse, participation in combat or atrocities, terrorism, and kidnapping; unintentional human actions, which include accidents, technological disasters, medical errors, and building collapses; and natural disasters such as hurricanes, earthquakes, wildfires, droughts or famines, and sudden illness.[5]

To suffer trauma, then, is to experience one of these events directly; witness it as it occurs; learn of it having happened to a close friend or family member; or be exposed repeatedly to "aversive details" of the event (e.g., by collecting human remains as a first responder or reviewing detailed evidence of abuse as a police officer or investigator).[6]

Though we have a fairly clear idea of what constitutes a traumatic event, identifying what it does—what constitutes the "trauma" itself, rather than its source—is trickier. Early psychologists like Sigmund Freud talked about trauma as a psychic wound, or a mental shock that damaged the mind's ability to protect itself from overstimulation, like a physical wound breaks the skin. Trauma thus became a moment where the brain was completely overwhelmed—by pain, noise and other sensory inputs, and strong emotions like fear—and rendered incapable of processing what had happened.

More recently, psychologists have framed trauma as a fundamental shattering of a person's assumptions about the world: that it is just or

---

Haven: Yale University Press, 2003), 6.

4 *Diagnostic and Statistical Manual of Mental Disorders*, 5th ed. (Arlington, VA: American Psychological Association, 2013), 309.81 (F43.10).

5 Schiraldi, *Post-Traumatic Stress Disorder Sourcebook*, 5.

6 *Diagnostic and Statistical Manual of Mental Disorders*, 309.81 (F43.10).

benevolent; that it is safe or predictable; or that they are worthy and able to act effectively in self-preservation.

In this framing, trauma doesn't just cause distress or strong emotion, but damages a person's sense of who they are and how they fit into the world. This attack on identity or purpose can be enough to have substantial psychological consequences, even if it's unaccompanied by physical pain or injury.[7] This latter definition can also help explain how people can experience trauma not only from being directly involved in a traumatic event, but also from seeing it or hearing about it.

Taking both definitions into account, we can think of trauma as a psychological injury that affects how the brain interacts with the world around it and how a person understands their place in that world.

The consequences of this injury are reasonably well understood. Probably the most interesting thing about the DSM-5's treatment of the topic is that it uses nearly identical lists of symptoms for acute stress disorder, PTSD, and an ordinary response to trauma. The major difference is in the duration and severity of those symptoms. Symptoms fall into four major categories, and can be summarized as follows:

- **Intrusion symptoms**, in which elements of the traumatic event disrupt a person's everyday life. These include:

  - Recurrent, involuntary, and intrusive memories of the event

  - Recurrent distressing dreams related to the event

  - Dissociative reactions such as flashbacks in which the person behaves or feels as if the event were happening

  - Intense or prolonged distress in response to internal or external cues that symbolize or resemble an aspect of the event (triggers)

  - Intense physical reactions to triggers

---

7 Brewin, *Malady or Myth?*, 4–5.

- **Persistent avoidance** of stimuli associated with the traumatic event, including:

  - Avoiding or trying to avoid distressing memories, thoughts, or feelings tied to the event, or external reminders (e.g., people, places, objects, situations) that arouse those distressing memories, thoughts, or feelings

- **Negative changes to cognition and mood** associated with the traumatic event, including:

  - Inability to remember an important aspect of the event

  - Persistent and exaggerated negative beliefs or expectations about oneself or the world (e.g., "I can't trust anybody," "I can't take care of myself," or "My life has been ruined forever")

  - A distorted understanding of the causes or consequences of the event that drive the person to blame themself or others

  - A persistent negative emotional state (e.g., fear, anger, or shame)

  - A loss of interest in pleasurable or important activities

  - Feelings of detachment or estrangement from others

  - Persistent inability to experience positive emotions (e.g., happiness, satisfaction, loving feelings)

- **Major changes to arousal and reactivity** associated with the traumatic event, including:

  - Irritability and unprovoked angry or aggressive outbursts

  - Reckless or self-destructive behaviour

  - Hypervigilance

  - An exaggerated startle response

- Problems concentrating

- Sleep disturbance[8]

Not everyone exhibits all of the symptoms on this list (for example, only one or two from each category are required for a diagnosis of PTSD), and some people won't experience any at all, even in response to a serious traumatic event.

According to the DSM-5, experiencing many or all of these symptoms for up to three days following a traumatic event is considered normal, and is not sufficient for any diagnosis. Experiencing a substantial number of them for three days to one month following the event may be sufficient for a diagnosis of acute stress disorder, and a duration over one month may lead to a diagnosis of PTSD. The majority of people who experience a traumatic event will not be diagnosed with a disorder, and someone might experience a couple of these symptoms for an extended period of time without it having a substantial effect on their life.[9]

I include this list not as a diagnostic tool or a suggestion that everyone who suffers trauma will be diagnosed with a disorder, but to highlight the breadth of effects that trauma can have on a person's life, regardless of whether it's sufficiently disruptive to qualify for a medical diagnosis.

Trauma can affect everything from our emotional regulation and arousal patterns, to our overall emotional state and view of the world and

---

8 *Diagnostic and Statistical Manual of Mental Disorders*. 309.81 (F43.10). This abridged summary does not constitute the full diagnostic criteria for either PTSD or acute stress disorder, and this book should never be used as a diagnostic tool.

9 The prevalence of acute stress disorder varies by traumatic event type. Rates are below 20 percent for people who experience traumatic events that do not involve interpersonal assault; 13 to 21 percent for motor vehicle accidents; and 20 to 50 percent for events involving interpersonal, deliberate violence such as rapes and physical assaults. *Diagnostic and Statistical Manual of Mental Disorders*, 308.3 (F43.0). For PTSD, the projected lifetime risk is just under 9 percent for US adults, despite the overwhelming majority of Americans reporting one or more experiences of traumatic events in their lifetime. *Diagnostic and Statistical Manual of Mental Disorders*, 309.81 (F43.10); Brewin, *Malady or Myth?*, 8–9.

events around us, to fundamental cognitive processes like memory and perception. Understanding the general shape of its effects is essential to building strategies for addressing and accommodating them.

It's also worth remembering that the highest incidence rates for both PTSD and acute stress disorder are in people who have been exposed to the "intentional human actions" category of traumatic events. Rape and sexual assault, physical assault, and events of mass violence such as acts of terrorism and mass shootings all top the list for traumatic events that are the most likely to result in a stress disorder or other complex response to trauma.

These acts of interpersonal violence are also among the most likely to drive students to self-defence or martial arts training. As instructors in those fields, we are very likely to encounter a higher-than-average proportion of students with PTSD and acute stress disorder, as well as students without trauma-related disorders who have experienced interpersonal violence and may still have some trauma-related symptoms.

Trauma is a psychological injury. It's a wound that may heal quickly or slowly, have a straightforward or complex recovery, and have a large or small effect on its subject. It might have all of the impact of a paper cut, or that of a major joint injury that still makes itself felt decades later. That variability doesn't make it any less real or quantifiable.

Being a physical instructor has required me to become familiar with a broad range of physical injuries and their effects on my students' ability to train. It should be the same with psychological injury. Just as I've learned to recognize the symptoms of a broken toe, a concussion, or a ligament tear—all of which are fairly common in the arts I teach—I need to be familiar with the effects of trauma, and how it might affect a student's ability to train. If I know that someone I teach has experienced trauma, or if they tell me that they've got a trauma-related disorder, then that information will have just as much of an effect on how I teach them as knowing they have asthma or a bad knee.

The Instructor's Role

I'd like to stick with the physical injury analogy for the moment, because it's very useful for understanding how to best interact with psychological trauma as an instructor. We are not medical professionals, nor are we mental health professionals, and it is never our job to fix our students. Instead, we need to watch for, prevent, and accommodate injuries to provide the best instruction we can and to avoid harming our students. We do not need to diagnose or treat those injuries, and attempting to do so is a distraction at best, and harmful at worst.

There are two main paths that I follow when managing injury in my school: one for students who have a prior injury that affects their training, and one for cases where an injury happens during class. Both apply equally well to trauma, and it's worth looking at them in more detail.

Past Trauma

There are a lot of different ways to find out if a student has a past injury that's relevant to their training. Many students disclose these on our waivers, which include a section for listing any illnesses, chronic issues, and past injuries that might affect a newcomer's ability to participate in class.

Other times, I notice that someone is moving unusually: maybe they're clearly favouring one side of their body; or they've got uneven muscle development that doesn't fit with what I know of their activity levels and practice habits; or there are signs of compensation in how they bend, twist, or reach. I'll ask them if they've ever been hurt in a way that might explain what I'm seeing. This often uncovers old injuries that students weren't even aware were still affecting them.

Sometimes the realization will be more acute, as a student tries a new technique or movement pattern and feels sudden pain. When they bring it up with me, I always ask if they have a history of injury to, or near, the area that's suddenly uncomfortable. Once I know what the issue is, I can make informed decisions about how I'm going to teach that student going forward.

Trauma is no different. Some students will mention PTSD or other stress disorders on their intake paperwork, or talk about a history of trauma when they first reach out to me for training (the latter is especially common with self-defence students). With others, I'll notice unusual patterns of behaviour: they might avoid certain training partners, positions, or types of contact; they might have unusually strong emotional reactions to some situations or people; they might have sudden outbursts of anger or fear, or have an oversized startle response. If there's a clear pattern or a big anomaly compared to how they usually conduct themselves in class, I'll ask them if there's anything behind their reaction.

Acute, surprising trauma reactions happen as well. The nature of martial arts and self-defence training means that students are likely to encounter situations and pressures that they don't face in their daily lives, and triggers might pop up after not having been an issue for many years—if at all. If a student has a sudden and dramatic emotional reaction to a new drill or technique, the follow-up conversation can often point toward trauma as a source.

Once we realize that there is an injury (either physical or psychological), we need to come up with a plan of action that allows the student to participate as much as possible while reducing the risk of further injury and helping with rehabilitation within the very limited scope of their fighting practice. Building that plan requires answering a number of key questions, with as much input as possible from the student:

- **Is the injury acute or chronic?** Are we dealing with a short-term problem like a sprain, break, or muscle pull? Or a long-term issue like tendinitis, joint degradation, or a pain condition?

  Was there a recent trauma that is being sharply felt right now but is likely to run its course quickly? Or are we dealing with the lingering after-effects of abuse, or a long-ago traumatic event that's left the student with PTSD or minor but occasionally intrusive symptoms?

The timeline of the injury affects everything from the expected recovery period—are they expected to recover in a few days, weeks, or months? Or is complete recovery unlikely?—to the student's level of knowledge and relationship to the injury. Acute issues are often new and strange, and the student might benefit from more active input from an instructor on how to best manage things. People with chronic conditions, on the other hand, have already learned how to live with them and are usually the experts on how their condition affects them.

Acute and chronic injuries also often follow different recovery trajectories. Acute issues start out needing a lot of support, and need less and less accommodation until the issue has resolved itself; chronic ones often fluctuate, and "resolving" them might mean successful management and mitigation rather than a cure.

- **How is it currently being treated?** Is the student using any assistive devices or physical supports? Are they taking pain-killers or anti-inflammatories? Are they in physiotherapy?

  Are they taking anti-anxiety medication or antidepressants? Attending talk therapy or counselling?

  Do they have any training habits built around managing their injury, such as stretches and strengthening exercises, or mindfulness habits like meditation?

  Understanding the existing treatment plan means we won't accidentally interfere with it, and may suggest additional accommodations that need to happen. If a student with a rotator cuff injury has been told by their physiotherapist not to lift loads above shoulder height, then we probably shouldn't be having them fence from guards that require them to hold a sword over their head. If their antidepressants can become toxic without proper hydration, then we should give them extra water breaks even on heavy conditioning days.

- **What activities make it worse?** There's an old joke about a man going to the doctor, and saying, "Doctor, it really hurts when I do this." And the doctor tells him, "Well, stop doing that." We can't avoid everything that causes a bit of discomfort—especially if that discomfort comes from underused muscles or mental pathways being gradually pushed to do their share of the work—but we should be careful with activities that cause a lot of discomfort or that we know can cause a student's condition to get worse. Both physical and psychological injuries have their triggers.

  Most importantly, knowing a student's triggers allows us to act before they become an issue. If a student has a knee problem that causes pain and swelling whenever they go past a ninety-degree bend, and our workout plan for the night includes a few dozen pistol squats, we can add an alternate exercise or warn them in advance and let them make the choice to participate if they're feeling up to it.

  If having an arm placed across their throat can trigger flashbacks or severe emotional distress in a student, and the menu for the night is choke escapes, it's worth giving them ample warning and letting them opt out, prepare themselves in advance, or take a role in class that doesn't involve the upsetting stimulus (e.g., peer coaching, safety monitoring, or taking the lead in a discussion).

- **What activities make it better?** Do they need to strengthen complementary or stabilizing muscles as part of their rehabilitation? Are there some exercises or patterns of movement that help their mobility?

Do certain kinds of drills get them into a headspace that makes managing emotional triggers easier? Are there certain partners they feel safer working with when a class' subject matter overlaps with their trauma?

The more we can incorporate things that help—and not just things that don't harm further—into our training, the more useful it becomes to the student. Look for places where training can complement (but not replace) their existing treatment. If they feel like training is actively contributing to their recovery, they'll stay motivated and engaged even through tough periods, and they will get a lot more out of class.

- **What do we need to refer out to a professional?** Does a physical injury need surgery or other direct medical intervention? Is the student struggling with an element of their strength or range of motion that needs the support of a physiotherapist, massage therapist, or other rehabilitation professional?

  Is the student looking for emotional support or advice that would be better provided by a counsellor or psychiatrist?

  We need to be very aware of the limits of our expertise, capacity, and time. Trying to address issues that fall outside of our knowledge can be dangerous for students, and overextending ourselves to provide support that falls outside of the teacher-student relationship can be stressful, exhausting, and ultimately unhealthy for both parties. Knowing when to call in the cavalry is an enormously useful skill to cultivate, and a key part of professionalism.

The plan that comes out of the answers to these questions is going to vary from instructor to instructor and from injury to injury. Some of us have a lot of experience with common injuries, and use it to build rough blueprints of training plans that can be adapted on the fly for a given student. Others prefer to let the student and the professionals they're already working with take the lead no matter what, and keep their own input to a bare minimum.

Some will happily work with every student and every injury, no matter how challenging, while others draw hard lines around the accommodations they're willing to attempt and are comfortable letting students know that they're not a good fit for the training space.

> ## Exercise: Build a Blueprint for Assessing and Addressing Past Injuries
>
> Make a general model for dealing with past trauma that affects a student's training. Use the above questions as a guide, and include how you will identify past psychological injuries, and how and when you will discuss them with students.
>
> Make sure to identify which kinds of cases you will refer out to qualified professionals, and write down the contact details of any counsellors, therapists, or other professionals you know and trust.
>
> If you don't have a similar plan for dealing with physical injuries, make one now.

Every one of us ends up settling into an approach that fits with our own experience and knowledge, the needs of our student body, and our teaching priorities. The only universal rules for an ethical instructor are to acknowledge that the injury exists, and to be very clear with the injured student about what adjustments we are and are not able to make, and what our expectations will be for their future participation in training.

This holds true for both physical and psychological injuries, and gives the student the basis they need for informed consent to continue (or begin) their training. If both the instructor and student are operating in good faith, there's lots of room to learn and adjust over time.

New Trauma

The process for dealing with injuries that happen during training is a little different. We still need to build a plan for accommodating the injured student after the fact, but we also need to identify the injury correctly and address its cause. For that, I use a second set of guiding questions:

- **What is the injury?** Here's where familiarity with the diagnostic criteria for common injuries becomes extremely useful. Can you spot the symptoms of a concussion? Do you know the difference between a muscle strain and a tear, or between a twisted and a sprained joint?

  Can you monitor for signs of trauma after a sparring match or stress test goes sideways?

  The faster we can accurately identify what has happened, the better we'll be able to care for our students and get them to more competent help when needed. If there are certain kinds of injuries that are common to your martial art or competition scene, everyone who teaches in your space should know what they look like. We can't provide a medical diagnosis, but we can do triage.

- **What immediate care does it need?** Can you provide adequate first aid, or is immediate professional intervention required? If the injury affects the student's brain in any way (whether that's via the physical mechanism of traumatic brain injury, or the psychological mechanism of trauma), can they be left to make their own decisions about whether to keep going? Can the student safely return to training after a quick time-out, or do they need to stop for the night? Do they need to be sent to the hospital or referred to other follow-up care?

Staying up-to-date on first aid certification should be a given for any of us teaching physical skills.[10] Experience also plays a big role in helping us make good decisions, especially when it comes to deciding what first aid equipment to keep on site or when to call for external medical assistance.

If you find yourself not knowing what to do in the aftermath of an injury, err on the side of caution and call in backup (whether that's a more experienced member of your school or an ambulance). It's very useful to know which of your students have first aid training, or are doctors, paramedics, mental health professionals, or other people qualified to help in an emergency.

These kinds of incidents are also a good indicator of where you might need more training. Keep track of what makes you freeze and set aside time to educate yourself about those kinds of incidents in the future.

- **How did it happen?** Was the injury caused by an interaction between students or staff? By an equipment issue? By an element of the environment? By a combination of some or all of those factors?

Get as accurate a picture as possible of what happened, including statements from the injured student, anyone else involved in the incident, and any witnesses. This doesn't have to be complex—sometimes all that's needed is "I cut my finger on my training blade" and a quick follow-up inspection to find a burr on the blade's edge—but it should be thorough

---

10 Along with standard first aid programs, professionally delivered mental health first aid training is available in many regions. Canada has a nationwide program, as do the United States, United Kingdom, and Australia. These programs aim to give the general public solid tools for providing immediate, short-term support in a mental health crisis, and can be a great starting point for instructors who are unsure of how to spot trauma-related distress or other acute mental health issues, or are uncomfortable providing support to students in psychological distress.

enough to understand all of the major contributing factors to the incident.

This is especially important for psychological injuries, as the factors that can trigger a trauma-related response are often less immediately obvious than a sharp edge.

- **How likely is it to happen again?** Are some or all of the factors leading to the injury endemic to your training environment? Was the equipment flaw a common failure point, or a freak accident? Is there an environmental hazard present (e.g., an unpadded wall corner or an uneven patch of floor that's easy to trip on) that might injure more people?

  If there was an interpersonal conflict, how likely are tempers to flare or egos to clash in the same way? Is there a student or staff member who keeps being the source of injuries through inattention, inexperience, or malice?

  Physical hazards like equipment and environment issues are easiest to identify after an incident, but interpersonal patterns are just as important. Especially in cases of psychological injury, we need to be able to identify patterns of behaviour, gaps in partnership skills, or issues with the school atmosphere (e.g., excessive pressure to "suck it up" under stress, or bullying of fighters who are seen as timid) that make it likely that more students will be injured.

  Once might be an accident; twice or three times is a pattern that needs to be addressed. Keeping a record of in-class incidents is enormously helpful here. It's a lot easier to spot patterns if you have written records, especially if the incidents are spread out over months or years.

- **How can we reduce that likelihood?** Do you need to change the equipment requirements for certain activities, or switch to a better gear supplier? Can environmental hazards be re-paired or removed?

Does a problem student need to be disciplined, removed from class, or given additional training to make up for gaps in their ability to practise safely? Does a staff member need more practice with heading off certain kinds of conflict, or more training in spotting low-level harassment and abuse?

A space where injuries are common is a space where it's hard to train well. This is just as true of psychological injuries as physical ones, and if students are regularly ending up with trauma after certain drills, tests, or events, then there needs to be a change. Once you understand the mechanism of injury, it's not hard to figure out where that change should happen—whether that's repairing an ongoing equipment issue or an ongoing social issue.

Exercise: Build an Immediate Injury Response Plan

Make a plan for dealing with psychological injuries that happen in your training space, using the above questions as a guide. Make sure to address record-keeping, and put together a list of current students and staff who have relevant training and can help with incidents. Identify any gaps in your skills, resources, or knowledge and set a timeline for addressing them.

If you don't have a similar plan for dealing with physical injuries, make one now.

Physical and psychological injuries often have different mechanisms and require different solutions, but they are equally real, and the same general decision-making process works to address both. If it seems like I'm belabouring that point a bit, it's because I think it's critical to demystify psychological trauma. Many of us treat it like a wholly unique thing that is impossible to deal with or understand without extensive training or firsthand experience.

When we make trauma exceptional, we take away our own power to engage usefully with students who've experienced it, and we cut ourselves off from using the skills we already have. Worse, we disempower those very students by treating them as too broken to get the basic consideration and accommodations that we'd give someone with a sprained ankle.

When we visibly shy away from engaging with trauma, pretend it's not real, or assign it its own special category, that sends a very clear message to the people dealing with it that they are beyond help, and that their very presence is upsetting and uncomfortable.

To some people, trauma creates a special social category for "victims" or "survivors" as humans who have experienced something so exceptional that no ordinary person can possibly understand them. That kind of othering can be an enormous impediment to recovery, and it can disrupt the classroom by drawing lines between students who've experienced trauma and everyone else.[11]

The truth is that traumatic experiences are common, as are trauma-related disorders, and that we need to be able to handle them with the same calm and care that we do other injuries and illnesses. After all, the incidence rate for PTSD in the United States is comparable to that for asthma, and we don't treat students who occasionally use an inhaler as uncoachable anomalies.[12]

---

11 For a longer discussion of the development of such a "stalled victim" identity that impedes progress, see Anna Valdiserri, *Trauma-Aware Self-Defense Instruction* (San Bernardino, CA: CreateSpace, 2016), 26–27.

12 In the 2005 National Health Interview Survey of the United States, prevalence of asthma was around 9 percent. The lifetime risk of developing PTSD for US adults is just under 9 percent (see note 9 above for discussion of this statistic). Barbara Bloom, Achintya N. Dey, and Gulnur Freeman, "Summary Health Statistics for U.S. Children: National Health Interview Survey, 2005," *Vital and Health Statistics* 10, no. 231 (Dec 2006): 4.

Stigma

While we can use many of the same strategies to address trauma and related disorders as we do physical injury, there are challenges that are unique to training students who have experienced trauma. Psychological injuries—like all mental health challenges—are heavily stigmatized in many cultures, and can be particularly hard for students to talk about or instructors to engage with in environments that prize toughness and strength.

The nature of triggers and the psychological symptoms of PTSD and related disorders also means that accommodation often requires dealing with complex social interactions rather than just padding a wall or buying better boxing gloves. Because of this, school culture and our own attitudes play an enormous role in our ability to be good teachers for students who've experienced trauma. Making sure that both are healthy is what enables the straightforward problem-solving approach I advocate in the previous section.

In the last twenty years, studies of trauma-related disorders have expanded well beyond military veterans (the first subjects of study for "shell shock," a very early model of PTSD). Two groups that have received a lot of attention in the psychiatric community, and that are of particular relevance to martial arts and self-defence, are police officers and sexual assault survivors.

Police officers have a high risk of both trauma-related disorders and suicide due to the high level of personal risk in their job and the frequency with which they are exposed to traumatic events. They are also less likely than the general population to seek out mental health support and more likely to develop unhealthy coping strategies such as avoidance and substance abuse.[13]

---

13 A 2006 study of Norwegian police officers, for example, found that less than 10 percent of those who reported anxiety, depression, or suicidal ideation had sought the help of a psychiatrist or psychologist. A study of the South African Police Service, which has a suicide rate five times that of other police services internationally, found that officers who used avoidance as their primary coping strategy—instead of engaging directly with the source of trauma or seeking

While individual reasons for avoiding treatment and using poor coping strategies vary, the social environment of law enforcement plays a big role in increasing stigma around seeking help and discussing trauma openly. Many officers view seeking help as a sign of cowardice, incompetence, or weakness, and worry that admitting to having been affected by trauma will damage their future job prospects.[14]

Different researchers have various explanations for these views. Some attribute these attitudes to the emotional demands of the job, which requires that officers remain calm and controlled even in moments of extreme stress and that they limit their overall emotional expression.[15] Others think the cause is stereotypes of officers as "heroic" or "invincible"; these are often reproduced by recruiting and training programs and parroted by management.[16] Other researchers feel the cause is the pressure to fit traditionally masculine traits such as emotional control, physical and mental strength, and the ability to act independently and solve problems without external support.[17]

The net effect is an environment where officers feel a substantial amount of both self-stigma (a loss of self-esteem and negative attitude toward themselves for experiencing trauma or needing help) and public

support in a social or religious community—had the highest rates of suicidal ideation. Anne Marie Berg, Erlend Hem, Bjorn Lau, and Oivind Ekeberg, "Help-Seeking in the Norwegian Police Service," Journal of Occupational Health 48, no. 3 (May 2006): 151; Jacobus Pienaar, Sebastiaan Rothmann, Fons J. R. van de Vijver, "Occupational Stress, Personality Traits, Coping Strategies, and Suicide Ideation in the South African Police Service," Criminal Justice and Behavior 34, no. 2 (Feb 2007): 255.

14 Louise Watson and Leanne Andrews, "The Effect of a Trauma Risk Management (TRiM) Program on Stigma and Barriers to Help-Seeking in the Police," International Journal of Stress Management (May 2017): 2, http://dx.doi.org/10.1037/str0000071.

15 Heather Stuart, "Mental Illness Stigma Expressed by Police to Police," Israel Journal of Psychiatry and Related Sciences 54, no. 1 (2017): 18.

16 Watson and Andrews, "Effect of Trauma Risk Management," 2.

17 Stephen R. Wester, David Arndt, Sonya K. Sedivy, and Leah Arndt, "Male Police Officers and Stigma Associated With Counseling: The Role of Anticipated Risks, Anticipated Benefits and Gender Role Conflict," Psychology of Men and Masculinity 11, no. 4 (2010): 287–288.

stigma (negative perception of officers with trauma- and stress-related disorders by their peers and superiors, including the belief that they are less competent, less worthy of promotion, or malingering).[18] As a re-sults, many refuse to seek treatment and experience high rates of PTSD, long-term stress disorders, substance abuse, anger management issues, and suicide.

So what does this have to do with our teaching environment? Most martial artists and self-defence students aren't cops and don't face the same levels of occupational stress and exposure to traumatic events as a first responder. The similarity between police officers and martial arts students lies not so much in their job descriptions but in their social environments and personal values.

If we look again at the pressures that contribute to stigma in policing—especially the valourization of strength and heroism, the emphasis on emotional control and independent problem-solving, and the fear of failure or weakness—we get something that looks awfully similar to many traditional training environments. Fighters can be just as prone to perpetuating stigma against those who are upset or harmed by their experience of violence.

One of the core arguments of this book is that fear of failure is both en-demic in martial arts and self-defence environments, and a serious bar-rier to effective learning. When we consider that fear of failure—and of being seen to fail—can prevent people from seeking life-saving help, the harm caused by this fear becomes even more apparent. A student who is too scared of being ostracized—or too unwilling to see themselves as a "failure"—to tell their instructor that they've got trauma-related symp-toms is putting themself at risk of further psychological injury.

---

18 A 2017 Canadian study was the first to record peer-to-peer public stigma directly, and found that the majority of officers believed that "most police officers" would not disclose to managers (84.9 percent) or colleagues (85 percent) that they suffered from mental illness, would expect to be discriminated against at work if they disclosed a mental illness (62.4 percent), and believed that being treated for mental illness was a sign of personal failure (59.4 percent). Stuart, "Mental Illness Stigma," 21.

Depending on the nature of those symptoms, they may also be putting others in the class at risk of psychological or physical injury (especially if they have difficulties with emotional regulation and anger management, tend to engage in self-destructive or risk-taking behaviour, or have an unpredictable startle reflex).

An environment that penalizes failure too heavily isn't just unpleasant and counterproductive—it's downright dangerous.

So we know that stigma can prevent students from seeking professional help and from disclosing their experiences and symptoms to their instructor. That's bad. What's worse is that this is only one of the ways in which stigma negatively affects their ability to recover from trauma. It doesn't just make it harder to get professional help, but actually contributes to the development of trauma-related disorders in the first place.

A 2003 meta-analysis of studies related to traumatic events found that the single greatest risk factor for developing PTSD after a traumatic event was lack of social support. This risk factor had a substantially stronger effect than trauma severity or post-trauma life stress.[19] Specifically, subjects who had negative reactions to their trauma from friends and family (e.g., coldness, lack of sympathy, criticism, and blame) were the most likely to develop PTSD, and the most likely to have poor treatment outcomes.[20]

The practice of "blaming the victim," in which a victim of a traumatic event is held responsible for either causing the event, being unable to prevent or stop it, or not putting it behind them quickly enough, has been most carefully studied in relation to survivors of sexual assault. It's heavily implicated in the development of self-stigma, which in turn affects the severity of PTSD symptoms.

One study differentiated between three types of stigma around sexual assault: cultural stigma (myths and negative stereotypes around sexual assault that are widely held in the US, such as "Husbands cannot sex-

---

19 Brewin, *Malady or Myth?*, 47.

20 Brewin, *Malady or Myth?*, 57–58.

ually assault their wives," and "Women ask to be sexually assaulted"),
public stigma (negative or unfair treatment by others in the aftermath
of sexual assault), and self-stigma (the shame, embarrassment, and de-
valuation that comes from internalizing cultural or public stigma).[21] It
found that self-stigma had a strong, positive correlation with severity of
PTSD symptoms, while public and cultural stigma were not consistent
factors when self-stigma was removed from the equation.[22]

In other words, survivors who believed that the public and cultural stigma they experienced was true and justified were a lot more likely to have
serious symptoms and a difficult recovery. Simply knowing that negative stereotypes exist, or having been treated badly by others, wasn't
necessarily enough to move the needle. It took absorbing those negative
messages into one's self-image to make things worse.

That mechanism is incredibly important to understand in a teaching
environment. While no instructor can control what cultural messages
a student gets about a traumatic event they experience, or how they are
treated by family and friends outside the school, we do have an influence over what ideas they take to heart. We have a lot of power to help
students mould and re-mould their identities, especially when they're
participating in training as part of their recovery from a traumatic event.

How we talk about violence and trauma—and most especially how we
talk about those who come out on the losing end of a violent encounter—has a big impact on how all of our students negotiate their own
relationships with violence. We may not be authorities on medical or
psychiatric issues, and they won't necessarily look to us for general life
advice, but we are their personal authorities on violence and how to
deal with it.

If we talk about violence as something that happens to people who deserve it, or as a game with clear winners and losers who derive their

21 Mandi F. Deitz, Stacey L. Williams, Sean C. Rife, and Peggy Cantrell,
"Examining Cultural, Social, and Self-Related Aspects of Stigma in Relation
to Sexual Assault and Trauma Symptoms," *Violence against Women* 21, no. 5
(2015): 601–602.

22 Deitz and others, "Aspects of Stigma," 608–609.

social capital and moral standing from the outcome, we're pretty likely to set our students up for self-stigma if they ever become victims of violence. If they've already experienced it, then we might become the catalyst for turning cultural and public stigma into self-stigma, or deepening existing self-stigma into something that makes recovery extraordinarily difficult.

Fixing the Conversation

How, then, do we talk about violence without contributing to stigma and screwing up our students' healthy responses to trauma? And how do we create an environment where they're willing to talk about the challenges they face without fear of being socially excluded?

Many of the teaching and culture-building strategies that I've laid out earlier in this book are very helpful for reducing stigma and addressing some of the common issues that students who've experienced trauma face, and can be made even more effective with a few tweaks. Let's take a look at the most useful approaches, and how they interact with trauma recovery and stigma.

Public-Facing Policy

For any student who has experienced trauma in a martial arts environment, and for many students who have experienced sexual violence specifically, codes of conduct and other public-facing policies are a first test of whether a school is likely to be safe. Unless they have received a referral from someone they trust—and often even if they have—students whose trust has been violated are usually very careful about who they'll allow to exert power over them in the future.

They're rightfully picky about where they'll train, and may avoid entire communities if they've had bad experiences within them. Clear, visible policies that define what sorts of behaviours will not be tolerated are a critical first step to establishing that your school might be worthy of trust. I know a good number of students with these experiences for whom the absence of a public policy is reason enough not to attend an event or visit a school.

Consent

Respecting the consent and boundaries of our students is integral to winning and maintaining their trust. Once again, this becomes even more critical when they've suffered serious violations in the past, and many will disappear if they see that consent is not valued or that boundaries are disrespected in a school.

This is also one area where it is easy to trigger trauma-related symptoms: touching someone without their consent (especially if that touch comes from behind or in a blind spot, or is otherwise a surprise), or violating a boundary (whether that's by pushing them to do things that they've stated they're not comfortable with, pushing them to ignore pain or discomfort, or ignoring them when they ask you to stop or try to disengage from a situation) is very likely to fall within familiar patterns of behaviour for someone who has been abused or assaulted.

While some other kinds of contact or behaviour are extremely difficult to avoid in a martial space (e.g., striking, grabbing, adrenalized and/ or aggressive body language), these kinds of violations are completely avoidable.

Actively prioritizing consent and boundaries models safe behaviour for the entire student body and is a further signal of safety to students who are reluctant to trust. Establishing healthy boundaries is also often an integral part of recovering from PTSD, and an environment that models that behaviour can contribute positively to recovery.[23]

Good Partners

Teaching students to be sensitive to their training partner's psychological state and to calibrate their drilling behaviour accordingly is a great way to make everyone better at responding to adverse reactions to triggers and other trauma symptoms. It does so without explicitly centring trauma in class discussions or singling out psychologically vulnerable students.

---

23 Schiraldi, *Post-Traumatic Stress Disorder Sourcebook*, 59–60.

If the feeder views responding appropriately to the player's discomfort or distress as a basic courtesy that they owe everyone rather than a special accommodation for "weaker" or "lesser" students, then a player who reacts badly during a triggering situation is a lot less likely to develop self-stigma.

Emphasizing intrinsic, rather than extrinsic, feedback in drills also encourages all students to pay attention to their internal state and reactions. This creates natural opportunities for them to self-monitor their own symptoms, and to use techniques such as visualization or breathing control to manage their own level of emotional arousal.

Self-Regulation and Opting In

Empowering students to manage their own level of engagement with the class material is especially important when trauma is involved. Nobody knows a student's triggers and symptoms better than they do.

They need to be able to step out when they want to calm down or avoid a specific trigger, or opt in to a psychologically challenging activity when they feel prepared to deal with its effects. An environment where this is normal behaviour for any student goes a long way toward reducing stigma, and also avoids othering students who need to self-regulate or granting a special status to "survivors."

It also gives students who've experienced trauma the power to manage their own symptoms their own way, and ties the sense of agency and control they get from doing that to their training. If the training space is somewhere where they have power over their own recovery, their intrinsic and autonomous extrinsic motivation to keep training is likely to increase dramatically.

The opt-in model also creates openings for students to disclose a history of trauma when they're ready, and on their own terms. You may not hear from everyone right away, but you are likely to get a lot more information when it's needed if students feel like they're in control of the conversation.

Modelling Failure and Play

The combination of modelling failure and including play creates multiple examples every class of cases where failure isn't a bad thing. It shows students, rather than just telling them, that imperfection will not be penalized and that publicly failing doesn't disqualify anyone from a leadership position or high rank.

In combination with the trust-building, development of emotional sensitivity, and empowerment that comes from the other tools in this list, this creates an environment where disclosing a history of trauma is as low-risk as possible.

Most students will still be dealing with cultural and public stigma from other sources, and may well be fighting self-stigma as well, but they're likely to perceive a low level of risk in the training space specifically. That makes them far more likely to ask for help, and more likely to give you all the information you need to accommodate them and help them grow.

Talking about Violence

The other major factor in stigma and students' comfort with disclosing their psychological injuries is how we discuss trauma and violence. Whether we're teaching recreational martial arts, competitive combat sport, or self-defence, discussions of real-life violence and trauma are inevitable. And when they happen, we convey a lot of our personal views on survival, trauma, and recovery.

As professionals who work with and think about violence on a regular basis, it'd be absurd for us not to have strong beliefs about its use. We can and should talk about our own relationship to violence, and share as much of our own experience as we are able. That openness doesn't mean that we can't avoid the ways of speaking that are most likely to contribute to self-stigma. There are a few traps that instructors commonly fall into that either signal to students that disclosure won't be safe, or feed habits of thought that are likely to make recovery harder.

The first is creating a hierarchy of success in a violent encounter that differentiates between "good" and "bad" ways of surviving. This isn't the same thing as recognizing that some courses of action are less risky than others and suggesting that students prioritize those, if possible.

For example, you can absolutely tell students that it's safer to avoid a violent situation than to have to escape one, and better to escape or de-escalate than to have to fight. What isn't useful is talking about the outcomes of actual violent incidents in terms of what the victim should have done instead—especially if the victim survived.

I once had a student come to one of my self-defence workshops after having avoided any kind of self-defence training for many years. She had been violently sexually assaulted in the past, felt unsafe and uncomfortable with her existing skill set, and really wanted to develop more tools for dealing with violence, but could not bring herself to set foot in a class. I eventually found out that she had tried to take a self-defence course shortly after being raped. During that incident, she had chosen to comply with her much bigger and stronger attacker in order to avoid further violence and get out alive.

When she told her instructor what had happened to her, he told her off for not having fought back hard enough, and later publicly used her case as an example of someone making the wrong choice.

She was doing everything right at that point—she had survived terrible violence using the skills she had at the time, she'd decided that she wanted to have more options in the future, and she'd sought out training in order to build her skills—and her reward was public humiliation and an enormous helping of stigma that turned her away from training for many years and set her recovery back substantially. She'd come to that class in order to become stronger, and her teacher only made her more vulnerable.

Talking about her experience so disparagingly also sent a terrible message to other students. If there were any other sexual assault survivors in the audience with similar stories, they would have felt the full brunt of the instructor's words, and gotten the same message that they had done everything wrong. It also almost guaranteed that they would not disclose their own experiences to that instructor; instead, they would compromise the quality of their training for the sake of avoiding public shaming.

Everyone else learned that one of the possible consequences of surviving "wrong" would be facing the judgement and censure of the people they respect and trust to help keep them safe. That makes self-stigma a lot more likely if they're assaulted in the future. It also complicates their decision-making process in a violent encounter by forcing them to not only consider what response is legally, ethically, and tactically appropriate, but also which one will earn their teacher's and peers' approval. When there's often a conflict between what makes us look cool and what keeps us alive,[24] and when adding more factors to consider extends our reaction time by critical fractions of a second, that kind of pressure can put students in a lot of danger.

It's entirely possible to talk about risk and even debrief a real incident without doing this kind of damage. For discussions of risk, focus on the facts and frame your suggestions with an emphasis on the risks themselves, rather than on the behaviour of victims or potential victims.

> *Predatory attacks such as muggings, sexual assaults, and murders are most likely to happen in lonely places, because the perpetrator doesn't want witnesses.*

versus

> *Don't go out alone if you don't want to get raped or murdered.*

or

> *If she hadn't gone down that alley, she wouldn't have been assaulted.*

---

24 Take another look at the "avoid > escape > de-escalate > fight" hierarchy. All of the least risky options are the ones that are also the most likely to make you look like a "coward" or "loser" in the retelling.

When you're discussing an actual event, this same framework applies. You can point out elements of the environment, position, and body language of those involved that give students clues as to what is happening and how to avoid or deal with a similar situation, without mocking or criticizing the actual people involved. If you find yourself saying "should have" or "if only . . .," you're probably not helping.

Exercise: Double-Check the Message You're Sending

Make an audio recording of yourself telling a few of your favourite stories about violence. These could be personal anecdotes, examples you bring up while teaching, or even jokes—anything that you like to tell in public. Tell them exactly like you'd tell them to an audience or, better yet, record yourself telling them to a friend or group of friends.

Listen to each story from the perspective of a student who's survived violence. What messages are they getting about who violence happens to, what kinds of consequences people deserve, and how people ought to behave in a violent situation?

If you catch yourself saying things that are likely to contribute to stigma, re-write your version of the story to eliminate those features. If you can't tell a story without them, reconsider its appropriateness for the classroom.

The second trap is talking about trauma as something that always breaks people. Everyone is changed by trauma in some way, but the shape and magnitude of that change varies a lot.

We understand this pretty well when it comes to physical injuries: even the tiniest cut leaves a mark on our body. It changes our very shape. The mark left by a physical wound might go away after a few days, or it may turn into a scar that lasts forever. That scar might just have a cosmetic impact, or it might affect how our body moves. Muscle fibres that have been cut and stitched back together don't behave the same way as uncut ones. Soft tissue injuries often lead to shifts in which muscles, tendons, and ligaments work hardest during a given action, and can completely change your gait, posture, and range of motion.

Not all of these changes are negative. Broken bones can knit stronger than they were before. Muscle issues can push us toward better, more efficient movement. Being mindful of an injury can dramatically improve our proprioception and make us better motor learners.

It's the same with psychological trauma. The same incident can leave one person relatively unaffected, another with PTSD, and a third with a stronger sense of self and a renewed outlook on life.

Post-traumatic growth is a phenomenon that has been receiving more and more attention in psychiatry since the turn of the millennium. Researchers have now identified a cluster of positive changes that can follow trauma, including:

- Greater appreciation of life and a changed sense of priorities

- Warmer, more intimate relationships with others

- A greater sense of personal strength

- Recognition of new possibilities or paths for one's life

- Spiritual development[25]

When we tell our students that trauma breaks, we prime them for being harmed by experiencing violence. They expect not to be okay. If they are fine after a traumatic event, the disconnect between their experience and expectations can be enough to create serious self-stigma. What if they're a monster for not responding "correctly"? What if they really are damaged, but are unable to see it because they're too broken?

---

25 Richard G. Tedeschi, and Lawrence G. Calhoun, "Posttraumatic Growth: Conceptual Foundations and Empirical Evidence," *Psychological Inquiry* 15, no. 1 (2004): 6.

It can become a self-fulfilling prophecy that triggers intense enough feelings of self-recrimination and guilt to lead to genuine PTSD. We make damage inevitable by treating it as such.

This framing also doesn't do much for students who really were harmed by their trauma. It centres only the negative elements of their recovery and removes the potential for post-traumatic growth. Growth often occurs hand-in-hand with the worst parts of recovery and is most often recognized only after the fact.[26] A student who doesn't believe that they can get anything positive out of their trauma may fail to recognize or allow for growth and lose out on one of the most powerful components of healing.

The insistence on "brokenness" can also contribute to self-stigma around failure and make students less likely to talk about their experiences with us. Most people don't want others to see them as damaged. If they believe that their teachers and peers will look down on them or see them as lesser, broken people, they may choose to stay silent.

We don't need to oversell post-traumatic growth or the potential positive outcomes of trauma, but talking about trauma in a well-rounded manner that recognizes that responses to it can be positive, negative, or neutral helps us avoid negatively influencing our students' recovery.

The last trap is framing recovery as a return to the way things were before. We know trauma changes people. They may change a little or a lot, and that change may be more or less painful, but it's exceedingly rare for someone to be exactly the same after a traumatic event as they were before it.

If a student talks to us about their past trauma and we're making a plan of action to accommodate them in class, how we discuss the trajectory of their recovery matters a lot. Especially if we're helping an existing student return to training after a disruption, it can be very tempting to set "getting back to normal" as the goal. What we often mean is, "Getting the student back to their previous level of participation and competence." But it gets framed as a return the prior state of their body and mind in-

---

26 Tedeschi and Calhoun, "Posttraumatic Growth," 15.

stead. The former of these may be possible; the latter pretty much never is.

When we build our recovery plans around returning to a former version of our student that no longer exists, we set them up for disappointment. Every time they have to perform an action differently to account for changes in how they move, or use emotional regulation and mindfulness techniques to deal with a trigger, they're reminded of the fact that they're not fixed yet. That they feel different, and train differently than they did before they were hurt. Even when they're back in classes just as frequently, and are performing as well or better than they did before, they'll fixate on the pieces that aren't the same and view them as places where they're broken or deficient.

Our training, our minds, and our bodies change all the time, and it's unreasonable to expect that this won't be the case after trauma. When you plan your students' return to training, set new goals that take into account their current condition, and be open about the fact that you expect them to change. Looking forward to a stronger, more resilient future self can be an enormous source of motivation. Looking backward to an idealized past self will only hold them back.

Addressing trauma can be daunting for even very experienced instructors. The biggest challenge is often not accommodating a specific student's needs, but opening up the conversation in the first place.

Reducing stigma and building trust are the cornerstones of a healthy approach to trauma management in the classroom. If your students know that they can talk about their experiences without being looked down on or ostracized, they're a lot more likely to talk to you about what has happened to them. If they trust you to not only listen, but also to respect their boundaries and prioritize their safety, they'll actually come to your classes.

From there, it becomes a matter of accommodating their needs and figuring out how to help them get the most out of their training, the same as we do for everyone we teach. I've presented a model for thinking about trauma that aligns it closely with physical injury, and lets us tap into our existing strengths as instructors. We know how to work around injury—this is just a new kind of injury to learn about and get good at accommodating.

If you find yourself at a loss when it comes to the practical details of working with a particular student or type of experience, research is your friend. I've listed a few good starting points on page 244. They're fairly broad works that will help build up your basic stable of strategies for dealing with trauma in the classroom.

What's likely to be even more useful, though, is letting the student themselves be your guides. If you earn and maintain their trust, and focus on managing everybody's safety, the student is likely to do the heavy lifting of recovery on their own. Facilitating someone else's path to growth and learning is safer, easier, and more effective than trying to micromanage that growth, and the same principles of exploration and play that we use to teach motor skills can be used to facilitate psychological development.

Conclusion

In this book, I've presented a paradigm for thinking about the kinds of psychological growth your teaching environment facilitates and identifying where it gets in the way.

We began with an in-depth exploration of the concept of failure and its relationship to motor learning, the development of emotional resilience, and fear. While fear of failure isn't the only source of problems in martial arts training, understanding how it operates and closely examining our own relationship to failure sheds light on many of the biggest cultural and practical challenges we face, including attracting and retaining vulnerable and minority students; managing physical and psychological risk; establishing and maintaining trust within our community; and challenging our students in ways that make them stronger, not more brittle.

The three pillars of policy, culture, and stress testing work together to create a healthy environment that nurtures and challenges all at once.

Policy works to eliminate unnecessary physical, psychological, and social risk that gets in the way of our students' training, and lays the groundwork for students to begin to trust us before they even walk through the door.

Culture makes that trust tangible, integrates it into every training relationship, and prioritizes our students' autonomy and agency. It also develops the soft skills of good partnership and self-regulation that make it possible to engage in the high-stress, high-risk training that pays the biggest dividends, and uses play to make even the most challenging training fun and intrinsically rewarding.

Stress testing is the heat that tempers our students' bodies and wills and makes them not just capable, but formidable. When it's done correctly, in an environment guided by the other two pillars, it is an agent of powerful transformation and growth.

Once all three pillars are in place, teaching even the most vulnerable students becomes much easier. I've focused on two populations that are often in the greatest need of effective martial arts and self-defense training, and of the resiliency that it builds, and that tend to respond poorly to traditional training environments: women and students with a history of trauma.

We've looked at how the three-pillar approach makes them psychologically and physically safer, more motivated, and a lot more likely to succeed. We've also explored specific challenges that come with teaching those groups in a way that gives us useful models for teaching all of our students, including those from populations not specifically covered in this book.

What you have now is a problem-solving framework: a method for looking at every aspect of your school's culture and structure and identifying how well it serves the needs of your community and how likely it is to facilitate the emotional growth that we all want for our students. It's not a replacement for your teaching methods, or the traditions of your art, or a call to set aside techniques that work for you, but a way of pointing all of those tools in the right direction and clarifying their purpose.

You probably have all the of the knowledge you need to implement most of the strategies I've outlined, and definitely have the knowledge to decide how best to fit them into the way your training space already operates. For the places where you're missing pieces of the puzzle or want to dig deeper into a topic I've raised, I've put together some starter resources in the following pages.

The "Sample Exercises" appendix contains a selection of exercises that I've found particularly useful for building essential soft skills, establishing trust, and introducing play, chaos, and stress into the training environment without losing control of the class.

The "Recommended Reading" appendix contains a mix of in-depth books and short, accessible articles that expand on concepts I've covered. It opens up avenues for deeper exploration of topics like violence dynamics, the science of motor learning, and the process of trauma recovery.

When I started approaching my own martial arts practice from the perspective that's outlined in this book, I was nervous. It required letting go of so many of my deeply held beliefs about what made people tough, and how resilience was built. I was scared of being too nice and too hands-off to really be able to push anybody—especially myself. But I was also tired of the shortcomings of my old training environments and desperate to find the fun in fighting again. This new approach offered that, and I was willing to try it for a bit and see what happened.

Imagine my surprise when I found myself pushed harder and tested more than I'd ever been—when I went from hoping to emulate my teachers to finding ways to surprise and surpass them on my own terms.

Teaching others this way has proven that my experience wasn't a fluke. My students laugh their way through workouts and drills that horrify visitors from other schools, and I've had more than one guest walk out of a drop-in class shaking their head in disbelief at the things they were willing to try and the fears they faced down. We've developed a reputation for having the most demanding training in our corner of the swordplay community, but you'd never know it from the atmosphere.

The safety and trust we've established is a source of immeasurable strength and tenacity, and I sincerely hope that you get to experience its power for yourself, in your own school.

Appendix: Sample Exercises

The following exercises are good starting points for integrating some of the core concepts from this book into your teaching. They've been organized by pedagogical goal to make it easier to find the exercise that serves your needs in a given moment.

Because of the breadth of this book's audience, you may come across exercises that work with tools (such as training weapons) that you aren't familiar with. Feel free to adapt these exercises to better fit with the arts that you practice, and don't give your students tools or challenges that you aren't comfortable handling yourself.

As with all other advice in this book, the exercises presented here are suggestions that experienced instructors can use to enrich their programming. They are not replacements for training with a qualified instructor, and you are ultimately responsible for your students' safety and the quality of their learning.

Unless otherwise indicated, all weapon exercises can be performed with the weapon held in the right or left hand. The hand holding the weapon is the "weapon hand", and the other hand is the "off hand". You may also see references to the "weapon side" or "off-hand side" of the body, or the "weapon leg" and "off-hand leg". If a fighter is holding their weapon in their right hand, then their right side is the weapon side, and their right leg is the weapon leg. Any strike originating on the weapon side and travelling toward the off-hand side is a "forehand" strike, and any strike originating on the off-hand side and travelling toward the weapon side is a "backhand" strike.

Exercises

Getting Comfortable with Contact and Hitting

1. Solo Force Calibration

The goal of this exercise is to help students control the amount of force they bring to bear against their partner and to give them concrete reference points for what it means to hit "hard" or "lightly" in training. It can be used as an introduction to impact calibration for beginners, or as a remedial tool for helping students with poor force control become safer training partners.

This exercise can be performed with unarmed strikes or with any kind of weapon. It can also be followed up with the partnered calibration exercise on page 139.

Equipment: whatever weapons students normally fight with; a heavy punching bag hung up with lots of space to move around it, or a large plastic bottle (two-litre capacity or larger) that has been filled with water and placed at about torso height

Goal: teach students to deliver safe, consistent force

Secondary skills developed: ability to switch between different levels of force, ability to recognize what different impact levels feel like from the perspective of the fighter throwing the attack

Exercise progression:

1. Player starts facing their target (heavy bag or water bottle). They should be at their usual striking range and in a comfortable fighting stance.

2. Player throws a standard attack to the target, at the speed and level of force they are accustomed to using. This can be a punch or kick, a cut, a thrust, or anything else that they normally do in sparring.

3. Player repeats the same attack, at the same level of force, and observes the effects. How much does the target move? What does the hit sound like? How does it make Player's striking limb feel?

4. Player repeats the same attack at three different levels of force. Their speed and body mechanics should remain consistent no matter how hard they are hitting. They should throw at least ten hits per level, or enough that they have a good sense of what a hit at each level looks, sounds, and feels like, and can replicate it consistently. The levels are:

   a. **Touch**: the striking limb or weapon makes contact with the outermost layer of the target only. Think of a punch that reddens the skin but doesn't bruise any tissue beneath it, or a cut that slices along the skin without cutting deeper. The target should barely move in response to the strike.

   b. **Light Strike**: the striking limb or weapon aims to penetrate its target to a depth of one to two inches (two to five centimetres). This is the kind of hit that leaves no doubt in a fighter's mind that they've been struck. It may leave a bruise if it hits a sensitive area or if the fighter bruises easily, but won't cause a hematoma or risk breaking bones. The target will move noticeably in response to the strike, but should not travel very far.

   c. **Heavy Strike**: the striking limb or weapon aims to go all the way through the target. This is a decisive, debilitating blow that is struck with the intent to do serious harm to an opponent. The target should move a lot, and may swing to the edges of its range of motion (heavy bag) or go flying across the room (water bottle).

5. Player identifies where their "usual" striking force (demonstrated in step #2) fits on the spectrum from a touch to a heavy strike. Together with their instructor and/or training

partners, they identify the most appropriate impact level for drilling and adjust their striking force to match it.

6. Player chooses a new attack or type of strike, and repeats the exercise.

Possible variants: have Player alternate between all three impact levels with each strike instead of working them in blocks (improves parameterization ability by forcing frequent adjustments); have Player "break" a blow by turning a heavy strike into a light strike or touch at the moment of impact, usually by relaxing the striking limb (builds the ability to account for errors mid-exercise and bleed off excessive force); replace the target with a striking pad held by a feeder, and have both partners move around the floor as Player throws their strikes (puts strikes into a more realistic movement context)

2. Unarmed Strike Evasion

The primary goal of this exercise is to identify and address students' discomfort with hitting their partners, especially when targeting vulnerable areas such as the head. You can either explicitly point out its purpose, or frame it as an evasion drill to elicit more natural behaviour from the feeder, who will believe that they are not the focus of the exercise.

It's very important to manage impact force and to keep the atmosphere light and friendly in order to keep the player safe. Once students get comfortable with the basic format of the exercise, the focus can shift to improving the player's tactics and movement quality. For a longer discussion of this exercise as a diagnostic tool, see page 136.

Equipment: none

Goal: acclimatize students to hitting their partner with an empty hand

Secondary skills developed: evasion (especially use of timing and distance), footwork, ability to think/fight through unpleasant stimuli

Exercise progression:

1. Feeder and Player stand facing each other, an arm's length apart.

2. Feeder reaches out and hits Player on the side of the head or face with an open hand. They should make solid contact, and hit hard enough for the impact to be unpleasant, but not hard enough to move Player's head. They should avoid targeting Player's ear.

3. Feeder throws a handful of strikes like this, alternating which hand they hit with. Player allows each hit to land.

4. Once Feeder has landed a few hits with no reaction from Player, Player starts evading the incoming blows. They may use footwork, distance changes, level changes, slips, and any other techniques in their arsenal to avoid being hit.

5. Every few strikes, Player doesn't evade and lets the hit land. This will keep Feeder honest in their targeting and level of force.

6. Once Feeder is aiming all of their strikes true and Player has gotten a decent workout evading them, Feeder and Player switch roles.

Possible variants: restrict Player's tactical options to specific techniques or ways of moving (allows students to practice new skills in a more open context); let Player use their evasive actions to set up counter-strikes, grapples, or throws (forces Player to consider both offense and defense); make the exercise competitive by using timed rounds and having Feeder count successful hits (increases stress, and may improve targeting if Feeder has gotten sloppy with their strikes)

3. Weapon Strike Evasion

This exercise introduces one of my favourite inexpensive pieces of equipment: the golf tube. These plastic, 1.25-inch-diameter tubes can be purchased from any golf supply store for under five dollars each, and can be used as simple impact weapons with very little risk of injury. They make a hollow "bonk" sound upon impact (my students have christened them the "Tubes That Go Bonk" as a result), which makes it easy to tell when a hit has landed and adds a strong element of play and silliness to the exercise.

As with the previous exercise, this can either be presented to the students as a hitting and strike feeding drill for the feeder, or as an evasion drill for the player. The feeder must not only aim to hit the player, but must also throw clean, straight cuts that travel a consistent and predictable path.[1]

Equipment: one golf tube per pair, two sets of eye protection (optional)

Goal: teach students to feed strikes with good intention to hit

Secondary skills developed: targeting, cut line and angle consistency, evasion (especially use of timing, angle, and distance)

Exercise progression:

1. Feeder and Player start facing each other. Feeder is armed with a golf tube, standing with their off-hand leg forward. Player is unarmed and in a basic fighting stance. Feeder should be able to reach Player's nearest shoulder with the top third of the tube after taking a step forward with their weapon leg.

2. Feeder steps forward and throws a descending, diagonal forehand cut to Player's nearest shoulder. They should move at about half of sparring speed, and their cut should follow through past the target if it misses.

1 I was first introduced to the "Tubes that Go Bonk" and to this exercise format by Maija Soderholm.

3. Player evades by stepping towards Feeder's weapon side and moving below the plane of the cut. They touch Feeder's nearest shoulder and retreat to safety.

4. Once Player is successfully evading the majority of the cuts, Feeder may begin alternating between forehand and backhand cuts in a steady rhythm. Player may tag the weapon side or off-hand side shoulder, depending on the cut they are evading.

5. After two to three minutes of continuous movement, Feeder and Player switch roles.

Possible variants: allow Player to make a follow-up attack, rather than just touching Feeder's shoulder (forces Player to consider how their body position and movement set up an effective attack); change the cut angles, distance between partners, or speed and rhythm of cuts (adds difficulty and variety); swap Feeder's golf tube for a hard plastic, wooden, or metal training weapon (increases stress)

4. Pummeling

This basic wrestling game gets students comfortable with the high level of physical contact that comes with grappling work and teaches them the difference between performing a movement mechanically and working to achieve a goal.

As students become proficient in this exercise, make sure that they remain goal-oriented. It's easy to slip from pummeling as a setup for achieving a grip, to just alternating positions without the forward pressure or tactical intent that makes the exercise work. Both partners should maintain good wrestling posture throughout the exercise (feet far enough apart to create a stable base, torso bent forward from the hips, straight back).

Equipment: none

Goal: teach students to feed appropriate pressure and resistance into a grappling exercise

Secondary skills developed: countering strength/aggression effectively, familiarity with wrestling grips, sense of timing and rhythm

Exercise progression:

1. Feeder and Player start facing each other in standing grips. Feeder reaches their right hand under Player's left arm, grabs Player's left shoulder blade, and pulls their own head and right shoulder close to Player's left shoulder, gaining a single underhook position. Player does the same. Both students place their left hand on their partner's right elbow.

2. Feeder drives or swims their left hand under Player's right arm and attempts to get an underhook on Player's right side (completing a double underhook position). They will have to pull back slightly to create the space necessary for this movement.

3. Player may use Feeder's movement as an opportunity to attempt the same technique. If both students move simultaneously, they will end up in the mirror of their starting position: left hand in a single underhook, and right hand on their partner's left elbow.

4. Feeder and Player continue competing for double underhooks. They may move their feet and vary the timing and speed of their movement as needed. They should build a steady rhythm of continuous movement as they try to achieve the same position.

5. Once one student achieves a double underhook, they count it as a "win" and the exercise resets to the starting position.

Possible variants: add new goal positions or actions, such as a go-behind, single-leg takedown, or throw (teaches students to use pressure and timing to set up specific skills); vary the speed at which students work the exercise (increases/decreases stress, or shifts focus to a specific tactical element)

5. Nap Wrestling

Wrestling ground work is one of the most challenging contexts for inexperienced students because of the high degree of contact and the psychological challenge of feeling another person's weight pressing you down. Working at very slow speeds reduces stress and psychological arousal and allows students to acclimatize to the physical reality of grappling work and to build comfort with their partner.

The focus of this exercise should always be on exploration and learning, and not on competition. This is a practice framework, rather than a set pattern drill, and you can vary its goals and allowed techniques in order to fit with what you're teaching on a given day.

Equipment: mats or another suitable surface for wrestling on the ground

Goal: acclimatize students to the physical pressure of ground work

Secondary skills developed: breathing, setting up techniques via position and timing, pinning and submissions

Exercise progression:

1. Feeder and Player start on their knees, facing each other, about an arm's length apart.

2. They begin wrestling at very slow speed. You can use drumming or background music to set the tempo, or have students count in their heads. Each movement (e.g. reaching out to grab a partner's neck) should take a slow one-two-three count to complete.

3. If one partner achieves a dominant position or completes a submission (via a joint lock, choke, etc.), they hold it for a

single one-two-three count, and then release and move on to a new goal. Both partners should be moving continuously.

4. Wrestling rounds can be timed for two to three minutes of continuous movement. After each round, students switch partners.

Possible variants: change the start position to an asymmetric one such as guard or mount (increases challenge for one partner and increases stress); limit available techniques, or set a specific position or technique as the goal (adds a technical focus); give each partner a different, secret goal (adds asymmetry without substantially increasing stress)

Reading a Partner's Movement, Intention, and Mental State

6. Follow the Leader

Most students intuitively use visual cues to orient themselves in a drill or fight. This exercise teaches them to use the information transmitted through touch. Watch students' speed carefully: I often see students moving way too fast, or one partner accelerating suddenly if they feel like they're losing or falling behind. It may help to frame this as a semi-cooperative listening exercise rather than a competition. Students should think of their movement as a form of communication and their focus should be on the connection between themself and their partner.

Equipment: none

Goal: teach students to interpret communication via touch

Secondary skills developed: maintaining facing and posture during movement, reading and responding to subtle movement cues, setups and deception

Exercise progression:

1. Feeder and Player start facing each other, with each fighter's right arm bent and held in front of their body so that the backs of Feeder's and Player's forearms touch.

2. Feeder starts moving their right arm very slowly (no faster than half of sparring speed). They may add body movement and rotation to increase its range of motion. Their goal is to break contact with Player or take Player off-balance.

3. Player moves their own right arm in order to maintain contact with Feeder at all times, matching Feeder's speed. They may rotate their body and move their feet in order to keep their balance and facing.

4. After two to three minutes of continuous movement, Feeder and Player switch roles.

Possible variants: blindfold Player or have them work with their eyes closed (increases reliance on tactile input); change the contact point (increases/decreases difficulty of maintaining balance and facing); allow one or both partners to push/pull the point of contact in order to upset their partner's balance (shifts focus to using contact to set up an attack)

7. Cue Feeding

This exercise expands on the idea of communication through movement developed in exercise #6: Follow the Leader. It's a great tool for teaching students how to set up feints and deception and can be the first step in a more developed technical sequence.

I introduce this quite early in my students' training in order to get across that a fight or exercise is also a conversation, and to frame being a good partner in terms of being able to communicate clearly. It can be performed with any training weapon, but I prefer to use golf tubes because they allow for a large number of strikes to land without much pain or risk of injury.[2]

Equipment: two golf tubes per pair

Goal: teach students how to communicate with their partner via visual cues

Secondary skills developed: building and breaking patterns, reading and responding to visual cues, feeding consistent attacks

Exercise progression:

1. Feeder and Player start facing each other, each armed with a golf tube. Player stands square, with their tube held vertically in front of them along their centreline. Feeder should be able to reach either one of Player's shoulders with the top third of their tube.

2. Feeder aims a descending, diagonal strike at one of Player's shoulders. This may either be a forehand strike to the shoulder facing Feeder's weapon side, or a backhand strike to the other shoulder.

3. Player parries the strike by moving their tube toward the side that is being attacked and blocking the hit.

4. Feeder throws a mix of forehand and backhand strikes to Player's shoulders. They may vary their body movement, footwork, speed, and impact force, so long as the strike angle and line do not change.

5. Player parries every strike in the same manner as they parried the first one.

---

2 This exercise is adapted from an exercise in Maija Soderholm's *The Liar, The Cheat, and The Thief.*

6. Feeder's goal is to communicate their intentions clearly to Player with every attack. If Player parries on the wrong side, that indicates that Feeder has failed. Feeder can also observe which of their movement cues cause Player to react the most strongly (e.g., shoulder rotation, footwork, eye movement prior to the strike, etc.).

7. After two to three minutes of continuous movement, Feeder and Player switch roles.

Possible variants: allow Feeder to try to deceive Player, or use their communication to set up a feint (provides a tactical context for communication); change targets or allowed strikes (provides opportunities for new responses from Player and new data for Feeder)

8. Basic Pendulum

The pendulum is a footwork pattern drawn from Visayan Style Corto Kadena and Larga Mano Eskrima. It creates a simple framework for movement and improvisation that allows a ton of variation and controlled chaos, while keeping students' movement predictable enough that space and safety aren't really issues.

In order to really take advantage of the tactical opportunities the pattern provides, students must learn to separate their steps from their weight transfers. If you see them just stomping back and forth, pull back to slower movement with a focus on the weight shift or have them take smaller steps.[3]

Equipment: none

Goal: teach students how to build a shared movement rhythm with a partner

---

3 The Pendulum practice depicted in this exercise and exercise #14: Pendulum Flow is the invention of Maestro Sonny Umpad. The version described here is inspired by an exercise taught to me by Maija Soderholm, a lineage holder of Visayan Corto Kadena and Larga Mano Eskrima. It should not be taken as a canonical representation of the original.

Secondary skills developed: footwork, balance, reading intention and movement cues

Exercise progression:

Solo version (footwork pattern only):

1. Start in a profiled stance with your left foot and shoulder leading. Your knees should be bent and about shoulder width apart and your weight should be almost entirely on your right (rear) leg. You should be able to pick up your left foot without any change in posture.

2. Reach your left foot forward and place it about a foot's length in front of its original position, keeping your weight on the right leg.

3. Shift your weight over your left leg, allowing your shoulders to rotate so that your chest faces the direction of travel. Bring your feet together.

4. Reach your right foot forward and place it about a foot's length in front of your left foot.

5. Shift your weight over your right leg, allowing your shoulders and left foot to rotate until you end up in a profiled stance with your right shoulder and leg leading.

6. Reverse direction by shifting your weight back onto your left leg.

7. Reach back with your right foot, placing it about a foot's length behind your left foot.

8. Shift your weight onto your right foot, allowing your feet and shoulders to rotate until you return to your starting position.

Paired exercise:

1. Feeder and Player start facing each other. Feeder begins in the starting position described in step #1 above. Player begins in the forward position from the end of step #5 above. Player should be able to touch Feeder's lead shoulder with a simple extension of their right arm.

2. Feeder starts moving through the pendulum footwork pattern at a relaxed speed.

3. Player moves backwards through steps #6-8 of the pendulum, matching Feeder's pace.

4. Once Feeder reaches the forward position of their pendulum (end of step #5), they reach out to touch Player's left shoulder, hip, or knee with their right hand, ensuring that they are still at the same range.

5. Feeder and Player switch roles, and Feeder sets the pace for the next few steps.

6. The students continue moving back and forth through the pattern, taking the role of Feeder whenever they're moving forward (steps #1-5), and Player whenever they're moving backward (steps #6-8).

7. After both partners have gotten comfortable with the pattern, Player may start evading Feeder's touches every once in a while. They may use body voids, weight shifts, or footwork to do so, as long as they can keep up their part of the back-and-forth movement flow.

Possible variants: give both partners weapons, and have Feeder throw an attack instead of reaching out to touch Player (changes the contact distance and adds challenge and stress); allow students to circle as they work the pattern, instead of just moving back and forth along a straight line (opens up new angles and opportunities to improvise)

9. Mirroring

This progression of observation exercises is another way to build communication and empathy between partners. You can also use it as a tactical exercise for teaching students how to quickly build a working model of an opponent's movement and fighting style as a component of tournament preparation.

Here, its main function is to give students the experience of moving like their partner, and to build empathy and understanding of how fighting in a different body might work. It's also usually a bit awkward and silly and a good icebreaker or social bonding exercise.

Equipment: whatever weapons students normally fight with

Goal: teach students how to identify each other's movements and physical habits

Secondary skills developed: mimicry of observed actions, physical communication, understanding of body mechanics

Exercise progression:

Walking:

1. One student in the group is Feeder, and everyone else is Player. Feeder walks naturally across the training space, turns around, and walks back while the Player group watches.

2. Feeder walks back and forth across the space, with the Player group following a few steps behind and mimicking Feeder's gait and movement patterns as closely as possible.

3. Players, collectively, identify three distinctive traits of Feeder's movement and describe them to Feeder.

4. The group chooses a new Feeder and repeats the exercise.

Fighting:

1. One student in the group is Feeder, and everyone else is Player. Feeder stands at the front of the space, facing away from the group. The Player group spreads out behind them, facing Feeder.

2. Feeder starts shadow boxing (or shadow fighting with a weapon), moving like they would in a sparring match, but at about half their usual speed.

3. Each Player mimics Feeder's movement as closely as possible.

4. After two to three minutes, Feeder stops and leaves the floor. The Player group discusses their observations and identifies three distinct characteristics of Feeder's movement.

5. Feeder returns to the floor, and the Player group demonstrates their best imitation of Feeder's fighting style, guided by their prior discussion. Feeder chooses which Player is doing the best job of mimicking them, and tries to guess which three characteristics the group chose.

5. The group chooses a new Feeder and repeats the exercise.

Possible variants: turn the fighting version into a partnered exercise, with a single Feeder and Player facing each other and no discussion step (builds a closer connection between specific partners); have the Player group use their observations of Feeder's movement to make predictions about Feeder's preferred response to a given attack or opening, and then have Feeder demonstrate their actual response to test the theory (deepens understanding of the link between body mechanics/movement habits and available tactical options)

Integrating Play and Problem Solving

Observation Exercises

These exercises break a fight down into discrete pieces, allowing students to engage in more detailed tactical thinking than is usually possible during continuous movement. They are excellent for exploring the complexities of an unscripted fight and for building basic observation, analysis, and problem-solving skills.

10. Group Problem Solving

This exercise introduces a general problem-solving framework that students can apply to their practice going forward. It's a particularly good fit for self-defence training. The group discussion component pushes students to articulate their decision-making process, which is a critical skill for self-evaluation in all contexts and for debriefing and legal follow-up in self-defence.

If the conversation stalls or you have a particularly quiet group, you can re-frame your questions or guide the conversation a little, but try to avoid feeding the students answers. Guiding them too heavily will reinforce the idea that you're looking for a single, correct answer and can make them reluctant to speak up out of fear they'll guess wrong.

Equipment: whatever is appropriate for the tactical problem you'll be presenting

Goal: give students a practical problem-solving model

Secondary skills developed: articulation of decision making, thinking under stress, tactical application of skills/techniques

Exercise progression:

1. One pair of students is chosen to demonstrate the problem. Everyone else is an Observer.

2. The demonstration pair choses who will be Feeder and Player, and Feeder puts Player in a tactically disadvantageous position (e.g., a grappling pin, hold, or choke; a weapon bind or other position that compromises Player's ability to use their weapon; a grab that allows Feeder to stab or hit Player).

3. As a group, the Observers identify Player's final goal (e.g., escaping; hitting Feeder; gaining a dominant position).

4. As a group, the Observers identify the greatest immediate threat to Player (e.g., Feeder's weapon or striking limb; having their breathing restricted by Feeder's position; an object, wall or floor that they could be thrown into).

5. As a group, the Observers identify the most useful tools and opportunities available to Player (e.g., an opening to strike or step into; a limb that is free and able to act; a surface to push off of to generate power; an unstable or off-balance element of Feeder's position).

6. As a group, the Observers come up with a single action for Player to take that will leverage the tools/opportunities available to them in order to neutralize the immediate threat, and bring them one step closer to their goal.

7. Player executes the suggested action, and Feeder responds naturally.

8. The group repeats steps #4-7 based on the new position that Feeder and Player have arrived in. This continues until Player has achieved the goal identified in step #3.

Possible variants: remove the Observer group and have students perform this in pairs, with Player describing their decision process out loud through steps #4-7 (allows for more repetitions and independent practice); set a timer that limits discussion time within the Observer group, and incrementally reduce the available time with every run-through of the exercise (adds stress)

11. Count Fighting

This exercise breaks free sparring down into single *tempos*, or units of timing. A *tempo* is the length of time it takes a fighter to complete a single action, or the span of time between one moment of stillness and the next. Throwing a punch takes one *tempo*. So does a fencing lunge. So does a simple guard or position change. *Tempos* can vary dramatically in length, and understanding the relative timing differences between actions is crucial to making good tactical decisions.

In this exercise, students should be moving slowly enough that they can make contact with their partner without causing harm, and see and think about the timing dynamics of the fight.[4]

Equipment: whatever weapons students normally fight with

Goal: allow students to observe and understand the relative timing of their actions

Secondary skills developed: good body mechanics and structure, seeing and capitalizing on openings, tactical decision-making, linking movements into combinations

Exercise progression:

1. Feeder and Player start facing each other, as they would at the beginning of a sparring match or fight, a step ot two outside of striking range.

2. The instructor counts "One!" out loud, and Feeder and Player move simultaneously. They may make any movement that takes a single *tempo* to complete, and then freeze. Both partners should be moving at no more than about one quarter of sparring speed.

3. The instructor counts "Two!", and both partners move again, each taking a single *tempo*.

---

4 I was introduced to the basic form of this exercise by Cst. John Irving of the Vancouver Police Department's Force Options Training Unit.

4. The instructor keeps counting and the partners keep taking single-*tempo* actions until one partner has struck a decisive blow or achieved a dominant position, or until they reach a stalemate. Most rounds will last about seven to ten counts.

5. Students switch partners, and repeat steps #1-4. Once everyone has completed at least four run-throughs of the exercise, the timing rules change. Cycle through each of the following variations in order, allowing a few run-throughs for each:

   a. On every odd-numbered count, starting with "One!", both Feeder and Player move as usual. On every even-numbered count, starting with "Two!", only Player moves, taking an additional single-*tempo* action.

   b. On each count, Feeder may take one single-*tempo* action. Player may take up to two single-*tempo* actions. All of Player's movement must end at the same time as Feeder's (which means that they must use actions with much shorter *tempos* than that of Feeder's action if they want to move twice).

Possible variants: use this framework to explore multiple-assailant situations with two or more Feeders for every one Player (emphasizes the danger of such situations with little risk of harm to students, and teaches Player to prioritize efficiency of movement); restrict the kinds of movements that either fighter can make to specific techniques, or to either purely defensive or purely offensive actions (highlights the timing attributes of the specified actions and may set up a follow-up technical exercise that capitalizes on those attributes)

Mixed-Goal Exercises

This exercise format provides an alternative model for building partnered exercises. It is particularly good for encouraging good movement and mindset from the feeder. Telling them to "start pummeling" or "throw some jabs" tends to have a very different effect on their mental state and movement than "try to get double underhooks on your partner" or "hit your partner in the forehead five times".

Well-matched goals for both the feeder and player can create a call-and-response effect that naturally builds a drilling rhythm without external prompting. A goal-centred exercise also allows students to come up with their own solutions to the problem presented to them, or discover why a technique they've learned is the best choice for a given context.

12. Pummeling Progression

This exercise expands on exercise #4: Pummeling, and is an example intended to illustrate how this kind of exercise works. The general framework of giving each partner a different goal can be applied to any context (e.g., striking, grappling, swordplay, mixed martial arts), and the exercise can be modified to suit whatever you're working on.

When building a exercise of this nature, it's important to outline clear goals for each partner. It's also important to think about how both partners' goals will interact. Ideally, the feeder will naturally move through positions that give the player opportunities to achieve their goal, and vice versa.

Equipment: mats (optional; if none are available, don't allow students to complete their takedowns)

Goal: teach students to use their partner's movment and intent to set up their own techniques

Secondary skills developed: basic grappling skills, sense of timing, body mechanics and quality of movement, footwork

Exercise progression:

1. Feeder and Player start facing each other, and begin pummeling as described in exercise #4: Pummeling. Both students should be attempting to get to a double underhook position. If either one gets to their goal position, reset and start again.

After two to three minutes, change the students' goals. Feeder continues to aim for double underhooks. Player must now achieve a go-behind.

1. Both students use the basic pummeling framework to build a rhythm and set up their target techniques.

2. As Feeder reaches forward to gain an underhook, Player may duck under Feeder's arm and step behind them, grabbing Feeder around the waist.

3. If either student gets to their goal position, they reset and start again.

After two to three minutes of continuous play, change goals. Feeder tries to achieve a go-behind. Player tries to get a single-leg or double-leg takedown.

1. Both students use the basic pummeling framework to build a rhythm and set up their target techniques.

2. As Feeder leans or pushes forward to go under the arm, Player may drop to their lead knee, grab one or both of Feeder's legs, and drive forward to take them to the mats.

3. If either student gets to their goal position, they reset and start again.

After two to three minutes of continuous play, change goals. Both students may try to get either double underhooks, a go-behind, or a double- or single-leg takedown. Turn-taking is not required.

Possible variants: substitute different goals for Feeder, Player, or both (changes interaction between students and allows for practicing different skills); begin from a greater distance instead of pummeling (forces students to set up footwork entries to their techniques in addition to timing)

Flow Exercises

These exercises provide a semi-controlled framework for students to improvise within. The feeder's job is to provide consistent, predictable stimuli for the player, and the player uses the psychological safety of that consistency to allow themself to experiment. Neither of these exercises should have clear "win" or "loss" conditions, and risk-taking and failure should be encouraged.

13. Five Strikes

This exercise builds an improvisational framework from a few simple attacks. The feeder builds a steady rhythm of attacks that set the pace. The player should feel free to experiment with their responses and try techniques or movements that they aren't sure will work. If they try something that fails, they shouldn't stop and reset, but jump back into the flow and respond to whatever the feeder is currently doing.

Equipment: whatever weapons students normally fight with, sufficient safety gear to be able to ignore a glancing blow

Goal: teach students how to improvise and respond effectively to failure within a semi-controlled environment

Secondary skills developed: feeding good strikes, footwork and movement quality, evasions, blocks, and other tactical responses

Exercise progression:

Solo preparation (attack pattern):

1. Throw a forehand strike that is common in your fighting system (e.g., haymaker or hook, roundhouse kick, forehand cut with knife or sword).

2. Throw a backhand strike that is common in your fighting system (e.g., backfist or backhand elbow strike, hook kick, backhand cut with knife or sword).

3. Throw a descending strike that is common in your fighting system (e.g., hammerfist to the nose, stomp, icepick stab with knife or dagger, descending sword cut to the head).

4. Throw a rising strike that is common in your fighting system (e.g. uppercut, knee to the belly or groin, reverse grip cut to the belly with knife or dagger, rising sword cut to groin or armpit).

5. Throw a straight thrust or strike that is common in your fighting system (e.g., jab or cross, push kick or *teep*, stab to the centreline with knife or dagger, lunge or thrust with sword).

Paired exercise:

1. Feeder and Player start facing each other. Player assumes a neutral fighting stance. Feeder stands close enough that they can hit Player with the first strike in their attack pattern after taking a single step.

2. Feeder works through the full five-strike attack pattern, aiming to hit Player with every strike. Feeder takes a single step with each strike, and resets to their start position between attacks. They should move at about three quarters of sparring speed and pause as little as possible during their reset.

3. Player responds to each attack with an evasion. They may slip, void, step, or otherwise move to avoid being hit. After

each attack, they reset to their start position. They should match Feeder's speed and rhythm as closely as possible.

4. Feeder and Player switch roles, and repeat steps #1-3.

5. Feeder and Player switch back to their original roles. Feeder repeats the attack pattern, and Player responds in a new manner. Work through the following sequence of responses:

   a. Player responds to each attack with a block. Using a limb or weapon, they stop Feeder's attack from reaching its target. After a complete sequence of five strikes, Feeder and Player switch roles and repeat this step.

   b. Player responds to each attack with a sequence of two actions. The first action may be a block or grab, and the second action should strike, immobilize, or otherwise dominate Feeder. After a complete sequence of five strikes, Feeder and Player switch roles and repeat this step.

   c. Player responds to each attack with a counter-attack. They should move within the *tempo* of Feeder's action, hitting them with whatever strike they want, and using footwork and body position to avoid being hit. After a complete sequence of five strikes, Feeder and Player switch roles and repeat this step.

   d. Player responds to each attack with a grab. They may grapple Feeder's striking limb, body, head, or legs. Player should release their grip quickly to avoid accidentally throwing Feeder too far off balance and breaking the flow of the exercise. After a complete sequence of five strikes, Feeder and Player switch roles and repeat this step.

After a complete run-through of this exercise, each partner should have completed the attack pattern as Feeder five times, and should have completed five sets of responses as Player (evade, block, two-part response, counter-attack, grab).

Possible variants: increase or decrease both partners' movement speed (allows focus on body mechanics and more room to think if slower, adds stress if faster); change one or both students' starting position (provides new tactical challenges)

14. Pendulum Flow

Once students are comfortable with the pattern in exercise #8: Basic Pendulum, it can serve as a framework for improvisation and play. The footwork pattern acts as an anchor that students can return to whenever they make a mistake or get lost.

If a student tries something that knocks them out of the pattern, their partner should simply continue to move back and forth through the basic footwork until their partner can rejoin them. Remember that the roles of feeder and player switch very frequently in this exercise: whoever is moving forward is the feeder, and whoever is moving backward is the player. Managing these rapid transitions is part of the challenge and fun of the exercise.[5]

Equipment: see individual exercise progressions

Goal: get students comfortable playing within a constant flow pattern

Secondary skills developed: reading and setting up opportunities, rapid role-switching, footwork and movement efficiency, strike and counter quality

---

5 The Pendulum practice depicted in this exercise and exercise #8: Basic Pendulum is the invention of Maestro Sonny Umpad. The version described here is inspired by an exercise taught to me by Maija Soderholm, a lineage holder of Visayan Corto Kadena and Larga Mano Eskrima. It should not be taken as a canonical representation of the original.

Exercise progression:

The following progressions and play formats are a few options for using the pendulum as a flow exercise. You can choose your favourite, mix-and-match, or build your own.

Progression #1 (unarmed strikes and counters):

1. Feeder and Player begin moving through the Basic Pendulum footwork pattern together, as described in exercise #8.

2. Instead of reaching out to touch Player, Feeder throws a straight punch or open-hand strike to Player's chin with their right hand as they complete their forward movement.

3. Player uses the weight shift and profiled body position at the end of their backward movement to avoid Feeder's strike, and parries it with their left hand at the last possible moment.

4. After both students have gotten comfortable with this attack/parry pattern, Player may follow up their parry with either of the following counters:

   a. Player turns the parry into a grab, and pulls Feeder off-balance with a sharp tug on their striking arm.

   b. Player pushes on the outside of Feeder's elbow with their right hand, moving Feeder's striking arm aside, and then tags Feeder on the head, armpit, or ribs with a counter strike.

5. Player must complete their entire counter before they begin their forward movement and switch to being Feeder.

Progression #2 (cuts and counters):

1. Feeder and Player are both armed with a knife, machete, or other short-bladed weapon. They begin moving through the Basic Pendulum footwork pattern together, as described in exercise #8.

2. Instead of reaching out to touch Player, Feeder throws a forehand cut to Player's lead shoulder, waist, or knee as they complete their forward movement.

3. Player either evades the cut via body movement or parries Feeder's weapon with their own.

4. After both students have gotten comfortable with this attack/ defense pattern, Feeder may start throwing either forehand or backhand cuts. Player may follow up their evasion or parry with one or more cuts to Feeder's weapon arm. Player must complete their entire counter and any follow-up cuts before they begin their forward movement and switch to being Feeder.

Open Flow:

1. Feeder and Player begin moving through the Basic Pendulum footwork pattern together, as described in exercise #8. They may be armed or unarmed, depending on your preference and training goals.

2. Feeder may throw any strikes they like, to any target. They should keep contact light, and can move anywhere from half of sparring speed to full sparring speed, depending on their partner's comfort level and the safety affordances of their weapons and gear. They should be in control at all times, and should be able to pull a mistargeted or dangerous hit, if necessary.

3. Player may evade, parry, and counter-attack however they like. They should match Feeder's speed, and exercise equal control.

The students do not stop or reset after a hit is landed, and do not keep score. They simply spar continuously within the pendulum framework and use it as an opportunity to experiment with new techniques and tactics. They may vary their footwork to move off-line instead of just stepping straight forward or straight backward, and may occasionally take an extra step or two to complete an action — as long as they always return to the basic back-and-forth pattern of the pendulum.

Open Play

The following two exercises are not drills, but formats or add-ons for open sparring that allow for more observation and learning than unstructured fighting. Both are suitable for beginners. Their greatest value, however, often comes as observation and reflection exercises for experienced students who are able to self-assess as they're fighting.

15. Slow Work

The goal of Slow Work is to maintain as much fidelity as possible to the movement and timing of a full-speed fight, while moving slowly enough to let fighters spot, consider, and act on tactical opportunities they might miss at speed, and to observe the consequences of their actions in detail.

Common issues for students who are not experienced with this style of fighting include: suddenly speeding up to block or avoid an attack that would be successful at slow speed; stopping or changing trajectory mid-movement, when such a change would be impossible at full speed because of momentum. Playing background music with a slow, steady beat can help set and maintain an appropriate pace, and pairs with a tendency to speed up can be broken up and re-partnered until they get comfortable with playing this way.

Equipment: whatever weapons students normally fight with

Goal: allow students to experiment within sparring and observe the consequences of their choices

Secondary skills developed: maintaining a consistent speed and intensity under stress, setting up techniques via position and timing instead of speed or athleticism, fine motor control

Exercise progression:

Basic framework:

1. Player and Feeder start a step or two outside of striking range, and begin fighting at one quarter to one half of sparring speed. They complete every action before moving on to the next one (i.e., they must follow through on a cut or strike, and fully transfer their weight in a push, step, or grapple, just as they would at speed).

2. Hits are acknowledged but do not reset the fight, and no score is kept. Both fighters flow continuously without stopping or accelerating for two to five minutes.

Observation cues:

While fighting, students can be directed to think about what is happening in any of the following ways:

a. Player and Feeder should make mental note of every opening they see in their partner's movement, regardless of whether or not they are able to take advantage of it. Are there openings that show up consistently? Do these appear in combination with specific attacks, guard changes, or other distinctive actions?

b. Player and Feeder should look for patterns in their partner's movement. Are there attacks or defenses they favour? What conditions do those favourite actions show up under? Do they have a favourite guard? A favourite footwork pattern? Do they move in a consistent rhythm or direction while fighting?

c. Player and Feeder should make mental note of what makes their partner react most strongly. Which attacks make them flinch or draw the largest parries? Which openings do they reliably attack into? What forces them to break out of their usual patterns of movement?

Possible variants: restrict Feeder to a few specific techniques or give them different weapons from Player (gives Player a concrete problem to solve); give Player and Feeder concrete, distinct goals such as landing a specific technique or provoking a specific response (changes dynamics of play from more passive observation to pursuit of a goal); use this format to explore highly asymmetric situations such as armed vs unarmed, or multiple Feeders against a single Player (allows for sparring within a very dangerous context at a lower level of risk)

16. Plastic Mind

The name of this exercise and its core idea come from Rory Miller's self-defence teaching.[6] It's a very flexible tool that can be applied to martial arts or self-defence, and pairs very well with exercise #15: Slow Work, and flow exercises like the Five Strikes (#13) and Pendulum Flow (#14). It can also be worked into full-speed sparring and stress testing exercises. The basic principle is very simple: our mindset and identity affect how we move, and there's no rule saying that anyone has to be themselves when they fight.

Equipment: whatever weapons students normally fight with

Goal: allow students to explore how their mindset and fighting influence one another

---

6 I first encountered Miller's plastic mind exercises at his 2017 Violence Dynamics workshop in Vancouver. He lays out his version of these exercises in *Training For Sudden Violence: 72 Practical Drills.*

Secondary skills developed: self-regulation, emotional self-management, reading a partner's emotional state

Exercise progression:

As students are fighting in whatever format you have chosen, give Feeder and Player specific imaginative cues. They are to take on the role they are given as completely as possible, setting aside their image of how they usually or ideally fight. You may give Feeder and Player the same cue publicly, or different, secret cues. The following list provides a few starting cues to choose from. Feel free to add your own:

a. **Animals and fictional creatures:** fight as if you were a bear. Or a lion. Or a kangaroo. Or a mouse. Or an orc. Or a minotaur. Or a ghost. Make your movements so characteristic of the creature you've chosen that your partner can guess what you are after a few minutes of play.

b. **Elements:** build a new fighting style around the element of earth. Or water. Or air. Or fire. Embody the essence of your chosen element in every movement, in your tactical choices, and in your emotional attitude toward your partner.

c. **Character archetypes:** fight as your favourite movie hero, or as your favourite gaming character class. Be Bruce Lee. Or Wonder Woman. Or Black Panther. Or a rogue. Or a paladin. Or a barbarian. Embody what makes them unique, and what makes them most effective.

d. **Emotional responses:** we fight differently depending on what our opponent triggers in us. Fight against the person who has broken your heart. Or harmed someone you love. Or cared for and nurtured you your entire life. Or against the biggest, scariest foe you've ever seen. Or against a person so delicate that the gentlest touch will break them.

e. **Goals:** the emotional or social intention behind a fight is just as important as its technical goal. Fight in order to psychologically dominate your opponent and prove to them that you're better. Or to restrain and control them without serious harm. Or to show off for an imagined audience and make both of you look as cool as possible. Or play with them like an inanimate toy, with no regard for what they want or need.

Possible variants: use Plastic Mind cues to get a competitor into the right mindset before a tournament; use Plastic Mind cues to enhance the realism of a stress test

Introducing Students to Stress Testing

17. The Ladder

This series of escalating partnered exercises is a good way to introduce students to different kinds of violence and the different levels of stress that come with them. I prefer to use it as an introduction to the experience of stress testing, rather than as a test itself. This is a chance for students to practice good partner behaviour under stress, get a taste of adrenaline, and develop a good understanding of their current physical and psychological capabilities under pressure.

I recommend setting aside about two hours for the full sequence and follow-up. Keep your group small the first time you run it (no more than four pairs). This exercise works best with two facilitators who can demonstrate each exercise together, and then supervise and work together to control group emotional arousal once the students get going.

It should be treated with all of the seriousness of a stress test. Some of these exercises carry a considerable amount of risk, and they should only be run with students who have the technical and physical skills to participate safely. At minimum, all participants should know how to fall and be comfortable with standing grappling and basic wrestling ground work, including joint locks and submissions. Go through a full safety assessment, as described on page 115, before beginning.

The final exercise in this progression will integrate disabling and debilitating strikes as well as throws and takedowns. Strikes to fragile targets like knees can be indicated or retargeted for safety, and especially vulnerable targets such as the eyes and throat can be armoured. Use your knowledge of your students' experience, motor control, and overall ability to set rules for how they should handle these techniques.

Equipment: wrestling mats, one plastic or rubber knife per pair, safety glasses, throat and groin armour (optional)

Goal: build students' awareness of the different kinds of violence they might train for and allow them to experience adrenalization in a controlled environment

Secondary skills developed: good partnership practices, emotional and physical self-regulation, situational awareness

Exercise progression:

Because of its length and complexity, this exercise is laid out differently from others in this section. I've mapped out a series of partnered drills, and suggested discussion topics for the breaks between them.

The goal of each discussion is to allow enough rest time for students to return to a level of emotional arousal that is close to their baseline state, and to give them some context and guidance for how they should approach the next exercise. Feel free to vary the length of your rests or change the discussion scripts as needed, depending on the experience level and emotional energy of your group.

Instructions for the instructors/facilitators are presented in paragraph form, and exercises for students are laid out in the numbered lists.

Introduction: Provide a general overview of how to categorize types of violence (see page 97 for a full description of our model), and identify the four main types you'll be playing with for the purpose of this exercise — sparring (play, symmetrical, social violence), a game against a cheating or stronger opponent (play, asymmetrical, social violence), a social fight (earnest, symmetrical, social violence), and attempted murder (earnest, asymmetrical, asocial violence).

Have all of the participants choose a partner. They will stay in this pair through all four exercises. This is your chance to separate and re-partner students whom you know to have emotionally volatile training dynamics.

Sparring Game (play, symmetrical, social violence)

1. Feeder and Player start pummeling, as described in exercise #4 above. They can compete for double underhooks, or another goal such as a go-behind. So long as Feeder and Player's goals are symmetrical and they're both playing by the same rules, the goal itself doesn't really matter.

2. Both students reset to their start position whenever one partner achieves their goal, and the exercise ends after two to three minutes of continuous movement.

Discussion 1: Warn the students that they are about to enter a more stressful and risky context. Tell them to expect takedowns, throws, and joint locks, and give each student time to inform their partner of any injuries, physical limitations, or triggers that may need to be accommodated. If anyone isn't sure how to work within the limits their partner sets, this is your chance to offer guidance, change up partnerships for safety reasons, or allow students to step out.

Cheater Fight (play, asymmetrical, social violence)

1. Feeder and Player start playing the same pummeling game as before.

2. Feeder may cheat. They can outmuscle and stonewall Player and ignore Player's successful underhooks or go-behinds in order to get their own.

3. When they realize that Feeder is cheating, Player changes goals and aims for a more decisive finish, such as a takedown, throw, or joint lock. Their goal should be to either take Feeder to the ground or immobilize them, not to cause harm.

4. Feeder and Player switch roles after two to three minutes of continuous movement.

Discussion 2: Mark the transition from play to earnest violence and identify some of the most important features of an earnest fight. Talk about the performance element of social violence and remind students that these fights often take place in front of an audience and include a verbal lead-up.

Encourage both partners to roleplay a bit and add talking, shouting, and emotional expression on top of their physical actions. If the students are uncomfortable with roleplaying, give them a sample script to follow or have the group practice just shouting at each other before beginning the next exercise.

Social Fight (earnest, symmetrical, social violence)

1. Feeder and Player start facing each other, within arm's reach, with their arms at their sides.

2. Feeder reaches out and shoves Player, or grabs them by their clothing and prepares to strike them. They can shout and swear at Player as they move in, keeping their language appropriate to the context ("Hey buddy, do you wanna go? You wanna fucking go?" rather than, "I'm going to kill you!"). Their goal is to corner or immobilize Player and hit them. They should keep their force light and limit themselves to open-hand strikes.

3. Player's goal is to end the fight as quickly as possible by either putting Feeder on the ground, making a bit of space and escaping, or both. Give them a target for what constitutes "escape" such as reaching a door or tagging a specific wall.

4. After Player has achieved their goal once, Feeder and Player switch roles.

Discussion 3: Introduce some of the realities of a knife attack. Make sure to get across how unlikely it is for the target to see the knife coming in an asocial assault. This isn't a duel and the knife isn't there to intimidate. It's going to come out when Player isn't paying attention and they're going to notice it only once they've been hit.

You can talk about how we can use rapid, repetitive strikes to the same target as an indicator that we are being stabbed and not punched. This discussion should prime the students for a more stressful exercise by conveying the seriousness and scariness of the situation being simulated.

Make sure that you've got appropriate safeguards in place for disabling and debilitating strikes. If students are unarmoured, instruct them to indicate, retarget, or otherwise weaken the impact of their strikes. If they are armoured, make sure that the level of force that players are allowed to use is a good match for both the armour and experience level of the feeders. You can give the students another chance to discuss injuries, physical limitations, and triggers before continuing.

Attempted Murder (earnest, asymmetrical, asocial violence)

1. Feeder and Player stand facing each other, at close range. Feeder holds a training knife and hides it behind their back. They put their other hand on the back of Player's neck, or pull down on the collar of Player's training jacket or *gi*.

2. Within five seconds of the start of the exercise, Feeder starts stabbing Player repeatedly in the belly with the training knife.

3. Player must count at least three stabs before they allow themselves to respond, and then their job is to create the space and opportunity they need to escape. This will likely require disabling or debilitating strikes to Feeder, and/or a throw or takedown.

4. After Player has made one successful escape, Feeder and Player switch roles.

Discussion 4: Adrenaline will have spiked hard during the last exercise, so it's time for a longer discussion and cooldown. Invite students to sit down, give them a quick summary of the effect that stress hormones are currently having on their bodies, and let them quietly reflect on how they feel. Take at least ten minutes to settle down. Let students drink water and work them through a simple breathing exercise if needed.

Once everyone is a bit calmer, recap the progression that they've just gone through, drawing attention to the shift in emotional arousal that came with each new exercise. Give the students an opportunity to discuss their experiences and ask follow-up questions. Leave ample time for a cooldown before sending students home.

Possible variants: replace the exercises with ones you've designed yourself that are a better fit for your martial art style, making sure to match the types of violence outlined by the original Ladder (provides an experience that is more relevant to students of swordplay, stick fighting, etc.)

Appendix: Recommended Reading

The books and articles in this appendix are good starting points for digging deeper into some of the big topics I discuss in each chapter. They are all written for non-specialist audiences, in print (at the time of this book's publication), and widely available for purchase or online access. For academic articles and specific works referenced throughout this book, see Appendix III: Works Cited.

1. Failure: the Keystone of Learning

Schmidt, Richard A., and Craig A. Wrisberg. *Motor Learning and Performance: A Situation-Based Learning Approach.*

> This textbook provides a comprehensive summary of the current state of research on motor learning, and is a great resource for getting a handle on the discipline and tracking down key studies and primary sources. The most recent edition is the fifth.

Soderholm, Maija. *The Liar, The Cheat, and the Thief: Deception and the Art of Swordplay.*

> Part drill book, part summary of the principles that make deception work in any fighting context, Maija Soderholm's book explores the concept of contextual interference from the perspective of an experienced teacher in a system that has made training difficulty and chaos central to its methods.

2. Policies: Reducing the Cost of Failure

Valkyrie WMAA Code of Conduct: http://boxwrestlefence.com/
valkyriewmaa/rules-policies/

PAX Code of Conduct: http://west.paxsite.com/safety-and-security

ECCC Anti-Harassment Policy: https://www.emeraldcitycomiccon.
com/About/At-The-Show/Anti-Harassment-Policy/

> These three online documents provide solid examples of public-
> facing policy. All of them are living documents that are actively
> enforced and have been revised multiple times to address the
> changing needs of the communities they govern. The first is the
> Code of Conduct for my martial arts school, and the latter two
> govern large fan conventions in the United States.

3. Training Culture: Cultivating Self-Reliance

Hillis, Josh. "Betty Gilpin and the Two Best Kept Secrets of Working
Out." http://www.losestubbornfat.com/betty-gilpin-two-best-kept-
secrets-working/

> This fitness article by coach Josh Hillis breaks down the prin-
> ciples of Self Determination Theory as they apply to physical
> training. It's a fun, straightforward summary with pointers to a
> lot of good academic material in its reference section.

Gilpin, Betty. "'Glow' Star Betty Gilpin: What It's Like to Have Pea-Sized
Confidence With Watermelon-Sized Boobs." https://www.glamour.
com/story/glow-star-betty-gilpin-what-its-like-to-have-pea-sized-
confidence-with-watermelon-sized-boobs

> This short, first-person narrative was the inspiration for Hillis'
> more technical piece, and chronicles actress Betty Gilpin's ex-
> periences on the set of the wrestling series "Glow". It does an
> excellent job of conveying the mindset of many beginners when
> they first enter a fighting space, and of showing the psycholog-

ical and physical impact of a supportive environment that embodies the principles I discuss in this chapter.

4. Stress Testing and Stress Inoculation

Miller, Rory. *Facing Violence: Preparing for the Unexpected.*

This book is my favourite primer on violence dynamics, and on the essential components of good self-defence training. It's a great place to start if you're not familiar with the terms and concepts I address in the "Relevance" section of this chapter, and essential reading for every self-defence teacher.

Miller, Rory. *Training For Sudden Violence: 72 Practical Drills.*

Many of the drills in this book are suitable for stress testing students, and are good jumping-off points for generating your own ideas. In "C6: Scenario Training", Miller lays out his own approach to scenario work and addresses safety, realism, and relevance in the specific context of self-defence training.

5. Hitting Girls and Other Taboos

Nuckols, Greg. "Sex Differences in Training and Metabolism." https://www.strongerbyscience.com/gender-differences-in-training-and-diet/

This article by coach and powerlifter Greg Nuckols summarizes the effect of gender-specific physiological differences on sport performance. It covers body composition (the primary physical difference highlighted in the first part of this chapter), as well as muscle structure and metabolic function; includes a good quick-reference infographic; and provides ample references for all of its conclusions.

Yard-McCracken, Tammy. "recognize the bait - recognize the hook." http://dangerousrealities.blogspot.ca/2017/05/recognize-bait-recognize-hook.html

In this article, psychotherapist and self-defence instructor Dr. Tammy Yard-McCracken provides a breakdown of how some men will abuse the idea of "realism" to overpower female training partners, and digs into the motivations and social scripts behind this behaviour.

6. Dealing with Psychological Trauma

Miller, Rory. *Facing Violence: Preparing for the Unexpected.*

Section 7.3 of Miller's book covers the psychological aftermath of violence, and Miller's own perspective on trauma, recovery, and resilience. He draws from his own experiences dealing with violence and working with survivors, and his view is a useful complement to the research-based perspective in this chapter.

Schiraldi, Glenn R. *The Post-Traumatic Stress Disorder Sourcebook: A Guide to Healing, Recovery, and Growth.*

This comprehensive volume offers a primer on many aspects of PTSD and its treatment, from a detailed breakdown of the history and diagnosis of the disorder to summaries of both professionally-delivered and self-guided treatment approaches. It's a good starting point for instructors wanting to learn more about how to approach the condition.

Valdiserri, Anna. *Trauma Aware Self Defense Instruction.*

This short, focused book is a primer on teaching self-defence to students with a history of trauma. Anna Valdiserri writes compellingly from the perspective of a trauma survivor and self-defence student. It is full of clear (and sometimes disturbing) examples of harmful teaching practices, and offers good practical tools for teaching vulnerable students safely.

Appendix: Works Cited

Abe, T., C.F. Kearns, and T. Fukunaga. "Sex Differences in Whole Body Skeletal Muscle Mass Measured by Magnetic Resonance Imaging and its Distribution in Young Japanese Adults." *British Journal of Sports Medicine* 37, no. 5 (2003): 436+.

Berg, Anne Marie, Erlend Hem, Bjorn Lau, and Øivind Ekeberg. "Help-Seeking in the Norwegian Police Service." *Journal of Occupational Health* 48, no. 3 (May 2006): 145-153.

Bernstein, N.A. *The Co-ordination and Regulation of Movements.* Oxford, NY: Pergamon Press, 1967.

Bloom, Barbara, Achintya N. Dey, and Gulnur Freeman. "Summary Health Statistics for U.S. Children: National Health Interview Survey, 2005." *Vital and Health Statistics* 10, no. 231 (Dec 2006): 1-84.

Brewin, Chris R. *Post-Traumatic Stress Disorder: Malady or Myth?* New Haven, CT: Yale University Press, 2003.

Brunette, Michelle K. and Norman O'Reilly. *Women in Sport: Fuelling a Lifetime of Participation.* Toronto, ON: Canadian Association for the Advancement of Women and Sport and Physical Activity, 2016.

Channon, Alex. "'Do You Hit Girls?' Some Striking Moments in the Career of a Male Martial Artist." In *Fighting Scholars: Habitus and Ethnographies of Martial Arts and Combat Sports*, edited by Raúl

Sánchez García and Dale C. Spencer. New York, NY: Anthem Press, 2013.

Deitz, Mandi F., Stacey L. Williams, Sean C. Rife, and Peggy Cantrell. "Examining Cultural, Social, and Self-Related Aspects of Stigma in Relation to Sexual Assault and Trauma Symptoms." *Violence Against Women* 21, no. 5 (2015): 598-615.

Diagnostic and Statistical Manual of Mental Disorders. 5th ed. Arlington, VA: American Psychological Association, 2013.

Dias, Roger Daglius, and Augusto Scalabrini Neto. "Stress Levels During Emergency Care: A Comparison Between Reality and Simulated Scenarios." *Journal of Critical Care* 33 (2016): 8-13.

Harper, Joanna. "Race Times for Transgender Athletes." *Journal of Sporting Cultures and Identities* 6, no. 1 (2015): 1-9.

Ifedi, Fidelis. *Sport Participation in Canada*, 2005. Ottawa, ON: Culture, Tourism and the Centre for Education Statistics, 2005. http://www.statcan.gc.ca/pub/81-595-m/2008060/t-c-g/tbl6-eng.htm.

Lee, Timothy D., Laurie R. Wishart, Sheri Cunningham, and Heather Carnahan. "Modeled Timing Information during Random Practice Eliminates the Contextual Interference Effect." *Research Quarterly for Exercise and Sport* 68, no. 1 (1997): 100-105.

Lindle, R.S., E. J. Metter, N. A. Lynch, J. L. Fleg, J. L. Fozard, J. Tobin, T. A. Roy, and B. F. Hurley. "Age and Gender Comparisons of Muscle Strength in 654 Women and Men Aged 20–93 Yr." *Journal of Applied Physiology* 83, no. 5 (1997): 1581-1587.

Magill, Richard A., and Kellie G. Hall. "A Review of the Contextual Interference Effect in Motor Skill Acquisition." *Human Movement Science* 9, no. 3-5 (1990): 241-289.

Martiny, Sarah E., Ilka H. Gleibs, Elizabeth J. Parks-Stamm, Torsten Martiny-Huenger, Laura Froehlich, Anna-Lena Harter, and Jenny Roth. "Dealing With Negative Stereotypes in Sports: The Role of Cognitive

Anxiety When Multiple Identities Are Activated in Sensorimotor Tasks." *Journal of Sport & Exercise Physiology* 37 (2015): 379-392.

Miller, Rory. *Facing Violence: Preparing for the Unexpected*. Boston, MA: YMAA Publication Center, 2011.

Miller, Rory. *Meditations on Violence: A Comparison of Martial Arts Training and Real-World Violence*. Boston, MA: YMAA Publication Center, 2008.

Miller, Rory. "The Progression." *Chiron* (blog). February 10, 2014. accessed March 28, 2018. http://chirontraining.blogspot.ca/2014/02/the-progression.html.

Miller, Rory, and Lawrence A. Kane. *Scaling Force: Dynamic Decision-Making Under Threat of Violence*. Wolfeboro, NH: YMAA Publication Center, 2012.

Pienaar, Jacobus, Sebastiaan Rothmann, Fons J. R. Van De Vijver. "Occupational Stress, Personality Traits, Coping Strategies, and Suicide Ideation in the South African Police Service." *Criminal Justice and Behaviour* 34, no. 2 (Feb 2007): 246-258.

Roelofs, Karin. "Freeze for Action: Neurobiological Mechanisms in Animal and Human Freezing." *Philosophical Transactions of the Royal Society B* 372. no. 1718 (2017): 1-10.

Rowling, J.K. "The Fringe Benefits of Failure, and the Importance of Imagination." *Harvard Magazine*. June 5, 2008. accessed March 28, 2018. https://harvardmagazine.com/2008/06/the-fringe-benefits-failure-the-importance-imagination.

Saunders, Terri, James E. Driskell, Joan Hall Johnston, and Eduardo Salas. "The Effect of Stress Inoculation Training on Anxiety and Performance." *Journal of Occupational Health Psychology* 1. no. 2 (1996):170-186.

Schiraldi, Glenn. *The Post-Traumatic Stress Disorder Sourcebook: A Guide to Healing, Recovery, and Growth*. 2nd ed. New York: McGraw-Hill, 2016.

Schmidt, Richard A. *Motor Learning and Performance: A Situation-Based Learning Approach*. 4th ed. Champaign, IL: Human Kinetics, 2008.

Schmidt, Ulrike and Stefan Pollak. "Sharp Force Injuries in Clinical Forensic Medicine—Findings In Victims and Perpetrators." *Forensic Science International* 159 (2006): 113-118.

Soderholm, Maija. "Random Flow and Why." *His Dark Side* (blog). March 08, 2011. accessed March 27, 2018. https://darkwingchun.wordpress.com/2011/03/08/random-flow-and-why-by-maija-soderholm/.

Somlyo, Andrew. "Coaching in Theory and Practice." Lecture, Swordsquatch, Seattle, WA, September 9, 2017.

Stuart, Heather. "Mental Illness Stigma Expressed by Police to Police." *Israel Journal of Psychiatry and Related Sciences* 54, no. 1 (2017): 18-23.

Sport Participation 2010. Ottawa, ON: Canadian Heritage, 2013. http://publications.gc.ca/collections/collection_2013/pc-ch/CH24-1-2012-eng.pdf.

Tedeschi, Richard G., and Lawrence G. Calhoun. "Posttraumatic Growth: Conceptual Foundations and Empirical Evidence." *Psychological Inquiry* 15, no. 1 (2004): 1-18.

Teixeira, Pedro J., Eliana V. Carraça, David Markland, Marlene N. Silva, and Richard M Ryan. "Exercise, Physical Activity, and Self-Determination Theory: A Systematic Review." *International Journal of Behavioral Nutrition and Physical Activity* 9, no. 78 (2012): 1-30.

Valdiserri, Anna. *Trauma Aware Self Defense Instruction*. San Bernardino, CA: CreateSpace, 2016.

Watson, Louise, and Leanne Andrews. "The Effect of a Trauma Risk Management (TRiM) Program on Stigma and Barriers to Help-Seeking in the Police." *International Journal of Stress Management* (May 2017): 1-9. http://dx.doi.org/10.1037/str0000071.

Wester, Stephen R., David Arndt, Sonya K. Sedivy, and Leah Arndt. "Male Police Officers and Stigma Associated With Counseling: The Role of Anticipated Risks, Anticipated Benefits and Gender Role Conflict." *Psychology of Men and Masculinity* 11, no. 4 (2010): 286-302.

About the Author

Kaja Sadowski has been a physical instructor since 2004. She taught figure skating, rock climbing, and mountaineering before coming to martial arts in 2010. She joined the coaching team at Valkyrie Western Martial Arts Assembly in 2012, and is the school's co-owner. She teaches group and private lessons to students of all experience levels, and has traveled extensively to teach at events across Canada, the United States, and the United Kingdom.

Her primary weapon is the rapier, and she also teaches unarmed striking, grappling, knife combat, and self-defence. Kaja has been a civilian auxiliary with the Vancouver Police Department's Force Options Training Unit since 2015, participating in realistic tactical training scenarios and providing guest instruction to their Special Municipal Constable program.

She holds a Master of Arts in English Literature, and did the majority of her graduate work on medieval English and French chivalric romances. She has presented at a number of academic conferences, and has taught at the undergraduate level in literature, history, and medieval studies. She regularly leverages her academic training to serve her martial arts research.

Kaja lives in Vancouver, Canada. When she's not punching people in the face, she enjoys embroidery, board games, and powerlifting.